25⁰⁰

D1520027

Christianity and Traditional
Religion in Western Zimbabwe
1859–1923

Christianity and Traditional Religion in Western Zimbabwe 1859-1923

Ngwabi Bhebe
Senior lecturer in history
University College of Swaziland

 Longman

Longman Group Limited
London

Associated companies, branches and
representatives throughout the world

© Longman Group Ltd 1979

First published 1979

ISBN 0 582 64237 X

Printed in Great Britain by
Western Printing Services Ltd
Bristol

Contents

List of maps   vi
Abbreviations   vi
Glossary   vii
Preface   xi
1. Ndebeleland: society and religion before 1859   1
2. The Ndebele and the first missionaries, 1859–68   27
3. Christianity and western Zimbabwe under Lobengula,
   1870–89   47
4. Religious institutions and the fall of the Ndebele
   kingdom, 1888–97   75
5. Missions and the traditional societies, 1897–1923   105
6. Christianity and education in western Zimbabwe before
   1923   129
7. Conclusion   157
   Note on archival sources   170
   Bibliography   174
   Index   184

List of Maps

1. Distribution of peoples of western Zimbabwe   facing p. 1
2. Mission stations   facing p. 105

Abbreviations

C.N.C.	Chief Native Commissioner
For. Sec.	Foreign Secretary
H.C.	High Commissioner
J.A.H.	*Journal of African History*
J.A.S.	*Journal of African Studies*
L.M.S.	London Missionary Society
R.N.A.	National Archives of Rhodesia
S.J.	Society of Jesus
S.O.A.S.	School of Oriental and African Studies
T.T.L.	Tribal Trust Land
U.C.L.A.	University of California, Los Angeles
W.M.M.S.	Wesleyan Methodist Missionary Society

Glossary

SHONA AND NDEBELE WORDS REPEATED IN TEXT

abafundisi – missionaries
abathakathi – witches, male and female
enkosini – the king's place
hosana – boy spirit mediums
Hole – people of Shona origin incorporated into the Ndebele state
idlozi – spirit
ilitshe – literally stone, but used to describe a Mwari shrine
indaba – meeting
indunas – chiefs
inyanga – medicine man or doctor
Inxwala – annual religious festival
imikhobo – ghosts
isanusi or *isangoma* (sing.), *izanusi* or *izangoma* (pl.) – diviner/ diviners
inyanga (sing.), *izinyanga* (pl.) – medicine man/men
kuzwarira – to give a female child in marriage
lobola – bride wealth
manyusa – messengers, intermediaries
Mnali – teacher
Modimo/Molimo – high god
mbonga – female spirit-mediums
mtontiso – rituals preceding the Inxwala
mutoro (sing.), *mitoro* (pl.) – rainmaking ceremony
Mwari – high god

Nhla – people of Sotho/Tswana origins incorporated into the
   Ndebele state
Nkulunkulu – high god
nyusa – messenger/intermediary
Shumba – a Kalanga cult and also a spirit medium of the cult
Somandla – another name for Nkulunkulu
ukubuyisa – bringing home of an ancestral spirit
ukucela imvula emakhosini – royal rainmaking ceremonies
ukuhlanziswa yinyanga – to be cleansed by a doctor
umbuyiso – the bringing home of an ancestral spirit ceremony
vadzidzisi – teachers
vanyai – messengers, intermediaries
Zansi – the Ndebele of Nguni origin
wota – to pay respects

To Rangarirai, Mzingaye and Tazviona Muluge

Preface

African religions have so far been conceptualised in static terms with changes being seen as dating only from the introduction of Christianity. Indeed, most of the outstanding work in this field of African studies has been produced by anthropologists,[1] whose methods naturally lead them to look at cultures as they are rather than at their dynamic aspects. For a long time historians apparently avoided addressing themselves to the study of pre-Christian African religious practices, beliefs and rituals because of sheer lack of documentary evidence, a disadvantage which has, however, since been overcome by the use of oral evidence. Yet even the introduction of this methodological technique does not seem to have encouraged historians to search for the genesis, expansion and other aspects of African religious systems. Some of the complaints made by J. F. Ade Ajayi and E. A. Ayandele about neglected themes in African religions in West Africa could be generalised to include southern Africa as well. The chief neglected area is the historical dimension in studies of traditional religions.[2]

This study, however, tries to see African religious systems in western Zimbabwe as living and developing, even though their origins are beyond the scope of the book. The growth goes on before and after the introduction of Christianity. Spectacular changes in the people's beliefs are first brought about by the coming together of different ethnic groups – the Shona, the Nguni of Mzilikazi, the Sotho, Tswana, and Venda – incorporated into the Ndebele state in the Transvaal. These diverse groups, though having similar two-tiered cosmologies of high gods and lesser spirits, differ greatly in the powers and functions they assign to either of the tiers. Their differences lie chiefly in the existence or non-existence of a 'supreme being' centred cult. The Shona possessed a fairly developed cult centred around their high god *Mwari*, while the other groups, with the exception of the Venda, had their systems of worship revolving around the ancestor spirits. When these systems were brought together in the early nineteenth century they amalgamated, with the result that the Nguni and other ethnic groups included in the Ndebele state began to acquire the notion of an active high god. The fusion took the form of super-imposition of Shona beliefs, practices and rituals associated with Mwari, the supreme deity, on the Nguni ones so that the Ndebele religious leaders worshipped their own ancestor spirits as much as they worshipped the Shona god.

The amalgamation process that predated Christianity continued after the arrival of the first missionaries in 1859, this time with the religious officials sometimes borrowing ideas from the new faith to elaborate their own systems. The process appears to have been a form of resistance against conversion to Christianity for the continually developing religions were able to meet the needs of their adherents. The resistance was rendered more effective by the belief in witchcraft that made it possible for Shona and Nguni diviners to 'smell out' people showing signs of interest in the western religion as evil practitioners, who were then executed. There were only a few people who managed to defy the system and to embrace Christianity. Before the establishment of colonial rule these Christians were outcasts in their own society and managed to adhere to their new faith by living with the missionaries at the mission stations or by migrating to South Africa.

The situation changed with the fall of the Ndebele kingdom and with the failure of the risings in 1896-7. The destruction of the Ndebele state led to the removal of the king, who had acted as the chief priest, while the unsuccessful attempts to throw off European domination produced a marked desire among the people to come to terms with Christianity and western technology. But the tenacious hold of beliefs, rituals and practices prevented the African societies from flocking to the missions. Consequently, the old people, feeling secure in the old world, encouraged their young ones to accept the missionaries' teachings. Perhaps one of the most interesting aspects of this period before 1923 is that the old religious systems continued to borrow ideas from Christianity, while most of the converts carried their old beliefs to the new faith, a situation portending the growth of independent churches. From an intellectual point of view, although mission schools were of the rudimentary type, a start was made in the spread of literacy among Zimbabwe Africans during this period.

This work has grown out of my doctoral thesis, 'Christian Missions in Matabeleland 1859–1923', successfully submitted to the University of London in 1972. I wish to express my gratitude for the valuable suggestions, comments and other assistance received from many scholars and institutions, and in particular the following: Dr George Metcalf, formerly of King's College, London University, whose patience, warm friendship and careful supervision enormously contributed to the success of my thesis; Messrs Anthony Atmore, S.O.A.S., and Richard Brown, University of Sussex, both of whom helped me to settle on the subject of missionaries in Zimbabwe; Professor Stanlake Samkange, Harvard University, whose lively correspondence with me in the initial stages of the work was of assistance in locating some of the data that I have used; Professor Richard Gray, S.O.A.S., Drs A. F. Madden, Oxford, and P. Marshall, King's College, London, my examiners, who made the first contributions towards the reshaping of the thesis for publication; my colleagues in the faculties of Arts and Social Studies, University of Rhodesia, whose seminar groups I used as a kind of 'testing ground' for some of my ideas appearing in this work; Drs P. O. Esedebe and E. Fashole-Luke, Rev. P. Thomson, University of Sierra Leone, who read either the whole or parts of it and made substantive comments and infused some of their West African experience into the work.

My thanks also go to the Commonwealth Scholarship Commission in the United Kingdom for the award to read at King's College, London University, and to the University of London Research Funds for the grant in 1971 to carry out field work in Zimbabwe.

For sheer lack of space, I cannot mention by name the various librarians, their assistants, and archivists, both in Britain and in Zimbabwe, some of whose collections are indicated in my Notes and 'Note on Archival Sources'; to all of them I am indebted for their full co-operation without which my work could never have gone forward.

To my mother, Valentina Mathombi, who not only shouldered the greater part of the financial burden of educating me but also taught me that good results come out of hard work, I owe a debt beyond expression.

Finally I am indebted to the University College of Swaziland for their contribution towards the publication of this book.

UNIVERSITY COLLEGE OF SWAZILAND   NGWABI BHEBE
1978

Notes

1. For instance Monica Wilson, *Communal Rituals of the Nyakyusa*, London, 1959; E. E. Evans-Pritchard, *Nuer Religion*, Oxford, 1956; see also works cited by J. F. Ade Ajayi and E. A. Ayandele, 'Emerging Themes in Nigerian and West African Religious History', *Journal of African Studies* (U.C.L.A.), i, 1, 1974, pp. 31–2.
2. See Ajayi and Ayandele, 'Emerging Themes', pp. 30–4. The most recent attempt at this is the collection of papers in T. O. Ranger and I. N. Kimambo (eds.), *The Historical Study of African Religion with Special Reference to East and Central Africa*, London, 1972.

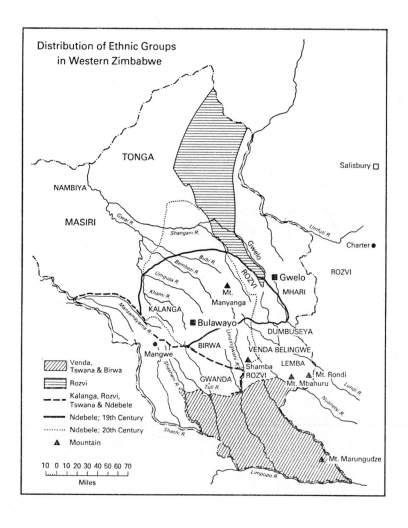

Distribution of Ethnic Groups
in Western Zimbabwe

TONGA

NAMBIYA

MASIRI

Salisbury □

Gwai R.

Shangani R.

Umfuli R.

Charter ●

Bubi R.

ROZVI

Gwelo

ROZVI

Bembezi R.

Umguza R.

MHARI

Khami R.

Mt.
Manyanga

KALANGA

Manzamayama R.

■ Bulawayo

DUMBUSEYA

Umzingwani R.

BIRWA

VENDA BELINGWE

Mangwe ●

LEMBA

GWANDA

Shamba
ROZVI

Mt. Rondi

Shashani R.

Tuli R.

Mt. Mbahuru

Lundi R.

Nuanetsi R.

Shashi R.

Venda,
Tswana & Birwa

Rozvi

Kalanga, Rozvi,
Tswana & Ndebele

Ndebele; 19th Century

Ndebele; 20th Century

▲ Mountain

Mt. Marungudze

10 0 10 20 30 40 50 60 70

Miles

Limpopo R.

I

Ndebeleland: society and religion before 1859

Religious and intellectual changes in Ndebeleland in the nineteenth century resulted from a complex process of interaction of ideas and institutions of diverse ethnic groups brought together by historical circumstances. Even before 1859, the year of the introduction of Christianity which in many parts of Africa was a powerful stimulus to religious change if not revolution, the people of Ndebeleland were already amalgamating, reshaping, reconstituting and elaborating their beliefs, practices and institutions to meet the demands of their altering political, social and economic environment. The complex socio-economic and political systems making possible this religious behaviour were themselves a consequence of two major events: the Zulu revolution in south-east Southern Africa, and the fall of the Rozvi confederacy in what is today Zimbabwe (formerly Rhodesia). The rise of the aggressive Zulu military state caused the emergence of states modelled upon similar principles. The result of the new political arrangements – and this is crucial for the present study – was that people of different religious beliefs and practices were brought together. The fall of the Rozvi polity on the other hand seems to have transformed the Mwari cult, hitherto closely associated with it, into a somewhat universalistic monotheism. Before examining the religious phenomena, it is necessary to take a brief look at the events leading to the coming together in Ndebeleland of the different ethnic groups and at their social, political and economic relationships.

The Ndebele kingdom, which had its origins in Zululand, was the dominant factor in the integration of the peoples of western Zimbabwe. In 1828 the twenty-six-year-old Mzilikazi Khumalo, a regimental commander under the Zulu King Tshaka, and a warrior statesman, broke away from the nation of the overlord with a following of about three hundred people and settled west of the Rustenburg mountains in the Transvaal in 1830. The military organisation and discipline as well as tactics and weapons inherited from the Zulu nation together with Mzilikazi's military acumen and strong leadership gave his nascent state a superior power far above that of most of the Sotho, Tswana and Venda polities it encountered. Mzilikazi used this military strength to conquer and absorb into his following many of the local peoples. Moreover, refugees from Zululand continued to join him. His following increased by leaps and bounds and in 1829 his subjects were estimated at from sixty to eighty thousand.[1]

By the later 1830s, however, the young kingdom was facing serious problems of insecurity posed by the sudden appearance of Boer Trekkers. These white settlers of Dutch origin were disgruntled with British rule in the Cape Colony and were therefore seeking fresh lands for settlement. Furthermore, the Zulus, itching as ever to punish Mzilikazi for his secession, had finally caught up with him. After a series of bloody encounters with the two groups of invaders from October 1836 to November 1837, Mzilikazi finally gave up trying to defend what had become his homeland and led his people to modern Zimbabwe. The Ndebele, as Mzilikazi's people were now called, finally settled on the watershed of the Limpopo and the Gwai river systems, having been foiled in their attempts to cross the Zambezi by the tsetse fly.

Zimbabwe was then the home of the Shona speakers. So far there is no agreement as to how Mzilikazi extended his rule over most of the Shona living in western Zimbabwe – the territory roughly coinciding with Ndebeleland. Some people think that the Ndebele easily overran the Shona. One of their chief arguments is that when the Ndebele intrusion occurred, Shona resistance had already been seriously undermined by the warlike activities of the Nguni of Zwangendaba and the Swazi of Queen Nyamazana, both Nguni precursors of the Ndebele.[2] It appears, however, that the ravages of these two groups, though highly destructive to the Shona central political structure (the Rozvi dynasty), were confined to the narrow routes of their northward migration.[3] Moreover, a large number of Shona chiefdoms managed to remain independent of Ndebele rule throughout the nineteenth century.[4] Apart from minimising Shona resistance, commentators have also tended to overemphasise the bloody aspects of Ndebele-Shona relations.[5] A thorough correction of these impressions is beyond the scope of this study; only a characterisation of the extension of Ndebele rule over and the reactions of the Shona is possible.

The Rozvi confederacy, the long established Shona political system, incurred a severe shock in about 1837 as the result of a defeat by the Swazi Queen Nyamazana. During the fighting at Manyanga, the residence of the Rozvi rulers, the ruling Mambo Chirisamhuru was fatally wounded. In later years some Shona groups attributed the fall of their confederacy to a divine punishment inflicted upon them on account of one of their rulers who had rejected the traditional beliefs.[6] The religious dimension of this story will be discussed later. Its political significance, however, may well be that the Shona religious authorities were trying to curry favour with the new rulers by accepting them as god-sent.

The demise of Mambo Chirisamhuru was neither followed by a complete collapse of Rozvi hegemony nor by a state of anarchic chaos, as has been implied.[7] What happened was that Tohochipi succeeded to the tottering dynasty and continued for many years to resist the Ndebele. Secondly, other agnates of the Mambo assumed unilateral independence by establishing themselves as chiefs of the provincial areas they had governed under the Rozvi confederacy. But by far the greater task of dealing with Ndebele intrusion and their expansionist ambitions fell upon the paramountcies or chiefdoms – formerly the basic territorial units of Rozvi local government run by hereditary leaders. As soon as it became evident that the central authority was crumbling, the chiefdoms simply reasserted their independence and organised their own resources to meet the Ndebele political and military challenge.[8]

In his approach to the various Rozvi political legacies, Mzilikazi pursued a policy that was at the same time violent and pacific. Fortunately for him, jealousies and rivalries hindered the Shona from uniting against him. Even Mambo Tohochipi failed to mobilise the chiefdoms into a common front against the intruders.[9] Mzilikazi was thus left to pick up the different Rozvi successor states one by one and force them either into submission or into abandoning the original centre of their country. Tohochipi himself retreated to the Duma country in the south-east, where he successfully resisted Ndebele incursions until 1866, through clever and skilful use of the mountain fastnesses and firearms.[10] Two other prominent Rozvi resisters were Mtinhima in the Malungwane mountains and Dyembewu in the northern part of the Doro range. The Ndebele besieged and defeated them, forcing some of their followers to flee farther east and the majority into submission.[11] The latter were part of a number of Rozvi communities, such as the Rozani of the Gwelo area, who quickly saw the futility of resisting the Ndebele and decided to collaborate with them. Such leaders were confirmed in their chieftainships and were given responsibilities such as looking after the king's cattle, collecting tribute from other subject chiefdoms, hunting for ivory and manufacturing iron weapons and implements for the Ndebele kings.[12] In this way the Ndebele eventually replaced the Rozvi as the rulers of western Zimbabwe.

But to understand the religious interaction between the invaders and the local peoples it is necessary to indicate some of the salient features of the exact relationships of the two groups. The Ndebele state superimposed itself on the local political units and was related to the latter through a complicated system of indirect and direct rule and through social assimilation. Such superstructural-subordinate arrangements suited well Ndebele political and social requirements and needs. Their army depended for its recruits on the incorporation of male youths from their subjects, as they could not assimilate whole chiefdoms without straining their administrative machinery. Moreover, incorporation of socially and politically intact groups might well lead to the accentuation of fissiparous tendencies. Controlled influx of Shona and indirect and direct rule, with a heavy emphasis on the former, also enabled the Ndebele state to maintain Nguni cultural traits for a long time. As will be shown, these relationships led to a complicated mixture of religious systems in the Ndebele kingdom.

The local communities that fell under direct Ndebele rule, such as the Nyubi of the Matopo area, and had lived in the area for a long time before the arrival of the Ndebele put up some resistance but were quickly defeated. Some of their chiefs were reduced to the status of headmen subordinate to Ndebele *indunas* (chiefs). There were also Venda chiefdoms that immigrated to the area of Ndebele settlement, and, like the Nyubi, were administered through their own chiefs. This also happened in the present Nata-Plumtree area, where there were Ndebele military units guarding the western border. These units were formed out of the local Kalanga youths with a very small proportion of men originally from the south, but commanded and administered by officials of Nguni, Sotho, Tswana or Venda stock. Apart from being required to furnish recruits for the local army, the Kalanga political systems in the area were left intact.[13] To be sure, the adjacence of the Kalanga country to the growing Ngwato power caused Ndebele kings to make frequent interventions in their internal affairs. Mischievous chiefs were deposed and replaced by loyal ones. Loyal groups were sometimes introduced into the area to neutralise it.[14] Farther away from the Ndebele area of settlement, in the present districts of Gwanda, Belingwe, Shabani, Selukwe and Que Que, the kings made no changes in the local political systems so long as the chiefdom supplied youths for the army, looked after the king's cattle, paid tribute according to their economic means, and refrained from collaborating with the enemies of the Ndebele. Thus, politically the immigrants and the indigenous societies were sufficiently close to each other to permit an interchange of cultural ideas.

It is also clear from the foregoing account that the establishment of the Ndebele kingdom greatly altered the ethnic composition and social structure of western Zimbabwe. In the centre of the country was the Ndebele state proper, composed of diverse ethnic groups and continuously expanding its population through incorporating Shona youths. Between the kingdom and the Shona communities in the east and south-east, the Virwa and Venda in the south, the Tswana in the west, and the Nambia, Nanzwa and Thonga in the north, was a transitional zone in which the Ndebele lived side by side with the original inhabitants, though not always under the same political control.

In the Ndebele state proper society was stratified into three main groups – the *Zansi*, *Nhla* and *Hole*. The Zansi were the original followers of Mzilikazi from Zululand. They formed a small but powerful portion of the society. Like any other Bantu people, they were vertically divided into clans each distinguished from the others by *isibongo* (totem). The clan leaders of this group formed the political elite of the kingdom. Some of them were the *izinduna*. But these chiefly authorities, unlike Shona chiefs, had no ritual functions, beyond acting as the priests of their immediate and extended families, just like any other male head of a household. Instead, their chief channel of communication with the supernatural world on such problems as droughts and epidemics was through the king. Thus major religious changes among the Zansi were not only noticeable in the behaviour of the king, but the latter, as the high priest of the nation, was constantly trying to solve religious problems caused by social and environmental changes. This point will be discussed later. Meanwhile it is necessary to look at the relationships of the different groups in the Ndebele state and how these were in turn related to the unincorporated Shona.

Below the Zansi were the Nhla, people conquered and incorporated into the Ndebele state when it was still south of the Limpopo. They were of Sotho, Tswana and Venda origins. They were more numerous than the Zansi, with whom they intermarried and shared political power in western Zimbabwe. Their religious impact on the Ndebele state is hard to establish. But as shall be shown, they not only furnished some of the *izinyanga* (medicine men) for the Ndebele kings, but they also provided people to run some of the Mwari cult shrines which the Ndebele consulted in the Matopo area.

The Hole formed the lowest but the largest class of the nation. They constituted a factor in the fusion of Nguni-Sotho-Tswana and Shona religious beliefs and practices. Two groups of Hole were identifiable in the Ndebele state. First, as already pointed out, there were chiefdoms that either were moved or voluntarily migrated into the central area of Ndebele settlement. Classic examples of these were the Nanzwa of the present Wankie area, the Nyai of Matopo, the Venda of the Gwanda-Beit Bridge and Shona of western Shonaland. With the establishment of the Ndebele kingdom, the Leya and Nanzwa found themselves insecure, as they lived between the Kololo of Sebitwane in the north and Mzilikazi in the south, both raiders. Most of their chiefdoms, unable to resist their enemies, chose to go and live under the protection of Mzilikazi. Their youths, together with the Kalanga young men, were formed into the Impande and Amabukuthwani *amabuto* (regiments). The elders were given land to settle under one of their chiefs.[15] Some time in the latter part of the nineteenth century, a Venda chief by the name of Tobela also had problems of insecurity because of harassment by raiders from the south, identified in oral traditions as the Swazi. Tobela and his followers sought sanctuary from the Ndebele king, who allocated to them the present Nswazi and part of the present Matopo Reserve. Although Tobela was probably placed under a Ndebele chief, he was given the position of the king's 'eyes and ears', equivalent to an intelligence agent. There were numerous groups of this type of Hole, who formed complete polities within the Ndebele state. Their distinguishing characteristics were that they were bilingual – speaking their own languages and Ndebele – and had a higher degree of social and economic intercourse with the conquerors than subject groups outside the Ndebele area of settlement. Today some of these groups have intermarried with the invaders and become somewhat indistinguishable from the latter.[16]

The second group of Hole consisted of captives and young men supplied by the subject chiefs for the Ndebele army. It was an accepted practice among Ndebele soldiers to bring back as many captives as possible from raiding expeditions. The incorporation system was so successful that by the time of the fall of the Ndebele kingdom in 1893, there were about three times as many Hole as the Zansi and Nhla put together.[17] It is important, therefore, to take a closer look at this huge Ndebele class which, though socially and politically subordinate to the other classes, exerted a cultural influence on the nation.

The word Hole seems to have been in use among the Ndebele from the Transvaal. W. F. Lye, who has made the most valuable study so far of Ndebele history south of the Limpopo, tells us that the name was applied to the Pedi, who, having been defeated, were brought home to perform manual labour for Mzilikazi. Hole, Lye goes on, 'became the Ndebele equivalent for "slave" '.[18] However, Nkani Sibanda, a former Hole, had another and interesting explanation for the origin of the word and its use among the Ndebele. The name Hole, Nkani maintained, did not acquire common usage until the advent of colonial rule. 'The Makalanga used to cover themselves with blankets, and when the Matabele asked them why they wore blankets in the hot sun they replied: We are used to dragging our blankets about with us – *holi ngubo*.' Therefore, Nkani concluded, the Kalanga suggested the name for themselves, and the Ndebele called them by it.[19] Nkani, however, was inaccurate about the time when the word was first used for it was current before 1893.[20] Moreover, it seems it was rarely used because of its derogatory connotations; indeed, from the general relationship between the Ndebele and their Shona captives it is most unlikely that they would have used such an unpleasant name for them.

When the soldiers captured people during a raid, the captives were brought and paraded before the king.[21] The females who were old enough to be married were immediately distributed among their captors, especially the indunas. But any soldier who wanted to have a young captive, female or male, asked for permission from the king, which was only granted on the full understanding that the applicant had the means of looking after a captive. If the soldier's request was successful, he then took the Hole to his own home where the latter became to all intents and purposes a member of his 'master's' family. Today the Ndebele claim that the Hole were relatively well looked after by their masters.[22] It was always borne in mind that the Hole were *abantu benkosi*, the king's people. If the king suspected that a man was ill-treating the Hole he was looking after, he would order the Hole to come and live at *enkosini* under the royal care. As an example of how the Ndebele valued and cared for their Hole, the wife of Machina Ndiweni of Hope Fountain showed me a scar in her chest, incurred from her own father as a result of abusing his Hole.[23] Lobengula certainly set a good example of looking after his Hole, and he was even notorious for always feeding them with beef:

> Lobengula never starved his slaves. He never gave them grain; but he gave them any amount of meat. They used to break out in sores on the legs through eating nothing but meat. One day someone said to the King: 'Why don't you give these boys grain?' and the King replied: 'No I want them to grow big and strong.'[24]

Some white people surmised that Lobengula was being deliberately stingy with carbohydrates to the Hole boys so that the weaker ones might die and the strong ones remain to be drafted into the army.[25] This, of course, was being unfair to Lobengula, whose idea of the best diet was unquestionably meat. He himself fed on it enormously; and he always affected to entertain his white guests to a dish of beef which would be washed down with some quantity of *utshwala* (Ndebele brewed beer). Unfortunately this latter beverage, which was nutritious and might have compensated for the farinacious elements the boys lacked in their diet, was, by Ndebele custom, not allowed to people under age. Thus, Lobengula fed his Hole on meat because he believed that it was the best food for people. Meat was not only thought to be excellent food, especially for men, but it was handy. The soldiers, on a raiding expedition, carried no grain for food, but the king gave them cattle to slaughter in the course of their journey.[26]

The social conditions of the Hole in Ndebele society were apparently reasonably good, judging from the way the Shona strove to identify themselves with their masters and conquerors. Some translated their totems from Shona to Sindebele, a process which has not ended even today: for instance, Shumba to Sibanda, Nyanga to Nkomo, Gumbo to Musipa, Shiri to Nyoni, Dziva to Siziba, Moyo to Nhliziyo, Shoko to Ncube, and many others. Others adopted the surnames of their masters. It must be stressed, however, that these changes did not affect the basic customs and taboos associated with these totems for, although the Shava, Ngwenya, Shumba, and Zhou adopted the Sindebele equivalents of their second names, they continued to regard the eland, crocodile, lion, and elephant respectively as taboo, the meat of which they could not eat.[27] Nor did the Remba izinyanga who were treating Mzilikazi for dropsy in 1854 abandon their practice of *kushinja* (cutting the throat of an animal before eating it).[28] It may well be that the Hole were induced to change their totems by social pressure, as even today the Ndebele tend to despise aliens who *kiliza* (cannot speak Ndebele properly). In other words captives may have been discriminated against socially until they had fully assimilated Ndebele ways. The assimilative process was facilitated by *umuhlehlo* (the Ndebele earmark) which they received on their arrival,[29] as a symbol of acceptance into the new society. Nevertheless, considering Mzilikazi's respect for some Shona customs,[30] and the way the Kalanga who had been in the Impande regiment were 'indignantly refusing to be styled Amakalanga',[31] it still seems that a great deal of voluntary self-identification with the conquering group was involved. The Berlin missionary C. Knothe, who travelled through southern Ndebeleland in 1888, pointed out that the majority of the Ndebele nation consisted of Ndebelised Shona, 'who have completely taken over the language, costume and customs of the Kaffirs and do not want to know that they are descendants of [the Shona] ... – although they keep visiting their [Shona] relatives'.[32]

Besides this apparently keen desire to be integrated with the master group and seemingly strong aversion to be associated with the places of their origin, both of which attitudes suggested favourable conditions for the Hole, it seems they enjoyed every opportunity that was available in the Ndebele kingdom. Perhaps T. M. Morgan, the L.M.S. missionary, may have painted a rosy picture of the conditions of the Hole, but his description gives us some indication of their state.

The practising of kidnapping may seem in one party to be cruel in the highest degree, and most painful to the other. But in Europe we have as much tyranny as there is in the interior of this continent for the African slave is almost his master's equal, and enjoys from the beginning the privileges of a child; and looks upon his master and mistress as being in every respect his parents again. Although a bondsman or a servant, in some respect he is not in bondage, neither does his servitude, especially in Moselekatse's country, convey the true idea of a slave; for he may any day with impunity leave his master, and go where he likes within the boundary of the kingdom; or he may soon become a master himself, and, instead of labouring for his own master, he may send his servant to do it; moreover, by diligence and care, he may become richer and more powerful than he who led him captive.[33]

Moreover, during the early years as the Hole grew up they were drafted into the army. They went through the same stages as any other Ndebele: starting off by looking after calves, goats and sheep, passing through the intermediate stage of herding cattle, and ultimately graduating by joining the regiments of their adopted parents or by being called to enkosini to form a new regiment.[34] Nevertheless some Ndebele informants insist that it was rare for a Hole to receive *ubuqawe* (the honour of a hero), for this was always given to his master. Yet there were Hole who managed to rise to the position of induna.[35] The Hole girls were either married by their own adopted fathers,[36] or by boys given to them by their masters.

Even though the conditions of the Hole seem to have been generally favourable, it appears that the captives, as distinguished from the immigrants or the recruits from the tributary chiefs, suffered tremendous social disadvantages both on their arrival and in their old age. The Ndebele as well as the Shona, at this stage of their development, depended for their social security on the extended family. One example will suffice to illustrate the importance of the extended family. Ginyilitshe, who was born about 1868, and was himself a Zansi, says that his father, Sigojwana, died and left a widow with five children, including the informant himself. The widow took her children and went to live with her father Dlamlomo. When she married for the second time she did not have to bother about her five children, who remained with their grandfather.[37] Needless to say, the Hole who had been captured and therefore had completely been uprooted from their societies could never hope to enjoy such security. The trader who said that when the Hole became old and could not work for their masters they were either driven into the veld to die on their own or killed by the masters,[38] was grossly exaggerating the plight of these people. Yet this certainly was an indication of the insecurity of a people growing up in an alien society.

Moreover, however well the Ndebele might care for their captives, it cannot be doubted that the initial shocks suffered by captives involving the loss of their parents and family could be severe. Probably all the Hole in the Ndebele state were reminded now and again of their being second class citizens by some Ndebele laws discriminating against them, especially during the time of Mzilikazi. This is how the law operated with regard to capital crimes during this period:

> For instance, one of his slaves murdering a real Ilindebele would certainly be punished with death, – the former being a vassal, and the latter belonging to the aristocracy of the country. Should a real Ilindebele murder a slave, or an ilihole, homicide in this case would, most likely, be punished with the fine of a number of cattle to the king. But should one vassal kill another, then the punishment would be life for life.[39]

But these instances of legal discrimination were probably few in the life of an Hole man. In general, it is clear from the above account that the relations among the various ethnic groups were sufficiently amicable to permit cultural fusion.

It may be argued, however, that some of the Hole already described were brought into the Ndebele kingdom as youths and therefore could not be efficient transmitters of culture. Indeed, the account is not meant to give the impression that the incorporated youths 'Shonalised' the Ndebele, but to demonstrate the ambivalent attitudes of the conquerors to the vanquished and show how the state increased its receptivity to Shona influences through depending upon the Shona for its population expansion. Furthermore, a definite link with the Shona was formed by the army recruits that kept on visiting their Shona homelands. Moreover, it is conceivable that the incorporated Hole eased the social barrier that might have existed between the Zansi and Nhla on the one hand and the Shona polities within the area of Ndebele settlement.

It was not only the social and political forces that brought together the Zansi, the Nhla and the Shona. An equally binding force was trade. Although the Ndebele were pastoralists, they relied for their livelihood mainly on crop cultivation. But the area they chose for settlement suffered, and still suffers, from frequent droughts. It is also possible to have regional variations of rainfall in western Zimbabwe, so that in a single year parts of the country can be favoured with good rains while others receive none or very little. This peculiarity of the country therefore compelled its societies not only to trade for grain with the distant peoples, but also to barter for food among themselves.

The Kalanga, the Nyubi and Venda, being well acquainted with the climate and the soil of their country, far surpassed their conquerors in the production of grain. The Kalanga were reputed to be 'industrious and skilful . . ., in smelting, agriculture and even medicine'.[40] Their agricultural methods were described by E. A. Maund in 1886:

> The mealie gardens in the rich soil of these valleys produce good crops. Their method of cultivation is to cut down trees to within three feet of the ground or merely to strip the lower bark and so kill the trees. They thus obtain the necessary light; then with mattocks they raise the ground into ridge and furrow two feet high, and the same apart on the ridges they plant the corn.[41]

In fact the Shona showed this agricultural enterprise even when they were incorporated into the Ndebele nation. The areas dominated by the Amabukuthwani and Impande regiments – both predominantly Hole – were marked by extensive corn fields and agricultural prosperity; their people, moreover, were experimenting with new crops such as the potato.[42] Indeed, as one Rhodesian white official has observed: 'It is a known fact that the Amandebele admired the Mavenda and Manyubi, for their superior agricultural techniques which helped to fill the Ndebele grain bins.'[43] Thus in times of scarcity, both the Ndebele rulers and whites resident in the country depended for their food supplies on the original inhabitants of the country. Ndebele society also depended on the Shona for iron tools and weapons; its kings incorporated certain Shona chiefdoms into their state principally to produce iron for them. In short, the economic needs were just as powerful in bringing together the peoples of western Zimbabwe as the social and political factors.[44]

The social intermingling, economic interdependence and relatively orderly close political relationships of these peoples created above anything else a congenial situation propitious for the interaction of their different religious systems. All the western Zimbabwe societies had similar two-tiered cosmologies – a high god and lesser ancestral spirits. They also all believed in magic and in the power of diviners and medicine men. The differences, however, lay in the powers and functions each society assigned to either tier. The Shona peoples of western Zimbabwe had both ancestral and high-god (Mwari) cults, while the Zansi and the Nhla had only the former. As we shall see, perhaps the chief religious change in nineteenth-century western Zimbabwe was the acceptance of the Mwari cult by the two invading groups.

It is necessary to examine the different religious systems, particularly those of the Zansi and the Shona. The Nhla system will be brought in to show its similarities to the Zansi and to illustrate the openness of the latter to influences of the conquered peoples. The Zansi believed in a creator called *Nkulunkulu*. They thought of him as the first human being, who with his wife Mvelengangi emerged

> out of a marshy place where there were reeds, and found cattle and corn awaiting them in abundance. They lived together and children were born to them, and having brought them up, given them various laws, customs, habits and property, the old people went under the ground again, became snakes, and have remained there in snake-like forms ever afterwards.[45]

Although the Zansi, like their Nguni counterparts in the south, had some notion of the high deity being linked with the heavens, and a being particularly associated with the clouds, rain, thunder and lightning, as Professor Monica Wilson puts it, 'no rituals were celebrated for God, and he was not consistently distinguished from a first ancestor who dwelt beneath'.[46] Regarding the absence of a high-god cult among these people, one writer says: 'The old, old man of the Zulu myth, who made the earth and the people upon it, retired into impenetrable seclusion and well earned rest after he had finished his labours and has not been heard since'.[47] This, however, seems to be a rather extreme view of the distance of the high-god from the living and his inactivity in their daily life. The Zansi themselves, perhaps influenced by Christianity, Sotho-Tswana, and Shona religions, today insist that although the ancestral spirits, whom they worshipped directly, had power of their own, they chiefly acted as intercessors between the living and their high-god.[48] However, the most important point to be established is that the Zansi had no separate and institutionalised system of communicating directly with Nkulunkulu.

Religious activity of the Zansi, therefore, centred around the ancestral spirits called *amadlozi* and their cult was fully developed. The Zansi conceived of man as consisting of three aspects: the material and two spiritual beings. Right from birth to death a person lived with a spirit – almost the equivalent of his shadow (*isithunzi*) – which looked after him, and could bring good things or misfortune. This integral part of the person, but having extraordinary power, was also called an *idlozi* (spirit). Indeed, they spoke in terms of *idlozi lami* (my spirit) and *idlozi lake* (his spirit). The distinction between this type of spiritual power and the spirit that passed into the realm of ancestral spirits was frequently fine, and no useful purpose for the present work can be served by trying to analyse their separate identities. After all what appears to the modern mind as mysterious or unnatural, may well have not posed the same problem to the nineteenth-century Zansi.[49] Suffice it to say this third element of man was the equivalent, though not the exact copy of, the Christian soul.

When a person died his spirit, as in the Christian idea of the soul, lived after him. The exact dwellings of the spirit are somewhat difficult to establish. The myth of Nkulunkulu described above points out that his spirit and that of his wife went underground with them but later emerged and went into the bodies of snakes. The spirits of their descendants behaved in a similar manner. Although the Zansi believed in the transmigration and reincarnation of the spirits and actually showed a great deal of deference to the animals supposed to embody them, they also thought of them as having at once fixed and unfixed places of abode. The fixed abode was the graveyard, while their spiritual nature made them air-like enabling them at the same time to live with their descendants and guard them wherever they went.

The amadlozi were very powerful indeed and took an active interest in the welfare of their living families and descendants. They controlled the good fortunes and misfortunes of the living; they required of the latter to maintain proper relationships with them; they punished, sometimes mercilessly, wrong-doers and those who neglected them, and rewarded the good. They afforded a blanket protection over their surviving relatives against witches and other practitioners of harmful magic; but they could also, if neglected and not properly propitiated, expose them to such dangers.[50]

The Zansi amadlozi beliefs and practices coincided with social and political structures. Each lineage and family had its own amadlozi and the most senior living descendant of the lineage and head of the family acted as the high priest. But this set of spirits had parochial powers and interests, such as the health, the material prosperity and other familial or lineage successes. Only the amadlozi of the king exercised national guardianship. As one Zansi has portrayed their attributes and functions: 'They exercised protective influence and worked for the well-being of the whole nation. They commanded nation wide respect. The chief priest of the cult was the king himself.'[51]

The most important rites associated with family, as distinguished from the national, ancestral spirits were *ukuhlanziswa* (cleaning) and *ukubuyisa* (bringing home). When a person died, it was as if his death pervaded all his nearest living relatives, giving them a contagious effect, so that they could spread death to their neighbours or whoever they came in contact with, including their livestock. Thus it was necessary for the surviving relatives, soon after burying their dead, to call in a doctor to cleanse or purify them. In the meantime, the dead man's spirit would be roaming about homelessly. After a year or so it would manifest itself in several ways such as in the form of a snake or by inflicting sickness upon one of the living relatives, or through dreams. The people responded by carrying out the *umbuyiso* ceremony, during which the most senior surviving relative officiated and a cow or an ox was sacrificed. The 'priest' praised and prayed to the spirit as it was now an idlozi. The meat of the sacrificed animal was left overnight for the idlozi to partake of it. The following morning a feast was held for people to come and eat the meat and drink the beer brewed for the ceremony. People feasted not as guests of the living relatives, but of the spirit itself. At the conclusion of the umbuyiso the spirit joined other ancestors and became, like them, an object of worship.

There is no need to go into the details of the regular forms of individual, family or lineage ancestral worship. Suffice it to point out that a Zansi undertook no dangerous action without invoking or supplicating his amadlozi for protection, guidance, and luck together with the requisite strength demanded by the situation. Also when a man propitiated his ancestral spirits for his general welfare and prosperity he did it by sacrificing an ox or a goat. The animal was brought before his door and he presented it to his gods with a statement to the following effect:

O Our fathers, this is an ox which I consecrate unto you, in order that your heart may be white [you may be kind] towards us, that we may be permitted to walk the earth in good health and be prosperous, that the number of our cattle may largely increase, that our gardens may be fruitful, and that our enemies may fall before us.[52]

After this prayer the sacrificial procedure was the same as that of ukubuyisa.

At national level ancestral worship was essentially the same, except that the ceremonies assumed a grander scale and much more elaborate aspect. The most important festival was the *Inxwala* (wrongly translated into English as the Great Dance). It was the annual occasion during which the king prayed and sacrificed as many as sixty oxen to his amadlozi for national prosperity, welfare, and above all for victory against enemies. It was a religious festival, and not a war dance. But the king's amadlozi also acted as the providers of rain. Thus back in Zululand and in times of drought or other national disasters the kings conducted their rainmaking ceremonies at the royal graveyards. These were called *ukucela imvula emakhosini*.

But when the Zansi came to western Zimbabwe, they relied on the following approach to the amadlozi. A number of oxen were slaughtered, sweet-smelling plants and firewood collected, and a fire made by rubbing sticks together. The burning sweet-smelling plants gave an aromatic scent, which when mingled with the smell of cooking meat pleased the ancestor spirits – caused them to open up the clouds for rains. People feasted on the meat and danced joyously. Giving some corporeal presence of the amadlozi were the black oxen dedicated to them which were never killed. There were other minor ways of begging rain such as when the king asked the queens and other women to go and bury all the exposed bones in the bush. The second, the *ukugwabuli nxoza*, involved the sending out of chiefs and their men to go around the countryside knocking down the sticks, stones and other objects that the herdsmen may have left lodged among the branches of trees.[53]

Finally the Zansi believed in magic. Certain plants, parts of human and animal bodies were held to possess extraordinary powers. The izinyanga were able to employ these powers for good and for evil purposes. Both men and women practising evil magic were called *abathakathi* and were killed as soon as they were discovered. Witches also possessed *imikhobo* (ghosts) which they sent out to beat or frighten to death whoever they wanted. An *isanusi* (diviner) was employed to discover witches. The Zansi isanusi, unlike the Shona diviner, did not employ bones for his divination but used spirit possession and discovered the hidden causes by the *ukuvumisa* technique (asking leading questions from his enquirers). Frequently this belief was abused because people could, out of envy, jealousy or sheer hatred, accuse their fellow men of witchcraft in order to have them killed. Indeed King Lobengula, son and successor of Mzilikazi, used the belief for political ends. Furthermore, it was one of the chief weapons the Zansi used to frighten their fellow men from adopting Christianity, by accusing intending or actual converts of witchcraft.

There were features that rendered the Zansi religion open to penetrations. The fixed nature of Nguni sacred places or shrines in the form of graveyards meant that when the Zansi left Zululand an important part of their religion remained. It is, therefore, reasonable to assume that when the Ndebele kings and their followers performed Zansi rainmaking ceremonies in western Zimbabwe or, for that matter, in the Transvaal, they must have had a nagging feeling of the incompleteness and perhaps ineffectiveness of their way of approaching the ancestors. This may have had the effect of causing them to accept the secure and confident local cults. Secondly, the Zansi ukucela imvula emakhosini definitely had a high degree of success as long as the ceremonies were performed in Zululand. For the key to these practices was that the kings and their helpers had devoted much time to the study of clouds and other forecasts of the weather and had also been instructed in these matters by the old ones. All this body of knowledge and experience of Natal was inapplicable to the totally different climate of western Zimbabwe. Moreover, this part of southern Africa was notorious for its frequent droughts, so that the services of rainmakers were in constant demand. The novelty of the environment no doubt forced Mzilikazi and his advisers to rely upon the assistance of the local rainmakers.

In a very important respect, however, the ancestor worship of the Nhla-Sotho-Tswana was strikingly similar to the Zansi one. Both the Sotho and the Tswana believed in a high god, *Modimo*, who was more interested in the welfare of the people than Nkulunkulu. Nevertheless, the people believed that the chief's ancestral spirits were more actively interested in the welfare of their living subjects than Modimo. Professor Schapera, an authority on the Tswana way of life, tells us that: 'It was Modimo who sent rain, and the chief's role was essentially that of an intermediary seeking rain from him on behalf of the tribe.' But the deity, because of his distance from the people, 'could be approached only through the spirits of the dead (badimo); and the chief's task was to pray to his own ancestors, asking them to intercede with Modimo'. Indeed, Professor Schapera gives the impression that the Tswana believed in a rigid system of approaching the supernatural world, with the chief as the sole priest appointed to pray to his ancestors, who in turn interceded with god.[54] It is most likely that when some of these peoples were incorporated into the Ndebele state they simply substituted Mzilikazi and his ancestral spirits for their former chiefs and their ancestors. On the other hand it seems the Nhla were among the first people to influence Zansi thought, by making them believe in a more active high deity. In 1829 Mzilikazi discussed his religious beliefs with Robert Moffat, the Kuruman L.M.S. missionary, and mentioned that their name of God was *Molimo* (Modimo)[55] – a fact suggesting that even after six years of contact the Tswana were having an impact on Zansi religion. It may well be that these were the origins of the Ndebele theological view that the ancestors possessed no independent power of their own, but derived it from the Supreme Being Nkulunkulu or *Somandla* (another name for the same deity), with whom they interceded on behalf of the living.

Mzilikazi's conversation with his missionary visitor and friend, however, suggested a much more complicated process of conversion to the Sotho-Tswana religion than a simple acceptance of the deity. Moffat recorded that the king 'stated that he prayed to Molimo, but from what he said, it appeared that he prayed or spoke to the late *Machobane*, his father'.[56] Perhaps, with typical missionary prejudices concerning pre-Christian African beliefs and practices, Moffat may have misconstrued Mzilikazi's prayers as being directed to his father's idlozi instead of to the supreme god Molimo. Nevertheless Moffat's observation is suggestive of the fact that Mzilikazi must have been merely adopting the Tswana name Molimo for Nkulunkulu, who as we have seen was often indistinguishable from the first ancestor. In that case, the Zansi's apparent acceptance of Nhla beliefs may be interpreted as a process of activating Nkulunkulu. It would appear, therefore, that the Zansi were perhaps attempting to formulate a set of universalistic beliefs and perhaps moral principles hinged upon their high god Nkulunkulu to be used as a reference source in the conduct of their extensive relations with peoples of diverse religious backgrounds.[57]

The Shona, on the other hand, confronted the invaders with a highly developed cult of the supreme deity, Mwari, who had created the universe and everything in it and was governing it with his own laws. Nevertheless, he rarely concerned himself with the affairs of individuals choosing to concentrate upon national interests. He preferred to manifest himself in certain places in mountains through a voice which could be interpreted and communicated to the public only by his own specially appointed priests. These caves had by the time of Zansi-Nhla invasion developed into esoteric shrines, run by Venda, Rozvi and other Shona priestly families.

The organisational structure of the priest colonies of the shrines is only beginning to come to light. It is now clear that the office of the high priest of each shrine is hereditary and that apparently the succession system is a collateral one and also sometimes alternates between two families – a fact accounting for frequent succession disputes as well as for the proliferation of shrines in the Matopo area. The high priest, however, runs the shrine with the assistance of junior priests drawn from the various segments of his extended family. One of the most important positions in the priestly hierarchy is that held by the late high priest's wife. This widow sits in the cave and impersonates the voice of Mwari, and his inquirers are not supposed to know that she is the one speaking. So during consultations, the voice-impersonator goes into the cave; next to the mouth of the cave sit the eldest sister of the high priest and his wife (who perhaps may be in the process of being trained to succeed her mother-in-law); after them follow the male priests and finally the inquirers. The whole group sits facing east, where Mwari is supposed to have come from originally. The voice addresses people in archaic Rozvi, the language of the former Mambo rulers, and the priests translate the messages into Ndebele, Kalanga or Shona, depending on the language or dialect of the inquirers.

Below this inner circle of priests, however, is a huge number of *mbonga* (women) and *hosana* (men) who are dedicated to Mwari by their specially inspired parents. When these boys and girls are in the process of growing up they are subjected to a strict moral code regarding sex and life and to a number of taboos concerning foods. The mbonga girls keep the entrances of the shrines clean and raise crops in their gardens. The hosana boys are taught dancing, all in preparation for the festivals held in honour of Mwari. From time to time the hosana may be sent into the country with special messages and they are required to dance in every village they pass through. When the girls are ready to get married, Mwari gives them husbands, who may be either priests or ordinary men in the country. Both the mbonga and hosana are susceptible to two types of spirit possession. They can be possessed by the senior spirits of their home chiefdoms or by some of the numerous spirits of the shrine complex of Matopo (Matojeni). Many hosana become mediums of *Majukwa* – spirits believed to have directly emanated from Mwari himself. When the mbonga can no longer bear children they qualify to become brewers of beer for the annual Mwari ceremonies and become eligible for the office of impersonating the voice.

The Matojeni shrine complex is, however, linked to the various chiefdoms by *vanyai* or *manyusa* (messengers or intermediaries). These are chosen by the chiefs after receiving a special call from Mwari. How exactly this happens we still do not know. But their role is to carry requests and offerings from chiefdoms and to bring back answers or orders from Mwari. Through these messengers as well as through the hosana, Mwari maintains a firm hold on his adherents and can proselytise the unconverted.[58]

During the time of the Rozvi confederacy it seems that the Mwari cult was a sort of state religious system, closely associated with the Mambo rulers and perhaps having one of its chief shrines at the headquarters – Great Zimbabwe.[59] Near the fall of the confederacy a breach seems to have occurred between the ruling elite and the religious authorities. As already pointed out, one Mambo is supposed to have discarded his faith in Mwari, upon which the latter is reported to have said:

> You have doubted me, you have flouted me before your people. You have shut ears and heart against my call, you have hunted me from place to place. I am therefore leaving you never to return; and my voice will no more be heard in the land, but instead of my voice will come my warriors [Nguni] wearing skins, and you will learn too late that Mwali has a spear.[60]

As we shall see later, similar messages are said to have been delivered to Lobengula during the scramble for Ndebeleland, when Mwari identified himself with the Christian God and viewed the white invaders as his sons come to punish the Ndebele king for his raiding activities.

The above tradition, as well as similar ones to come, has to be interpreted in the context of the need of Mwari's intellectual philosophers, the priests, to preserve their cult from being smothered by invading cults. For the Mwari priests, a situation was then impending in which their cult would be only one of many – with all of them carrying out the same functions as itself. In the coming plurality of cults the god or set of gods to win the struggle for primacy would be not the one associated with centrilocal interests and functions, but a universalistic deity – a father of mankind and not of the Rozvi Shona or Zansi. In short, the Mwari priests may have been abandoning parochial, Rozvi or Shona centred attitudes and sentiments and perhaps elaborating the responsibilities of their high god to include the invading groups. In the event the, cult, with its redefined high god, with its highly organised system of priesthood and its incredibly efficient rainmaking rituals, gradually gained an influential position in western Zimbabwe in the nineteenth century.

It now appears, however, that when the Zansi and the Nhla invaded Zimbabwe Mwari sent out his junior priests, the manyusa or vanyai and the hosana to tell the invaders about Mwari and his powers. The message was to the effect that Mwari controlled rain and that, if propitiated with black oxen, tobacco and other useful articles, he would cause a downpour even if there was drought.[61] More miraculous powers of the god were preached about:

that he lived in a huge mountain where stones were always crashing together and trees always waving without wind, that he could kill a man without visible cause and could make that which a man held in hand pass away without knowing it.[62]

Although the Zansi king Mzilikazi seems to have immediately grasped the importance of the cult's priesthood as an intelligence system in his raiding activities on Shona peoples, it apparently took some time for him to believe in it, and he was said to have at one time persecuted the hosana.[63]

Yet by 1859, when missionaries arrived, the belief in Mwari was growing rapidly in the Ndebele kingdom. The hosana were roaming around the country and were regarded with considerable awe. One of the missionaries who came to the country in 1859 described, perhaps with some exaggeration, the hosana's activities and how they were treated by the villagers:

In order to increase his Mwari's influence and the people's awe of him, he has trained up his sons and other relatives, and sent them forth into various parts of the land to dance and feast. They are also said to be rain-doctors. One of these young men, covered all over with ornaments, which consist of buttons, beads, bangles, shells, and various kinds of charms, entering into a village or town, so overawes and allures the inhabitants, that they are soon entirely in his power. That his favour may be secured, presents are heaped upon him, while he in turn, finding that he has become the real lord of the place, does as he likes, – commands, orders, sends, or calls whomsoever he pleases, and even eats their food without scruple. A night dance and feasting complete the entertainment and the visit.[64]

Furthermore, those who went to consult Mwari were approaching the sacred shrines with proper reverence, taking care not to violate the rules and regulations hedging their sanctity.[65]

It is important to understand how the Zansi and the Nhla were adopting the local beliefs and practices. The Mwari cult did not supplant Zansi and Nhla ancestor worship and systems of divination; but it became a superstructural layer. Moreover, no rigid division of functions was established between the cults, so that Mwari was consulted as an additional means of divination and as a bringer of rain. Thanksgiving offerings were made annually by both Mzilikazi and Lobengula to both the Zansi amadlozi during the Inxwala ceremony and Mwari at the shrines.

Thus, when there was a drought Mzilikazi first prayed for rain to the amadlozi. When these failed, he would summon the Mwari priests to come and perform the *mutoro* (rainmaking) ceremony. These priests would make a huge fire with various kinds of plants to produce thick billows of smoke in order to charm the clouds. The treating of the sky was accompanied by the blowing of *wamada* (horn trumpets). The doctors never failed to bring down the rain mainly because of 'their accurate acquaintance with signs of the season; so that they will seldom venture to commence their course of cloud-treating until they are pretty certain rain is not far off'.[66] It is interesting to note that the rainmaking ceremonial procedure was a mixture of Zansi and Shona – the charming of the clouds with billows of smoke, as we have seen, was the Zansi way of pleasing the amadlozi with aromatic smoke. Like Christianity, which in western Europe was forced 'to absorb and assimilate' some surviving beliefs and practices,[67] the Mwari cult was incorporating some of the Zansi ways of approaching the supernatural world.

Shona and Venda penetration of Zansi and Nhla religion was also manifested in the role and increase of Hole doctors. In 1854 Mzilikazi himself employed Hole doctors who were treating him for dropsy. It is also said that the *izinyanga zemizi* (village medicine men) who were found in every town or village and knew much about the medicinal properties of wild animals and plants were nearly always Shona.[68] These professionals, who divined by means of throwing bones either to discover witches or causes of illness and its possible cure, charged fees for their work, yet they sometimes presented an exasperating challenge to the missionaries, who tried to outdo them by giving their medical advice and treatments free.[69] By the latter part of the nineteenth century Hole doctors had become so numerous in the Ndebele state that one missionary declared that he hardly saw one of these people who was not an *inyanga*.[70] It was, in fact, through their being among the prominent medicine men of the Ndebele kings that the Malaba family of the Obodo community in the Plumtree district acquired their chieftainship. Their oral tradition states that they were Venda of the northern Transvaal and migrated as a small family to western Zimbabwe in the nineteenth century under the leadership of one Mpangala. Mpangala soon found favour with the Ndebele king upon being discovered to be a proficient *nganga*. He was not only employed in this trade at court, but he was also given a portion of the country to rule.[71] The Venda-Shona diviners, of course, did not supplant the izanusi, but operated side by side with them.

Thus it is clear that the Zansi and the Nhla established fairly peaceful socio-economic and political relations with the local Shona peoples. The atmosphere they created was conducive to an exchange of cultural ideas and institutions, manifested particularly in the religious sphere. The form of religious interaction was one of mixing in which no one cult acquired primacy and with no clear division of functions between the two dominant cults. The aim of the following two chapters will be to show the continued mixing or amalgamating process and to examine the reactions and responses of the people involved in the process to missionaries.

Notes

1. W. F. Lye, 'The Ndebele Kingdom South of the Limpopo River', *Journal of African History* (*J.A.H.*), x, 1969, pp. 96–7
2. See A. J. B. Hughes, *Kin, Caste and Nation Among the Ndebele of Rhodesia*, Manchester, 1955, p. 7; this is also the opinion of some Ndebele traditionalists: see Mhlagazanhlansi (pseudonym of Neville Jones), *My Friend Khumalo*, Bulawayo, 1947, p. 10
3. L. H. Gann, *A History of Southern Rhodesia: Early Days to 1934*, London, 1965, p. 188
4. G. E. Oates (ed.), *Matabele and the Victoria Falls*, London, 1898, pp. 151–2; Alexander C. Bailie in 1876 said that it had taken twenty years to conquer the Shona they were then ruling: C.2220, A. C. Bailie to Administrator, 31 Dec. 1876, p. 56
5. A. Boggie, *From Ox-Wagon to Railway*, Bulawayo, 1897, pp. 7–8; W. Rayner, *The Tribe and its Successors: An Account of African Traditional Life and European Settlement in Southern Rhodesia*, London, 1962, pp. 32–4
6. The best account of the Nguni-Shona clashes is by D. N. Beach, 'The Rising in South-Western Mashonaland, 1896–7', unpublished Ph.D. thesis, London, 1971, pp. 115–19; his 'Ndebele Raiders and Shona Power', *J.A.H.*, xv, 1974, pp. 633–51; see also T. O. Ranger, *Revolt in Southern Rhodesia 1896–7*, London, 1967; A. W. Elliott, *Gold From the Quartz*, London 1910, p. 20
7. Elliott, *Gold*, p. 23
8. Beach, thesis, pp. 58–70; Ranger, *Revolt*, pp. 13–16; F. T. Posselt, *Fact and Fiction*, Bulawayo, 1935, pp. 147–50; H. N. Hemans, 'History of the Abenanzwa Tribe', *Rhodesia Science Association*, xii, 1912, pp. 85–112
9. Beach, thesis, p. 117
10. *Ibid.*, p. 118; Thomas Morgan Thomas, *Eleven Years in Central South Africa*, London, 1873, p. 340; J. P. R. Wallis (ed.), *The South African Diaries of Thomas Leask 1865–1870*, London, 1945, p. 102
11. R.N.A. NB6/1/1, S.N.J. (Belingwe N.C.) Report, 31 Dec. 1898
12. Beach, thesis, p. 126; Delineation Report on The Malisa Chieftaincy: Silombela T.T.L. Que Que District, 4 Aug. 1963, p. 1; Report on the Kanda Community: Chief Lukuluba: Silombela T.T.L. Que Que District, 14 Aug. 1963, p. 4
13. Delineation Report on the Mathe Bafana Chieftainship: Matopo T.T.L. Essexvale District, 27 Feb. 1964
14. C.8547, p. 34; James Chapman, *Travels in the Interior of South Africa*, 2 vols., London, 1868, ii, pp. 252–3; Delineation Report on Mpini Chieftainship: Nata T.T.L. Plumtree District, April 1965, pp. 27–64
15. David Livingstone, *Missionary Travels and Researches in South Africa*, London, 1858, pp. 73–6, 443; Chapman, pp. 98–107, 180–3, 186; *The Zambesi Mission Record*, iv, 1910, pp. 35–9
16. Delineation Report on the Mbetshi Community: Chief Mathe Bafana: Matopo T.T.L. Essexvale District, 27 Feb. 1964, pp. 1–2
17. R.N.A. NB6/1/1, Jackson's Report, 31 Dec. 1898; C.8130, p. 9

18. Lye, p. 90
19. R.N.A. WI8/1/1, statement by Nkani
20. See for instance C.5918, p. 125; Thomas, p. 249
21. This paragraph is based in part on conversations with informants after each main recorded interview
22. Interview with Tshabangu, 17 June 1971
23. Interview with the wife of Machina Ndiweni, 14 June 1971
24. R.N.A. FR2/2/1, reminiscences of Ivon Fry
25. C.5918, p. 123
26. R.N.A. WI8/1, statement by Ginyilitshe; Edward Tabler, *The Far Interior*, Cape Town, 1955, p. 108
27. *The Missionary Magazine and Chronicle*, xxviii, 1864, p. 284
28. J. P. R. Wallis (ed.), *Matabele Journals of Robert Moffat*, 2 vols., London, 1945, ii, pp. 230, 250, 269, 371
29. R.N.A. FR2/2/1, reminiscences of Ivon Fry
30. Wallis, *Matabele Journals*, p. 369
31. *The Zambesi Mission Record*, iv, 47, 1910, p. 39
32. R.N.A. BE2/1/1, C. Knothe, Diary of a Journey to Bonyai, entry for 24 July 1888
33. *The London Missionary Magazine and Chronicle*, xxviii, 1864, p. 283
34. J. Mackenzie, *Ten Years North of the Orange River*, Edinburgh, 1871, pp. 327–9; Oates, p. 153
35. E.g. Dagamela Ncube of Babambeni, Sindisi Mpofu of Impande, Nkatiwo Sibanda of Mbuyazwe, Uwini and Lozani
36. Interview with Tshabangu
37. R.N.A. WI8/1, statement by Ginyilitshe
38. Frank Mandy, 'Matabeleland: The Future Gold Fields of the World. Its People and Resources', 1891, *Rhodesia Pamphlets*, i, 1, pp. 20–1
39. Thomas, pp. 248–9
40. J. P. R. Wallis (ed.), *The Matabele Mission of J. S. and E. Moffat 1858–78*, London, 1945, p. 206; Elliott, *Gold*, p. 23
41. C.4643, p. 110; see also R. Moffat, 'A Visit to Moselekatse's country, King of the Matabele', *Royal Geographical Society Journal*, xxvi, 1859, p. 91
42. C.4643, pp. 110–1; Mandy, p. 27
43. Delineation Report on the Mathe Bafana Chieftainship: Matopo T.T.L. Essexvale District, 27 Feb. 1964, p. 2
44. N. M. Bhebe, 'Ndebele Trade in the Nineteenth Century', *Journal of African Studies* (U.C.L.A.), i, 1974
45. Thomas, p. 281
46. M. Wilson, *Religion and the Transformation of Society: A Study in Social Change in Africa*, Cambridge, 1971, pp. 32–3
47. P. Nielsen, *The Matabele at Home*, Bulawayo, 1913, p. 36; see also E. J. Krige, *The Social System of the Zulus*, Pietermaritzburg, 1950, pp. 280–1
48. Mhlagazanhlansi, *My Friend Khumalo*, p. 32
49. See Emile Durkheim, *The Elementary Forms of the Religious Life*, trans. J. W. Swain, New York, 1965, pp. 39–43.
50. Cf. *Worker and Workers*, Oct. 1896, p. 422; Krige, p. 284; for a succinct mention of the indeterminate abode and nature of the 'soul' in the early

stages of the development of religions, see Max Weber, *The Sociology of Religion*, 4th ed., Boston, 1963, p. 5
51. Mhlagazanhlansi, *My Friend Khumalo*
52. *The London Missionary Magazine and Chronicle*, xxviii, 1864, p. 284
53. See, for instance, Mhlagazanhlansi, *My Friend Khumalo*, pp. 32–3; Thomas, p. 275
54. I. Schapera, *Rainmaking Rites of the Tswana Tribes*, London, 1971, pp. 17–19
55. Wallis, *Matabele Journals*, i, p. 16
56. *Ibid.*
57. For a much more elaborate discussion of this type of conversion, see R. Horton, 'African Conversion', *Africa*, xli, 1971, pp. 101–7
58. Literature on the Mwari cult is extensive: see N. M. B. Bhebe, 'A Critical Review of Our Knowledge of the Mwari Cult', University of Rhodesia, Henderson Seminar, 22, 1973; R. Mwanza, 'Mwari, the God of the Karanga', Lusaka Conference, 1972; J. M. Schoffeleers, 'An Organizational Model of the Mwari Shrines', paper presented to University of Rhodesia, Faculty of Social Studies, 1973; M. I. Daneel, *The God of the Matopo Hills*, The Hague, 1970; Ranger, *Revolt*; H. von Sicard, 'Die Initiation in Mono-mutapa-Reich', *Ethnos* (Stockholm), vi, 1941, pp. 42–7; 'Karangemas Maniskouppfatting', *Svensk Missionstidskrif* (Uppsala), xl, 1952, pp. 84–92; 'Mwari, der Hochgott der Karanga', *Kolomane Volkerkunde* (Viener Bei-trage Zur Kulturgeschichte und Linguistik. Herunsgeg. vo. H. Bauman), i, 1944, pp. 133–91.
59. R. Summers, *Zimbabwe: A Rhodesian Mystery*, Johannesburg, 1963, pp. 101–2; D. P. Abraham, 'The Roles of "Chaminuka" and the Mhondoro-cults in Shona Political History' in E. Stokes and R. Brown (eds.), *The Zambesian Past*, Manchester, 1965, pp. 28–46.
60. Elliott, *Gold*, p. 21
61. Interviews with the wife of Machina Ndiweni, Tshabangu, Khumalo, 1971; D. G. Lewis, 'Molimo', *Nada*, 1934, p. 84
62. J. P. R. Wallis (ed.), *The Northern Gold Field Diaries of Thomas Baines*, 3 vols., London, 1946, i, p. 251
63. J. P. Richards, 'The Mlimo Belief and Practice of the Kalanga', *Nada*, 1942, p. 54; Thomas, p. 277
64. Thomas, pp. 288–9
65. *Ibid.*, pp. 289–90
66. *Ibid.*, p. 276
67. Durkheim, p. 51
68. Mhlagazanhlansi, *My Friend Khumalo*, p. 22
69. R.N.A. MISC/SY1/1/1, W. E. Sykes, Journal 1887–9, p. 10; L.M.S. B1/F2/JD, W. A. Elliott to For. Sec., 7 Oct. 1884; *The Diamond Fields Advertiser*, 27 May 1889
70. L. M. S. B1/F3/JB, Joseph Cockin to For. Sec., May 1879
71. Delineation Report: The Madimabi Community under Tshitshi, 1965, p. 55

2

The Ndebele and the first missionaries, 1859–68

Both secular factors and traditional religion determined Ndebele reactions and attitudes towards the first missionaries. Indeed in 1857 Mzilikazi consented to the coming of the London missionaries purely for non-religious reasons. He hoped to use the missionaries as trading agents with white South Africa; the settlement of L.M.S. missionaries in his country might also draw nearer than ever before his personal friend Robert Moffat of the Kuruman mission station; the Ndebele might further exploit missionary technical skills in the mending and repairing of their firearms which they were buying in increasing quantities from white traders especially from 1860 onwards. But the settlement of the L.M.S. missionaries in the country in 1859 also raised serious political problems. Just before the arrival of the *abafundisi* (missionaries) Mzilikazi had instituted investigations regarding their background, their connections with the Boers and their teachings among the Tswana, especially among the Tlaping of Mahura and the Kwena of Setshele, both of which had had long contacts with L.M.S. missionaries. The results of these intelligence activities had not assuaged Ndebele fears of jeopardising their security by having whites living among them. Mahura in particular not only warned the Ndebele about the way missionary teaching conflicted with African ways of life but he further stressed that the white teachers were the precursors of the aggressive Boers; wherever the former went the latter were sure to follow and conquer. An Ndebele investigator had also gathered bad impressions about missionaries through his dealings with Setshele, chief of the Kwena and first convert of the famous missionary-cum-explorer, David Livingstone. Setshele, a professing Christian and preacher, condemned warfare and yet he himself engaged in military campaigns against his northern neighbours, the Ngwato. The Ndebele investigator discovered that Setshele never practised what he taught. In short, the Ndebele concluded, anything they said must be taken with a grain of salt.

Although these non-religious problems and many others exercised decisive influence in the Ndebele initial reactions to missionary intrusion, once the L.M.S. abafundisi settled at their first mission station, Inyati, and began to have regular contacts with the people most of the Ndebele political suspicions were eroded away. Diehard opponents of the missionaries were of course there throughout the nineteenth century. They mostly acted through the traditional religious system, which remained one of the chief obstacles to Ndebele acceptance of Christianity right up to the early twentieth century.

The traditional religious influence upon Ndebele reaction to the missionary presence was evident as early as September 1859, when Robert Moffat led the first group of missionaries into the country. On approaching Ndebeleland, the missionaries observed signs and symptoms of lungsickness among their draught oxen and immediately reported these to Mzilikazi. The king not only ordered the quarantining of the diseased animals, but also arranged for the medical treatment of the missionaries themselves. An inyanga cleansed them and their possessions by sprinkling them with medicines soaked in water.[1] Apparently the missionaries were ignorant of the whole significance of the cleansing ritual. One of them, William Sykes, had lost his wife at Kuruman and this was known to the Ndebele. To the Ndebele Sykes was carrying on his person the evil and contagious force of death which was already affecting the draught oxen and should he be allowed to come into the country untreated he might affect the whole nation together with all their livestock. During and after such a treatment, the bereaved person as well as his surviving relatives were supposed to stay away from the rest of society. In fact for almost three months Mzilikazi and his people treated their missionary guests as outcasts, refusing even to show them a place for settlement.

While the missionaries were still living in virtual quarantine, an incident occurred which to the missionaries was unworthy of any attention, but to the Ndebele was a grave act of witchcraft. A servant of the missionaries called Goliat grabbed an Ndebele boy by the hair – which was tantamount to bewitching the young man. The furious Mzilikazi went to the place where the missionaries were camping and tried the supposed evil practitioner in their presence. The missionaries admitted that the king could have imposed a severer penalty on Goliat had Robert Moffat not pleaded for mercy on his behalf. Even then the king impressed upon the minds of the apparently ignorant missionaries the gravity of the crime, and they were forced to try to appease him with a present.[2] Moreover, in taking this case so seriously the king may well have been intent upon making it clear to the newly arrived whites that if they wanted to live in Ndebeleland they should respect local religious systems.

Another early example of the way religion regulated Ndebele attitudes towards the missionaries occurred in late November 1859. This was the time for the Ndebele nation to prepare for their annual worship of the king's amadlozi. The national Inxwala assembly was preceded by the *mtontiso* rituals, during which the king was smeared with *intunga* (milk-cream) mixed with medicines by his inyanga, a process intended to render the king fierce and prosperous. It was *kwakuzila* (sacrilege) for anyone to engage in the normal daily activities during the mtontiso week, so that it was a national holiday. Thus even though the missionaries were running short of food and wanted to supplement their stores by hunting and fishing, they were banned from moving about the country.[3]

The religious clash between the missionaries and Ndebele became increasingly apparent when the former started preaching in the country. The problem was exacerbated by the diehard opponents of the missionaries, who, particularly between 1860 and 1862, became vigilant for any misfortunes befalling the nation and were ready to blame them on the presence of *amakhiwa* (Europeans). The missionaries, on the other hand, undermined their chances of gaining influence in the country by refusing to trade for the king. By June 1860 Mzilikazi was so disillusioned with the missionaries that he had lost his initial interest in their work. Up to that time he had taken the initiative to gather up people at his place for the missionaries to preach to, had supplied interpreters and attended the missionary services in person. The favourable behaviour of the king had indeed been greeted with general optimism by the missionaries.[4]

But the serious clash between Ndebele religious beliefs and Christianity as well as Mzilikazi's disappointment with the missionaries began to manifest itself in July 1860, barely a month after the departure of Robert Moffat, former leader of the young mission and personal friend of the king. On 15 July, John Smith Moffat, the son of Robert Moffat and one of the missionaries, preached about the equality of all men – regardless of age, sex, and position in society – before God. The king displayed his strong dissension from the sermon by suddenly flaring up in rage, ordering the interpreter to stop 'telling the people such stuff and lies'.[5] The following Sabbath Mzilikazi ordered the congregation to sit well away from the missionary preacher so that they could hardly hear the sermon.[6] The king's attitude terrified the missionaries to the extent that they began to talk of some 'approaching persecution'. At the same time the king desisted from attending the services and even abandoned his observance of the 'sacred day', arguing that 'it was the teachers' Sabbath' and not his.[7] A few months later he decided to go and live away from the missionaries.[8]

The king's anger with the missionaries was no doubt prompted by religious conflict and by unsatisfied material cravings. Mzilikazi may have taken fright at the missionary propaganda which, with its implied egalitarianism, challenged directly his supreme religious and political position in Ndebele society. There was indeed a genuine clash between, on the one hand, the Ndebele conception of the relationship of the living with the supernatural world which emphasised seniority and status in the intercession with the amadlozi, and on the other the Christian view that held anyone as having direct access to God through prayers and sacraments. Even in the case of the Mwari cult, which the Ndebele were adopting, only the chosen priestly hierarchy running the places of Mwari's manifestation interceded with the unseen deity on behalf of the community.

These religious misunderstandings were aggravated by a series of disasters that befell the Ndebele nation during the first two years of missionary settlement in the country. In July 1861 the long dreaded lungsickness made its appearance among J. S. Moffat's cattle. This disease had first broken out in Cape Colony and had gradually spread throughout South Africa. It had caused considerable poverty among the blacks and the whites; some black tribes had been stripped of all their livestock. 'If the visitation plays the same havoc that it has done elsewhere,' Moffat apprehended, 'it is impossible to speculate the results, for as you know, cattle are the great end of life in this country.'[9]

Moffat's fears did not take long to be realised. The disease broke out among Mzilikazi's cattle in the months of September to December and immediately began to kill them by hundreds. There was every prospect that it would 'make a frightful sweep in a few years'.[10] By January the death rate of the cattle had not abated at all.[11] The herds must have been enormous during these years; in the neighbourhood of the Inyati mission station alone there were no less than 100,000 cattle.[12]

Perhaps surprisingly, the Ndebele did not at first associate the disease with the coming of the missionaries. The king took the spread of the epidemic to his country as inevitable. Some people regarded the disease as supplying them with abundant beef which they might not have got under normal circumstances. In general people found no cause for alarm, believing that the king would sooner or later drive out the disease with magic. Apparently the izinyanga, who incidentally enjoyed the reputation of possessing 'a surprising knowledge of cattle remedies',[13] were employed in large numbers to prepare the appropriate medicines to fight the lung-sickness, but with little success.[14]

By July 1862 the missionaries were estimating that well over 10,000 cattle had perished during the previous ten months. Anger was fast mounting among the Ndebele against the rate at which the disease was taking toll of their cattle. The anger began to be directed against 'the presence of the Makiwa (white people)', especially against the missionary settlers.[15] The people knew that the disease had come with the traders, but somehow they 'wished to retaliate upon us [missionaries] the wrong done them by traders'.[16] Moreover it became common talk that the people were urging the king to expel the abafundisi or to persecute them; and the white teachers themselves were greatly disturbed by these threats. But Mzilikazi resisted these demands, arguing that the disaster brought about by the traders could not justifiably be revenged upon the missionaries.[17] Nevertheless, the following two lines from a poem sung at the time revealed how the missionaries and the epidemic had become linked in Ndebele minds:

> Umoya lo u vela 'pi na?
> Uvela gwo Mtshete enkulumana.
> (This wind whence comes it?
> From Moffat from Kuruman.)[18]

Clearly, then, the epidemic was blamed by many on the abafundisi.

Nor was the lungsickness the only disaster that befell the Ndebele in the years 1860 to 1862. Famine raged in the country for two years; and by 1862 the Ndebele had fallen into despondency. Although western Zimbabwe was, and still is, notorious for its frequent long periods without rain, the people were declaring that 'they have *never* known such seasons as the last three have been'.[19] On 5 October Loziba, the favourite wife of Mzilikazi, and *Unina weNyati* (the Royal Mother of the Inyati town) died of rheumatic fever.[20] Then smallpox spread from Botswana into Ndebeleland and crossed the Zambesi by December 1862.[21] Finally, there was the usual *ikwindla* (fever characterised by severe diarrhoea), which often attacked people in the months of the first fruits. In 1860 the Ndebele complained that this too had been unusually severe, although Robert Moffat could not find much evidence to support their claim.[22] The people seemed to blame all these disasters on the missionaries.

It is important to examine just how the Ndebele associated these misfortunes with the abafundisi resident in the country. Although the people often regarded reading and writing as part and parcel of the *amasalamusi abelungu* (miracles of the whites),[23] it is very doubtful whether they seriously attributed any witchcraft to the amakiwa. But there were two ways, one logical and the other purely religious, in which the missionaries could be linked with the successive catastrophes. First, the people observed that the lungsickness and the smallpox came to their country from the same direction as the abafundisi had come, and also not long after their settlement in the country. Therefore, it was easy to conclude that they had brought the epidemics. When the missionaries tried to argue that the lungsickness had come with black or Boer traders from the Cape, the Ndebele retorted that there was no distinction between the Boers and the missionaries. They also pointed out that the African traders came from Kuruman, the home of the Christian teachers.[24]

Moreover, the lungsickness, smallpox, droughts, fever and the death of Loziba were bundled together and attributed to the presence of the amakiwa, in a religious way. It has already been shown how the Ndebele believed that the amadlozi had power over their lives. Fortunes or misfortunes manifested the pleasure or displeasure of the amadlozi. The ire of the ancestral spirits could be aroused by a person or a group of people, foreign or indigenous, not conforming to the requirements of the proper relationship between the living and the dead. The missionaries not only committed a gross omission by not coming to terms with the *amadlozi ka-Mzilikazi* and the *Vene vevu* (Mwari),[25] but also sometimes acted in flagrant violation and contemptuous disregard of the vital Ndebele customs.

Two examples will suffice to illustrate the point. In 1860 the king ordered Loziba to conduct a parochial rainmaking ceremony. She was supposed to lead the women of Inyati to the mountains to bury all the exposed human skeletons and other remains, as these were believed to hold away the rain. A day for the ceremony was fixed and declared sacred, and no one was supposed to work. Thomas, however, disregarded the order and worked in his garden, contemptuously dismissing the whole affair as 'meaningless traditions and dreams'.[26]

The second episode came when Mrs Thomas and her child died on 10 and 12 June 1862 respectively. Among the Ndebele, as we have seen, when a person died the living relatives were required to retire into seclusion for *ukuyahlanziswa yinyanga* (cleansing by a doctor), for it was feared that the livestock at every place these relatives went, and the people they mixed with, would die, or some other calamity would overtake them. But again Thomas refused to comply; and the people were said to be 'highly indignant . . . that Mr Thomas does not conform to their heathen custom'.[27] Clearly then for a people who held that their happiness and prosperity depended on the proper relationship with the amadlozi and upon the observance of the customs governing the relationship, it is not difficult to see how they connected the natural calamities with the presence of the missionary settlers.

The Ndebele anti-missionary feeling perhaps reached its climax in 1862 when they put strong pressure on their king to reject the L.M.S. application for the accession of yet another missionary, and further successfully intrigued to kill Manqeba. The king told J. S. Moffat that if an additional missionary dared to come into the country the people would murder him. He also confessed himself as being subject to strictures upon admitting foreigners into the country, who had brought about the destruction of their cattle. He left no doubt that the aliens in question were the missionaries; the Ndebele claimed not to mind about commercial people who came and went.[28]

It was in May or July 1862 that the missionaries suffered another blow against their cause, in the form of the execution of Manqeba, their most influential ally, as well as Siama, one of their interpreters. Manqeba was a staunch supporter of the idea of opening up the kingdom to missionary enterprise. He seems to have been influenced in his modern ideas by his long-standing record of association with the Gospel. There was a story that the first person to acquaint the Ndebele with Christianity was Mtshete (Robert Moffat). It was later preached by Setshele, the then famous teacher and chief of the Kwena. After the evangelist-chief's departure, Mzilikazi, bent on keeping alive the new religion, appointed Manqeba chaplain, 'his recommendation being that he knew more about the white people than anyone else'.[29] Whatever the validity of the story, it shows that he was a well known and strong supporter of the aba-fundisi.

As soon as the missionaries had settled down, Manqeba is reported to have outdistanced his countrymen in mixing with the teachers and emulating their way of life. He took the lead in giving up going to the izinyanga, preferring western medical attention given by the missionaries, and in gathering up every piece of cloth he came across to clothe himself like the whites. By 1861 he could rarely be seen visiting his missionary friends except when dressed in clean clothes and riding on a horse. The missionaries reciprocated his favourable disposition by taking a keen interest in him and giving him gifts.[30] He was moreover a favourite member of the *Mpakhati* of Mzilikazi, who lavished on him gifts of horses, clothes, guns, beads, and many other western valuables.

Manqeba's fate was similar to that of Lotshe Hlabangana, who paid dearly with his life for showing interest in the people of the West two and a half decades later. While it is possible to say that Lotshe appeared friendly to the whites because he wanted to save his nation from being violently overrun during the scramble and to see some of the inhuman practices, such as witch-hunting, abolished, it is difficult to know why Manqeba showed such an interest in the missionaries to the extent that he was prepared to die for his friendship with them. Perhaps the story of his early association with the Christian religion was not a myth, so that both Setshele and Robert Moffat had convinced him that the survival of his people lay not in the rejection but in the embracing of the Western way of life.[31]

In any case, Manqeba's behaviour created many enemies for him, particularly among other indunas, who started to make slanderous remarks in the hearing of the king to undermine his most favoured position in the royal circle. Manqeba's enemies alleged that he wanted to usurp the kingship and that he made love with the *amankosikazi* (queens), both of which allegations the king dismissed apparently as being unlikely to be committed by his trusted induna. But when the king fell ill, Manqeba's conspirators came forward with more success. They alleged that Manqeba had slaughtered a crocodile in the Bembesi river, extracted its liver, mixed it with magic, and with the concoction tried to poison his majesty. At this point Mzilikazi consented to the killing of his favourite adviser, Manqeba. With him were killed his brother, Siama, and four leading men of his town, including most of his followers.[32]

Between 1860 and 1862, therefore, the L.M.S. totally failed to take root in Ndebeleland. In the first place, they refused to satisfy the Ndebele's material aspirations, arguing that Christianity must be accepted by the people on its own merits without any bribery. This deprived the missionaries of one of the easiest ways of gaining the confidence of the Ndebele. In fact this attitude of the L.M.S. embarrassed their local supporters who might have argued that the coming of the abafundisi would bring in its train material benefits. Moreover the settlement of the missionaries coincided with a series of calamities, which were seized upon by the anti-missionary element and interpreted as manifesting the displeasure of the amadlozi to the policy of accepting white foreigners into the country. The missionaries lent themselves to this by opposing Ndebele religious practices. The execution of Manqeba marked the zenith of Ndebele anti-missionary feeling, but the incident also showed exactly how that society was capable of eliminating Christian-influenced people without necessarily accusing them of apostasy.

It would indeed be misleading to give the impression that the Ndebele withdrew themselves behind a wall of anti-missionary bitterness which was totally impenetrable to the missionaries in the period 1860 to 1868. To some extent the abafundisi managed to retain links with the people and to impart their propaganda, although they dismally failed to realise any conversions.

They endeavoured to convert the Ndebele by the usual and obvious means of preaching. In early 1860, the king was willing to 'do all in his power to assist' the teachers in their 'great work'.[33] He took the initiative to call up people to gather in the Inyati cattle kraal or the *isigodlo* (the queens' residential section of the town) for service every Sunday. The impression gathered from the correspondence of the missionaries is that the congregations were large. But when the king eventually disagreed with the missionaries and removed from Inyati, the number of people going to church fell precipitously. Between July and December 1861, the regular service attendance did not exceed ten.[34]

The missionaries naturally thought of compensating for their losses at Inyati by going to preach in two other towns. This plan was started by Thomas, a man of distinguished industry, who, as early as October 1860, had already begun to preach in Ndebele and was contemplating translating the 'Life of Jesus' into that language.[35] One of these towns was four miles to the east, and the second was six miles to the south, of Inyati. The assiduous Thomas addressed the people of the first village on Wednesdays and of the second on Fridays, and he found his listeners eager to hear the Gospel.[36]

In 1862 the number of towns at which the missionaries preached remained at three; the average attendance at the newly opened places was between ten and thirty. The people were still showing a 'wish to be instructed and to understand'.[37] The average attendance at Inyati on the other hand had in the same year risen from ten to about eighteen to twenty.[38]

In 1863, however, they increased the preaching places from three to four, so that their field of operation now covered a total population of seven hundred, but the average weekly congregation was between one hundred and one hundred and fifty.[39] It would appear that the missionaries did not increase the number of towns where they preached beyond four until 1868. Apparently the reason was that J. S. Moffat went away in 1865, leaving only Thomas and Sykes to continue the work; an area with more than four centres of population settlement would have been too large for them.

A statistical summary of the situation of the mission work was given in July 1866, and it may be assumed that this did not change significantly up to 1868:[40]

At service, at Inyati, average number	65
At school, at Inyati, „ „	40
At one of the villages, at service, average number	50
At third village, at service, average number	29
At fourth village, „ „ „ „	48

At Thomas's house, morning prayers   29
„   „   „ evening prayers   9

Most of those that came to school, and to morning and evening prayers were employed by Thomas and their total daily wages cost him half a pound of beads. Thomas was to perfect his method of converting his employees at Shiloh, the mission station he built after his dismissal from the L.M.S.[41] Although his Directors and his colleagues vehemently disapproved of his ways, regarding them as bribery, there was nothing unusual about them. Indeed in other parts of Africa, missionaries got their first faithful converts from among the slaves they rescued from traders and among their household servants.[42]

So it is clear that to some extent the missionaries were kept busy by preaching to the Ndebele, however limited the number of their listeners. Further, from the number of people that they addressed it would appear that their repeated claims of there being silent converts in the Ndebele kingdom may after all have been true. On the other hand it is obvious that the mission work was scarcely a great success. The missionaries attributed the unpopularity of their work to Mzilikazi's influence. This becomes clear in another aspect of their work, formal education.

From the very beginning the missionaries felt the great need to spread literacy among the Ndebele, so that they could read the Bible for themselves. One of the most indefatigable teachers was the first wife of Thomas. In 1861 she was reported to be holding a class of about thirty pupils at her house. But she was much restricted by the complete lack of equipment – she did not have even a single book – although her husband was already planning to build a classroom for her.[43] The best way to attract people to school, as the missionaries soon found out, was to create employment at the station. In the morning, just before the workers went to their different tasks and at break time in the afternoon, they were taught how to read and write.[44] Apart from it being unpopular with Sykes, a strict observer of the L.M.S. regulations and principles, the resources of the missionaries were rather limited to maintain this scheme for any length of time. Moreover Sykes soon complained that the Ndebele were materialists, more interested in the daily bead-wages than in learning.

Without the material inducements, the zeal and enthusiasm of the abafundisi to establish anything of a regular school came to naught. They were soon convinced that Mzilikazi was actively exercising his influence against them. It was reported from hearsay that the king had said to those who had been attending school regularly in 1862: 'Yes I see you listen to the teachers more than to me; you love them more than me.'[45] Such rumours spread as far afield as Shoshong.[46] It was even alleged that people were afraid of learning lest they be killed if it reached the king's ear 'that they could read the white people's book'.[47]

Sykes communicated to the Directors what he thought was a clear proof of Mzilikazi's refusal of his people to be taught, and the report is interesting enough to warrant a detailed description. Sykes chanced upon a group of youths sitting together after a Sunday service. One of them was repeating the sermon of the service for the benefit of those who had not listened carefully. The missionary joined them and interrupted the narrator by reminding those who could not remember the preacher's words of the advantages of being able to read the Bible for themselves. He then asked them why they were unwilling to come to school. They replied, 'The chief ... that is the very thing or we would have learned long ago. The chief has never said we may learn and we dare not until the word comes from him.'[48]

Sykes, however, determined to find out for himself the true position of the king in relation to literary education. He found Mzilikazi surrounded by his numerous attendants. He addressed the monarch saying they had come a long way to live among the Ndebele with the hope of teaching them to read the Bible and explaining the scriptures on Sundays. He pointed out that it was the greatest wish of the missionaries to make the people literate so that they might see for themselves the message of God as revealed in the Holy Book. The king declared: 'I tell my people my own words.' The missionary replied: 'It is right, but God has spoken to all men in his book.' The idea provoked a roar of laughter from the king and his attendants; and when silence fell upon them the teacher resumed his petition. This again raised hearty laughter, more extended than the first. After a third attempt and meeting with the same response, Sykes gave up and stalked back to his wagon, more depressed than ever.[49] Besides illustrating what a cheerless task it was to evangelise the Ndebele, this case shows that the king attached little, if any, value to literary education.

Other evidence which the missionaries interpreted as pointing to the king's active influence against them was produced by John Mackenzie in 1864. This was connected with an ox Mzilikazi had at the time given Thomas as a gift, when the latter was preaching at one town under Monyakanya. Monyakanya was reported to have said in 1862,

> When the king heard that Mr Thomas was preaching in my town, he at once exclaimed 'I am glad; Thomas commits no fault. The teachers' hearts will weary if we grant them no favour whatever. Go – present Thomas with that ox, & tell him I am glad to hear that he teaches my people. But', added the Chief, 'remember there is to be only prayer to God' – meaning as Monyakanya explained it, – 'that they were not to learn anything, but just to come together while the teacher prayed'.[50]

All in all, therefore, the missionary claim that the king was firmly against the evangelisation of his people does not at first seem an unreasonable one.

Nevertheless, although Sykes and Mackenzie came to see the king as the chief obstacle, other evidence from the same period casts doubts on this assumption. For instance the story of the induna, Mnyakanya, does not agree with what Thomas himself reported in 1862. The recipient of the royal present said that when the king learned that he was addressing the people of Mnyakanya, he sent him an ox as a token of friendship, adding that 'he was very thankful to me for my diligence in teaching his people the word of God – that the whole of his country was before me that I might teach wherever and whosoever I pleased and that he wished me all the success'.[51]

Thomas in fact had a chance of reading Mackenzie's report before it was dispatched to the Directors, and it behoved him to challenge it as false and an unjust misrepresentation of Mzilikazi's attitude. He pointed out that Mackenzie had misunderstood Monyakanya, who most likely had said, 'the King told us, to attend the word of God; but we are afraid to become Christians lest we will be killed'.[52] Two things must be pointed out: first, the quarrels which culminated in the expulsion of Thomas from the L.M.S. were already causing serious division among the missionaries, with Thomas on the one side, and Sykes and J. S. Moffat on the other. When Mackenzie came in 1863 he sided with the latter group.[53] So his resuscitation of the already forgotten 'ox' case was to some extent an attempt to find evidence to indict Thomas as a trader or a recipient of gifts, and thereby prove that he violated L.M.S. regulations. Secondly,

Mackenzie was so obsessed by the idea that Mzilikazi's influence was against mission work that he turned down the king's grant to him to set up a second mission station on account of the fact that the Ndebele ruler had not given him 'permission to teach reading'.[54] So it would appear that he was perhaps over-eager to seize upon anything which seemed to give validity to his obsession. It was about this time that J. S. Moffat was telling the Directors that: 'There seems to Mr Sykes and myself quite enough work to justify an addition to the staff of the Society here.'[55] The fact that Mackenzie's report was written at the time when the missionaries in the country were optimistic about their work makes it highly suspect.

In the same year that Thomas wrote to correct Mackenzie's mis-representation of Mzilikazi's character, J. S. Moffat corrected what he thought was a misconception of the same subject. His letter is worth quoting at length because of its insight into Ndebele society and the real obstacle in the way of Christianity:

> allow me to correct a mis-statement on which great stress has been laid and which I myself have been led into making. Moselekatse has never to my knowledge nor to that of Messrs Sykes and Thomas formally interdicted the people from learning to read. No such interdict exists. The great obstacle and the one to be overcome by the usual means is the people themselves, in their habits and natural indifference to the truth. It is enough to state that from the commencement of the current year school has been uninterruptedly held at Inyati.[56]

Elsewhere the same missionary complained about the indifference of the Ndebele to Christian teachings.

> It would be a positive relief here to get hold of somebody who was sufficiently curious to ask a single question about religion. Our con-versations on this subject are invariably one-sided. The native listens out of respect and acquiesces in all you say with a most docile air, and there is the end of it.[57]

It appears then that for some time the missionaries were misled into believing that the king was the chief cause of their failure. Indeed, Mrs Mary Margaret Carnegie, the daughter of Sykes, later exon-erated Mzilikazi and explained what was the root cause of the Ndebele lack of interest in missionary propaganda. The old king, she said, 'did not actually prevent mission work being done and services were held regularly but little impression made. Witch-doctors and medicine men were in power, and no one would have dared to be different from anyone else'.[58] The point of the religious authorities being the chief obstacle to Christian penetration will be pursued later; for the moment, suffice it to say that Mzilikazi did not ban his people from being converted.

The slowness of the missionaries to comprehend the cause of their unsuccessful attempts to set up a regular school is amazing. In 1863 Sykes observed: 'Some have said that they would learn to read at once, but when they discovered it would take weeks, perhaps months, the resolution vanished.' This was a clear indication of either laziness, or lack of incentive, or both on the part of the Ndebele. He added: 'Others have said they would learn if we would give them something for learning, which I always decline to do'.[59] Unfortunately the great desire to come to terms with western culture which drove many young people to the missionaries in the early twentieth century did not as yet exist in the nineteenth century; and the ability to read the Bible was not sufficient inducement for the Ndebele to pursue the toilsome formal education. Moreover, to the Ndebele, reading and writing were certainly fascinating, and apparently useful, secrets of the whites, which they evidently associated with the white men's extraordinary skills, but which bore no relevance to their way of life. Indeed Dr John McCracken shows how material inducements provided by Livingstonia were crucial in attracting the Tonga and Ngoni to mission stations and in winning the friendship of the chiefs. Even when the Ngoni king, Mbelwa, refused the missionaries easy access to his people, the missionaries managed to reach a relatively large number of the Ngoni by providing employment at the mission station for as many as sixty or more labourers for periods ranging from three weeks to a month at a time.[60]

McCracken tells us,

> The majority of chiefs with whom Livingstonia had dealings behaved in a friendly manner towards it, partly, it would seem, because of the great wealth in calico and beads flowing from the mission, partly because of its obvious technological prowess.[61]

Such a close association of Christianity and material inducements was forbidden by L.M.S. regulations.

Deprived of this strategy, which proved crucial in the early days of Livingstonia, the missionaries in western Zimbabwe simply continued to nag at Mzilikazi for not allowing his subjects to be educated.

In 1867 the exasperated king finally gave the long awaited so-called permission. He summoned the induna of Inyati as well as his *abalisa* (headmen), and 'in the presence of several headmen from other villages' told them 'that they must learn the white people's book'.[62] It is interesting to see the effect of this action, as reported by Sykes:

> The first morning a large number attended. The second morning not so many. The third comparatively few. I began my week on the fourth morning with sixteen scholars, and ended the following Tuesday with four ... During the third week the morning school disappeared as people say they are too busy in their gardens to come at present.[63]

Of course the clash between schooling and indigenous economic activities was a problem that would beset the missionaries well into the twentieth century and was only partially solved when school holidays were made to coincide with the ploughing and harvesting seasons. Nevertheless, it is clear that the whole thing that had been hailed by the L.M.S. official publication as Mzilikazi's 'full permission for all his people to learn all that the missionaries wish to teach!'[64] made no lasting impression whatsoever on the naturally indifferent Ndebele. If Mzilikazi had been the real obstacle, his permission which was publicly announced should have led to some marked change in the missionary enterprise in Ndebeleland.

The Ndebele apparent rejection of Christianity arose to some extent from a genuine incomprehension of the white men's view of God. Thomas recorded a question posed by one of his audience about Jesus Christ:

> And when I had finished one of them with great indifference and cool-ness asked me how could I say that Jesus did only good things to us? Was it not he who sent the sun to burn their corn and grass and because of that they and their cattle were likely to die out of hunger?[65]

Indeed, Christians have their own way of reconciling the concept of a God of love with the natural disasters that befall mankind but to the Ndebele these would probably be more confusing than their traditional views. The Ndebele belief in the dangerous aspects of the Deity is clearly seen in one of their prayers, made during sacrificial rites: 'Here is the meat that you like. Come together all of you; eat and be filled, you and your children. Don't kill us tomorrow saying that we refuse you food.'[66] Thus when the missionaries portrayed the Christian God as the one who created the world and was still ruling it with his own laws, the Ndebele were confused to hear that he was full of love only, for who then was responsible for droughts and other disasters? In addition to the conflicting theological concepts of the local people and the abafundisi, Christianity did not show any potentiality of giving practical answers to Ndebele daily problems that were better than those offered by the Shona and the amadlozi. In 1863 when there was drought, the king called upon the Mwari priests at the Malungwana mountains to come and perform the mutoro at enkosini, making no reference to the missionaries.[67] However, in 1868 when drought was again threatening, he requested the white teachers to pray to their own God; but during the evening of the same day he took the special precaution of asking for it himself in the traditional way. The missionaries naturally complained that the crafty king wanted to take away the credit from them.[68] But this was a clear demonstration of the Ndebele religious mixing process, which, as we shall see, led many of those who professed to be Christian to persist privately in their traditional beliefs as well. This was partly due to a lack of complete confidence in the new religion and partly to fear of the supposed dire consequences attending the abandonment of one's traditional beliefs and practices.

Needless to say, the missionaries ran into even worse troubles when their preachings challenged vital indigenous institutions. In the Ndebele state, as throughout much of Africa, polygamy proved a formidable obstacle. This was condemned by the missionaries on religious grounds and also for being 'inhuman' and for degrading the woman to nothing better than a slave.[69] When Mzilikazi was asked why his people rejected the gospel, he answered briefly and to the point: 'We Matabele like many wives.'[70] The institution of polygamy will be the subject of a more detailed discussion later, but it is worthwhile emphasising at this juncture that the Ndebele saw no moral superiority in monogamy to polygamy.

Sometimes the missionaries went too far and condemned customs that were harmless, if somewhat bizarre from their point of view, such as mourning rituals. It was declared that this practice was a clear manifestation that 'they have no hope, any more than any other Gentiles'.[71] Such unwarranted assaults on customs could only alienate the people. Nor did the missionaries manage to overcome such resistance by identifying Christianity, as they tried to do throughout the nineteenth century, with western medicine. In point of fact the Ndebele were perceptive enough to distinguish between the two aspects of western culture; they eagerly availed themselves of the material benefits of the missionaries and stood aloof from the Christian religion.

Thus it is clear that the missionaries failed to influence the Ndebele during the period 1860–8, because the people were not interested in Christianity, which threatened their own culture, was largely incomprehensible to them, and did not offer better solutions to their everyday problems than their traditional beliefs. This Ndebele indifference to Christianity was reinforced during this period by the anti-missionary feeling unleashed by natural disasters, which were associated with the settlement of the abafundisi.

Notes

1. J. P. R. Wallis (ed.), *Matabele Mission of J. S. and E. Moffat*, London, 1945, p. 75
2. T. M. Thomas, *Eleven Years in Central South Africa*, London, 1873, pp. 66–7
3. Wallis, *Matabele Mission*, p. 80; Thomas, pp. 68–9; L.M.S. B2/F1/JA, Sykes to For. Sec., 2 Jan. 1860
4. L.M.S. B1/JC, Moffat to For. Sec., May 1860; Thomas to For. Sec., 30 April 1860; for the missionaries' refusal to trade for Mzilikazi and the latter's disappointment, see Wallis, *Matabele Mission*, p. 93; J. P. R. Wallis (ed.), *Matabele Journals of Robert Moffat*, 2 vols., London, 1945, ii, pp. 265–6; L.M.S. B1/F1/JD, Sykes to For. Sec., 20 Sept., 11 Dec. 1861
5. L.M.S. B1/F1/JC, Thomas to For. Sec., 10 Oct. 1860
6. Wallis, *Matabele Mission*, pp. 101–2
7. L.M.S. B1/F1/JC, Thomas to For. Sec., 10 Oct. 1860
8. *Ibid.*, Thomas to For. Sec., 16 Feb. 1861; B1/F1/JD, Thomas to For. Sec., 2 July 1861; Wallis, *Matabele Mission*, pp. 110, 135
9. Wallis, *Matabele Mission*, p. 150
10. L.M.S. B1/F1/JA, Sykes to For. Sec., 20 Sept., 11 Dec. 1861
11. Wallis, *Matabele Mission*, p. 164
12. L.M.S. B1/F1/JA, Sykes to For. Sec., 20 Sept., 11 Dec. 1861
13. Mhlagazanhlansi, *Early Days and Native Ways*, Bulawayo, 1944, p. 25
14. Wallis, *Matabele Mission*, p. 156; L.M.S. B1/F1/JD, Thomas to For. Sec., 18 Sept. 1861; Thomas, p. 230
15. L.M.S. B1/F2/JD, Sykes to For. Sec., 29 July 1862
16. Thomas, p. 230
17. *Ibid.*; L.M.S. B1/F2/JD, Sykes to For. Sec., 29 July 1862
18. Thomas, pp. 205–6
19. Wallis, *Matabele Mission*, p. 164; see also L.M.S. B1/F1/JC, Thomas to

For. Sec., 10 Dec. 1860; B1/F1/JD, Sykes to For. Sec., 20 Sept., 11 Dec. 1861

20. Wallis, *Matabele Mission*, p. 155; Thomas, pp. 318–19

21. Wallis, *Matabele Mission*, p. 176; L.M.S. B1/F2/JA, Thomas to For. Sec., 23 Sept. 1862; R. Moffat to For. Sec., 25 Dec. 1862

22. L.M.S. B1/F1/JC, R. Moffat to For. Sec., May 1860

23. L.M.S. B1/F4/JB, David Carnegie to For. Sec., 6 Sept. 1889

24. The lungsickness was first brought by Marupe's oxen; Marupe was Robert Moffat Junior's driver, who had brought food supplies for missionaries and had also remained in the country for some time trading with Mzilikazi.

25. T. O. Ranger tells us that it was customary for the people who conquered the country before the advent of colonial rule to make 'peace with the land', by which is meant the tribal religious authorities; T. O. Ranger, *Revolt in Southern Rhodesia*, London, 1967, p. 143

26. L.M.S. B1/F1/JC, Thomas to For. Sec., 10 Oct. 1860

27. *Ibid.*, Sykes to For. Sec., 29 July 1862

28. *Ibid.*, R. Moffat to For. Sec., 20 March 1860; Wallis, *Matabele Mission*, pp. 168–9, 179–89; Tabler, *The Far Interior*, p. 262

29. L.M.S. B1/F2/JD, Mackenzie to For. Sec., 8 March 1864; see also Wallis, *Matabele Mission*, p. 188

30. L.M.S. B1/F1/JD, Thomas to For. Sec., 18 Sept. 1861; Thomas, p. 251

31. See N. M. B. Bhebe, 'Christian Missions in Matabeleland 1859–1923', unpublished Ph.D. thesis, London, 1972, pp. 159–62, 187

32. L.M.S. B1/F2/JA, Thomas to For. Sec., 23 Sept. 1862; Moffat to For. Sec., 25 Dec. 1862; Thomas, pp. 251–3; J. Mackenzie, *Ten Years North of the Orange River*, Edinburgh, 1871, p. 326

33. L.M.S. B1/F1/JC, Thomas to For. Sec., 30 April 1860

34. *Ibid.*; L.M.S. B1/F1/JD, Sykes to For. Sec., 20 Sept., 11 Dec. 1861

35. L.M.S. B1/F1/JC, Thomas to For. Sec., 10 Oct. 1860

36. L.M.S. B1/F1/JA, Thomas to For. Sec., 10 Dec. 1860

37. L.M.S. B1/F2/JA, Sykes to For. Sec., 29 July 1862

38. *Ibid.*

39. *Ibid.*, Sykes to For. Sec., 3 Aug., 17 Sept. 1863; Thomas to Robert Moffat, 24 Sept. 1862; Thomas to For. Sec., 23 Sept. 1862

40. 'Papers respecting the Matabele Mission', pp. 56–63

41. See Ch. 3

42. Cf. R. Oliver, *The Missionary Factor in East Africa*, London, 1952, pp. 50–65; R. I. Rotberg, *Christian Missionaries and the Creation of Northern Rhodesia*, Princeton, 1965, p. 42; M. Wright, *German Missions in Tanganyika*, Oxford, 1971, pp. 87–8

43. L.M.S. B1/F1/JC, Thomas to For. Sec., 16 Feb. 1861; B1/F1/JD, Sykes to For. Sec., 20 Sept., 11 Dec. 1861

44. L.M.S. B1/F2/JA, Sykes to For. Sec., 25 Sept. 1862

45. L.M.S. B1/F1/JD, Sykes to For. Sec., 3, 10, 20 March 1862

46. *Ibid.*, R. Price to For. Sec., 6 April 1862

47. L.M.S. B1/F2/JA, Sykes to For. Sec., 29 July 1862

48. *Ibid.*, Sykes to For. Sec., 3 Aug., 17 Sept. 1862

49. *Ibid.*

50. L.M.S. B1/F2/JB, Mackenzie to For. Sec., 8 March 1864
51. L.M.S. B1/F2/JA, Thomas to For. Sec., 23 Sept. 1862
52. L.M.S. B1/F2/JC, Thomas to For. Sec., 1 March 1865
53. See 'Papers respecting the Matabele Mission'
54. Wallis, *Matabele Mission*, pp. 213–15
55. L.M.S. B1/F2/JB, J. S. Moffat to For. Sec., 13 Jan. 1864
56. L.M.S. B1/F2/JC, J. S. Moffat to For. Sec., 10 Oct. 1865
57. Wallis, *Matabele Mission*, p. 210
58. R.N.A. MISC/CA5, Mrs Carnegie to Good, 1 Nov. 1937
59. L.M.S. B1/F2/JA, Sykes to For. Sec., 3 Aug., 17 Sept. 1863
60. K. J. McCracken, 'Religion and Politics in Northern Ngoniland, 1881–1904' in B. Pachai, *The Early History of Malawi*, London, 1972, pp. 220–1
61. K. J. McCracken, 'Livingstonia as an Industrial Mission, 1875–1900. A Study of Commerce and Christianity in Nyasaland' in W. M. Watt (ed.), *Religion in Africa*, Edinburgh, 1964, p. 10
62. L.M.S. B1/F2/JC, Sykes to For. Sec., 1 March 1867
63. *Ibid.*
64. *The Chronicle of the L.M.S. for the Year 1867*, p. 203
65. L.M.S. B1/F1/JC, Thomas to For. Sec., 11 Feb. 1861
66. *The Zambesi Mission Record*, iii, 35, Jan. 1907, p. 185; see also *The Missionary Magazine and Chronicle*, xxviii, 1864, p. 284
67. Mackenzie, p. 331
68. L.M.S. B1/F2/JC, Sykes to For. Sec., 19 March 1868
69. *The Missionary Magazine and Chronicle*, xxviii, 1864, p. 284
70. L.M.S. B1/F2/JB, Mackenzie to For. Sec., 8 March 1864
71. *The Missionary Magazine and Chronicle*, xxviii, 1864, p. 285

3

Christianity and western Zimbabwe under Lobengula, 1870–89

There was a growth in missionary interest in Ndebeleland between 1870 and 1889. The L.M.S., the Zambesi Mission of the Jesuits, and the independent and former L.M.S. missionary Thomas Morgan Thomas all worked in the Ndebele state proper. The Berlin Mission extended its activities from the Transvaal to the southern and south-eastern Ndebele tributary chiefdoms. But the attempts of the Paris Missionary Society under Francis Coillard to establish a mission in south-western Shonaland between 1877 and 1878 were frustrated by the Ndebele king.

In spite of the intensified missionary activity, very few converts were made. The Shona who were either under Ndebele rule or were engaged in resisting the Ndebele showed more interest in what the missionaries could offer for their struggle for independence or survival rather than in the Christian religion. Moreover, the Ndebele domination over the Shona offered very little chance for the missionaries to establish any systematic evangelical work.

In the Ndebele state proper, the merging process between Shona and Nguni-Sotho-Tswana religious ideas gathered momentum under Lobengula. He provided a congenial atmosphere for this process through his frequent use of traditional religious authorities and magical powers to rule the Ndebele. Much of his prestige rested on his reputation of being a good rainmaker. To be proficient in this art, he co-operated closely with the Mwari cult. His political authority and security in his office as king to some extent depended on the use of both Shona and Nguni diviners to smell out potential rivals and rebels as witches. As one traveller observed: 'For instance, when any of his indunas are troublesome and begin plotting rebellion, etc., should the news get to the king, what is easier than to give out that they are practising *illegitimate* art at the same time as they are killed.'[1] Indeed, it was the same frequent employment of the izinyanga, izangoma and the Mwari priests by Lobengula that was so succinctly described by Fr Depelchin, the Superior of the Zambesi Mission:

> [Lobengula] has had no other principle to guide him in his Government but divination and sorcery. In every important deliberation he consults the devil, and according to the answer, or inspiration, he is supposed to receive, he gives his orders to his ministers, who obey him with promptitude and faithfulness.[2]

This formidable alliance between the central authority and the religious institutions largely accounted for the Ndebele indifference to the Christian missions.

Much of Lobengula's reliance on traditional religious institutions, however, lay in the difficult circumstances of his coming to power. Mzilikazi died on 9 September 1868, leaving no nationally recognised heir to the throne. The heir-apparent, called Nkulumane, had long disappeared from the country and a thick mystery shrouded both the circumstances of his disappearance and his whereabouts. The triumvirate ruling the country during the interregnum, after much searching for the missing heir, finally made up its mind to install Lobengula, Mzilikazi's next son in line of succession. There was formidable opposition to Lobengula's succession mounted by Nkulumane's supporters.[3]

That Lobengula ultimately gained control of the Ndebele state in the teeth of formidable opposition to some extent depended on the work of Mncumbata, the leading member of the triumvirate. Mncumbata clearly saw that the Ndebele kingdom had greatly changed over the years and that the support of the Hole class was crucial in the decision of the kingship. He approached the Mwari priests and consulted them on the choice of the successor. They chose Lobengula for reasons that can only be guessed. Presumably their choice fell on Lobengula because they knew him better, as there was a story that they had once given him asylum when he escaped from the 1840 executions of the Thabayezinduna crisis.[4] A more likely reason, however, was that during the interregnum it was generally felt that Nkulumane, if he existed, had stayed too long with white people in South Africa and that he was likely to open up the country to western influences, if he came to power.[5] The Mwari priests may well have been concerned to forestall any westernisation of the country.

When Lobengula was installed king of the Ndebele, the Mwari priests accepted him into the priesthood by giving him the insignia of their 'order' consisting of 'a black cloth which he wore round his waist, and he was also given the nickname Ngwalongwalo'.[6] By this gesture, the officials of the cult conferred on Lobengula the authority to preside over the mutoro (rainmaking ceremonies).[7] Another dimension of the same gesture which has come to light through studies of the Shona societies is that by it the Shona religious authorities exercised a political role – the prerogative of installing a king's successor or conferring spiritual legitimacy on him.[8] But the most important point to be observed is that by inviting the Mwari institution to participate in the appointment of Lobengula, Mncumbata had finally integrated the Shona religious institutions with the Nguni beliefs in the person of the king. The immediate and practical significance of the consultation of the Shona religious authorities, however, was that Lobengula gained the support not only of most of the Zansi and the Nhla, but also of the Hole majority, enabling him to defeat his opponents in battle.[9]

Thus Lobengula owed his position to the people and the religious institutions. He could not exercise power as freely as his father, who had come to the throne by heredity. When in 1888 Lobengula, in his search for a peaceful solution to the white problem, signed the Rudd Concession, which turned out to be a European treacherous act forcing the king to sell the country to Cecil John Rhodes, the indunas, for instance, bitterly complained that Lobengula could not do such a thing without their consent because 'they put [him] in his position'.[10]

Another difficulty which confronted the young king was that he did not possess as much livestock as his late father. During the interregnum, many local powerful indunas and probably his half-brothers and cousins appropriated his father's cattle.[11] The resources of the Ndebele king had to be immense to meet all his obligations: he had to slaughter cattle for the annual national festivals and religious rituals, to feed visitors and his numerous attendants and dependants, to provide food for all the people who continually came to *wota* (pay their respects), and finally he had to distribute cattle among newly set up villages.[12]

Starting in such a weak position, Lobengula 'had to begin very cautiously and gradually strengthened his position'. Employing the diviners, he weeded out his enemies and also some of his father's indunas, replacing them with his own trusted men. 'And so as time went on he gradually consolidated his power and secured himself on the throne. But he never had, nor as long as he remains in the Matabele country, will he ever have the despotic power of his father.'[13]

The significance of his being the people's king and his possessing limited powers becomes apparent in his relationship with the missionaries. It was a well-known fact both to the missionaries and the whites in general that 'Though not a Christian [Lobengula] has a great respect for the white man's creed', and he often told Europeans frankly that

> he himself believes God makes the rain, though he may be coming straight from his medicine kraal, after being busy there for hours brewing mystic potions . . . for the purpose of making rain, or throwing bones to discover someone accused of witchcraft, or to ferret out who is to blame for the failure of an expedition, or for a trek ox falling lame.[14]

In fact on his accession the king gave hope to the missionaries that he might become a Christian king. William Sykes spent a great deal of time instructing him in Christian precepts and tenets and also in demonstrating the misery and degradation wrought by trying to govern his people 'by heathen laws, in which live the aweful friends of witchcraft, injustice, and cruelty'. Lobengula in fact heeded Sykes's persuasion in adopting European dress, observing the Sabbath, and permitting the missionaries to teach the Gospel anywhere in the country.[15] He also appears to have been influenced intellectually, for these early associations with the missionaries earned him at least among his subjects the reputation of being literate. Nkungusi, his wife and daughter of Mzila, declared during an interview with R. F. Windram in 1937 that her royal husband could read and write and that the reason he always had other people to read and write letters for him was simply because he was king.[16] Frank Johnson, a prospector and concession seeker, who was arrested and detained by the Ndebele for violating some of their laws, reported in 1887 how he was told of Lobengula's literacy. The court, consisting of indunas and izinyanga, accused him of having written to the Cape Colony maligning the Ndebele king as possessing 'two tongues in his head'. On inquiring how his majesty had got to know about all that, Johnson was informed that Lobengula had seen and read the letter himself, even though he had not bothered to open the letter. The king had simply looked at the envelope and had seen the words inside. The court further told Johnson that their king possessed as much common-sense, learning and wisdom as the white men and that he was equally able to read letters without opening the envelopes.[17] We now know that Lobengula never acquired literacy, but the reputation of his being literate was indicative of his people's acknowledgement of his apparently extraordinary intellectual talents which he had sharpened through learning from the missionaries.

In addition to his great respect for the Christian religion, Lobengula, in the face of the difficult circumstances of his coming to power, found it expedient to enlist the support of the missionaries. The succession crisis attracted the envious eyes of the Transvaal Boers and the Natal colonial officials, who saw in it possibilities of extending their power to western Zimbabwe.[18] The king, therefore, realised the wisdom of befriending the missionaries, who might use their influence with their white fellows to persuade them to keep out of Ndebele politics. Consequently the L.M.S. were allowed to open the second mission station called Hope Fountain.

The L.M.S. hopes of Lobengula becoming a Christian, or at least adopting Christian principles of government, were in part upset by the arrival of the Mfengu doctor, Mbulali and his son Hlegisane. When Mncumbata was busy trying to make Lobengula king, Hlegisane came into Ndebeleland on a hunting expedition from Waterboer's territory in the Orange Free State. He told Mncumbata that his father Mbulali 'can by the use of medicine and charms render any army invincible and that he can make a great chief of the meanest subject'. Mbulali was immediately invited to come and 'doctor the army, consecrate the king' and was eventually granted Ndebele citizenship and settlement in the country with his whole family as members of the Zansi.[19]

This tremendous doctor or magician, Mbulali, who apparently also had little respect for whites,[20] came with the doctrine that he possessed such powerful medicines as would make the soldiers' spears sharp and cause the *impis* to be always successful in war. He also warned Lobengula that the missionaries were people of peace, that they condemned war of any kind, and that if the king believed them he would never achieve the greatness of his late father, whose death had been likened to the fall of a mountain. He dissuaded Lobengula from adopting Christianity, which might revolutionise the Ndebele way of life. Eventually the king lost much of his earlier interest in the missionary propaganda.[21] It also seems quite probable that it was Mbulali and his son and successor, Hlegisane, who contributed much to keeping alive Ndebele martial spirit which otherwise was dying out. As Thomas, after recounting the savage and brutal mutilation of Chief Chibi for the initiation rites of Hlegisane, indignantly complained:

> If Cape people come here to teach the Amandebele such cruelties as the above mentioned when can we expect to succeed in persuading the heathen to put aside their barbarities and heathenish customs and sit down quietly and gently at the feet of Jesus?[22]

But Lobengula's final failure to adopt Christian reforms arose not only from the influence of the two Mfengu doctors. It also came from his clear understanding that he could not excite the displeasure of the religious institutions without losing much of his power and prestige. As the Jesuit missionary reported in 1879:

> But the people believe in the mountain gods [Mwari], they dread them as having intercourse with the spirits, and being able to do them great harm. Lobengula seems too clever for such superstitions, but wants the influence of these impostors with the natives. As long as he gratifies them he can easily rule the Matabele and tributary tribes. Without their support his prestige and authority might indeed be considerably diminished in the opinion of many people; their opposition might destroy his power. Therefore so long as the present rule lasts there is but little hope of converting the Matabele and much less the subjugated tribes.[23]

Ironically enough, Lobengula, in his difficult position of being something of a Christian at heart but a complete traditionalist in outward appearances and action because of his dependence on the traditional religion, evolved enlightened views and arguments for the traditional religion. Thomas Baines, a gold concession seeker, once remarked: 'I believe, however, that Lobengula's views on this point are far in advance of the popular theology and that the majority of the people look on the rain-maker and his sacrifices and the rain as literal cause and effect.'[24] Although Baines, like most of his white contemporaries, underestimated African understanding that it was not the priest's magical proceedings that caused the desired things to happen, but that the priest only used these things to pray to a supernatural being or beings who had power over nature, nevertheless Lobengula also does seem to have been very much above the rest of the people in understanding theological matters. As he himself said: 'We do not believe that the killing of an ox or burning particular herbs makes rain, but these are the means by which we ask it, just as you ask it by reading your book and saying prayers.'[25]

Because of his fairly good knowledge of Christian teachings and his insight into the indigenous religion(s), the king eventually came to challenge one of the basic notions of the Christians and of the justifications of the Christian mission to Africa. Christians believed that their own religion was the only true one, and Robert Moffat argued that the Africans had little knowledge of the true God. Moffat held that the black races of Africa were the 'sons of Ham [who] entered Africa, by way of Egypt'.[26] He also believed that these dark people, with the rest of humanity, acquired the knowledge of God through Divine Revelation, which had only been universal during two periods – at Creation and at the time of Noah after the great flood.[27] But the sons of Ham had lost nearly all their true religion through a degraded way of life and accumulation of super-stitions. The latter process, so he maintained, had reached a point where it was threatening to overshadow the vestiges of the true God. Therefore, the task of the missionary was to revive this glimmer of the divine light and to clear away the superstitions.

Lobengula, however, saw the traditional and the white man's religions as two separate and equal conceptions of the supernatural world and its relationships with man. These two systems, he believed, had been divinely willed at Creation; and therefore he argued it was against the divine will either for an individual to move from the one system to the other, or for one system to try to impose itself on the other. He was once reported as having said

> he believed in God, he believed God had made all things as he wanted them. He had made all people and that he had made every country and tribe just as he wished them to remain, he believed God made the Amandebele as he wished them to be and it was wrong for anyone to seek to alter them.[28]

In Lobengula, therefore, the traditional institutions had an articulate and enlightened defender.

Indeed, under this king's rule, the Mwari institution gained such wide and deep influence that the Europeans who came into the country sometimes thought that it was the only form of worship of the Ndebele, not at first perceiving the also firmly embedded amadlozi substratum. For instance, the Jesuits were informed by John Lee, a white settler, that, 'the worship of [the Ndebele] is nothing but a coarse fetishism. In the hollow mountain there is a gourd dressed up as a doll, which the people adore as the son of God.'[29] Since the exact nature of the Mwari shrines was unknown to anyone except the priests, the 'gourd dressed up as a doll' was nothing but a figment of Lee's imagination. Apparent, nevertheless, in Lee's derogatory description is the fact that the Ndebele were worshipping Mwari.

A few months of their stay in Ndebeleland, however, brought the Jesuits to discover that, 'there is a wretch about twelve miles from here [Bulawayo], who lives in a cave and calls himself God'.[30] A little later the same missionaries were talking of 'four or six gods (wicked impostors living in the mountains at several places)'.[31] Of the relationship between the Ndebele and these 'gods', the Jesuits observed that these 'two or three . . . gods, human beings living in the mountains are held in great fear by our heathens'.[32] Joseph Cockin, a grandson of one of the founders of the L.M.S. and who joined the Society in 1877, also described how the Ndebele viewed their adopted god: 'They say he is not a man but a spirit, that you can not see him, nor feel him. He dwells in a cave or a series of caves and when anyone approaches a strange sound is heard.'[33] Not only did the Ndebele profess profound faith in Mwari, but they demonstrated it by supplying the institution with quantities of grain and other forms of food, cattle, wives and useful articles. As the missionary observed, 'judging from the number of cattle and amount of corn they [the gods and goddesses] consume their appetites must be enormous'.[34]

Disregarding the obviously tendentious aspects of the missionaries' description, it is clear that the Mwari institution had become established in Ndebele society. It is also clear that the four shrines of the cult – perhaps Wirirani, in the Matopo hills east of Hope Fountain, Njelele in the south, Mkombo (Mangwe, Manyembe) in the south-west, and that of Inyati, run by Salugazana in the north – had become centres of much religious activity.[35]

By co-operating closely with the cult Lobengula greatly improved, or developed, his talent for making rain. In respect of this extra-ordinary gift, Europeans called the Ndebele king 'the clerk of the weather and the rain-maker general of the country'; they noticed that he enjoyed the 'reputation of being a remarkably good hand at a thunderstorm'; that if his subjects were asked, 'Do you think there is going to be rain?' they invariably answered, 'The king knows; we don't know.' The white visitors further considered him to possess a wonderful knowledge of the moon phases and to be 'as correct as an almanac'. On one occasion he surprised one of the white residents by making a thunderstorm 'in June – the one month when you least expect rain'. Whenever the dry season drew to an end, Lobengula withdrew into seclusion 'in the sacred goat kraal', where he made rain with the assistance of other doctors.[36]

The problem, however, is that although many sources suggest that Lobengula acquired much of his talent as an efficient rain-maker from his co-operation with the Mwari rainmakers, the exact nature of this relationship is far from clear. Of course there are numerous references to communications between the shrines and enkosini (the king's place). Perhaps the only piece of evidence that comes close enough to indicating Lobengula's kind of relationship with the Mwari cult officials is that by Lieutenant-Colonel Vaughan-Williams, which, however, should be accepted with caution as it was recorded more than half a century after the observation. Vaughan-Williams said that the most influential doctors in Ndebeleland were the Mwari priests, some of whom were permanently resident at enkosini and, with Lobengula, made rain in the sacred enclosure.[37] This suggests the present manyusa's relationship with chiefdoms in which the former commute between the shrines and their homelands and officiate during the mitoro (rainmaking ceremonies).

Mtompe Khumalo, who eulogised Mzilikazi's rule and con-demned Lobengula's for allowing the bastardisation of the Ndebele culture by Shona influence, described how Shona ideas superseded Nguni ones. He said that some influential Ndebele started to argue that Mwari was nearer than Somandla, whom the Ndebele had all along prayed to through the amadlozi. This was immediately fol-lowed by the appearance at enkosini of a number of Shona rain-doctors, Jukwa, Sihulukulu, Menzo, Nawa, Mankonyana, and Salugazana.[38]

Fortunately we have an eyewitness account of Jukwa at work at the king's place in 1879. Jukwa was an *ihosanah*, a male dedicated to the Mwari while still a child, a counterpart of the female mbonga. He was a medium of a *jukwa* spirit, one of the spirits 'believed to have emanated directly from Mwari'.[39] He was connected with the Thabazika Mambo shrine near Inyati, and he was perhaps usually sent to go and dance at Lobengula's place, as he was seen doing by Joseph Cockin. On this occasion Lobengula consulted him on the cattle disease, lungsickness.[40]

Apart from the rainmaking activities, the cult was used as a convenient means of getting rid of members of the royal family or influential indunas whom the king found troublesome or a menace to his position. In 1880, for instance, Mngcengence, the only sister by his mother and nearest living relative of Lobengula, was 'smelt out' by the *Ilitshe*, the Mwari. Mngcengence, usually called Nina by the whites, had acted as the *inkosikazi* of Bulawayo before Lobengula married Xwailile, Mzila's daughter. When Xwailile came, Mngcengence refused to give up her position. Moreover, it was common knowledge that she was 'very fond of white men and wished to marry a trader', perhaps an unfavourable prospect for an influential member of the royal family, as this might open the floodgates of Western influences. To get rid of her Lobengula referred her case to Mwari, where she was accused of bewitching her brother so that he could not have male children, and she was hanged. Also closely related to Mngcengence's case and probably more interesting was the death of the trader Clarkson. When the Ilitshe pronounced Lobengula's sister a witch, Clarkson, being present, flared up and abused the shrine. The trader was told there and then that he would not live long. A few months later he was struck by lightning and died. It was generally believed that Mwari had avenged the insult.[41]

More or less at the same time as Mngcengence was smelt out, Lotshe Hlabangana, chief adviser to the king, was referred to the Ilitshe, where he was also accused as a witch. But Lobengula managed to resist the demands for his execution until 1889.[42]

Besides the Mwari institution, Lobengula had at his disposal the izinyanga and the izangoma or the izanusi. Lobengula always kept two or three of these diviners at enkosini.[43] The izinyanga sometimes openly competed with the missionaries in medical treatments. A most illustrative case was that involving Thomas and one doctor Sitomo, which took place in 1880. Magatshana, a first cousin of the king, was taken ill suffering from a fever. Lobengula asked Thomas to cure him. As soon as the patient began to recover, he invited Sitomo to come and divine the cause of the ailment. The inyanga cast his bones and immediately diagnosed *umukuhlane* (fever). He proceeded to slaughter one of the patient's goats in order to mix some of the flesh with the medicines. Typical of the izinyanga, Sitomo sent most of the meat to his home with his wife. His strategy in the whole affair was that Thomas should continue to treat Magatshana so that if he recovered Sitomo would claim the credit and collect the fees. The missionary discovered the conspiracy well in time and refused to attend the patient as long as the herbalist interfered. Sitomo also refused to give up administering his herbs to Magatshana, and the stalemate was broken by the king himself, who persuaded the African doctor to leave.[44] To Thomas the incident was crucial as he was bent on demonstrating the superiority of the white man's medical science over that of the Ndebele.

The izangoma, unlike the izinyanga, excelled in the field of divination. They foretold future events and discovered causes of illness and other hidden 'facts' through spirit possession, and by the ukuvumisa process (make-agree).[45] Lobengula retained full control over this class of religious authorities by exercising the power of sanctioning the initiation of any new members. On their initiation day, they received 'robes' consisting of monkey skins, a head-dress of feathers, python skins, necklaces of snake-bones, and a horn of medicines[46]. Certainly the izangoma, when in full attire, presented an awe-inspiring sight. Their singular advantage over the Shona izinyanga was that they did not hesitate to name a person a witch Even today, 'the isangoma is the most respected of the various diviners of witches amongst the Ndebele'.[47] Logengula's favourite isangoma was called Zondo.[48] And many a man was executed by the king as the result of Zondo's activities.

The missionary task of evangelising the Ndebele was, therefore, rendered near impossible by the powerful hold on the people and their king of the religious practices and beliefs, which were being rejuvenated and inspired with confidence through amalgamating with the Shona institutions. Indeed, Ndebele headquarters epitomised this very ganglion of resistance to missionary influence. J. S. Moffat, who revisited Ndebeleland for the purpose of negotiating a treaty with Lobengula, gave a vivid picture of the situation at enkosini. The centre of resistance to Christianity was, he declared, 'here "enkosini" '. Enkosini, he observed, was the heart of the nation, throbbing and sending its pulsation to extremities. Here you have the great indunas who are to a large extent . . . the controlling power, who regulate much of the chief's action and therefore have his responsibility. Here is the *harem*; which dislikes us with a . . . sensual repugnance, here are the wizards who hate us fiercely with the keen interest of their coming downfall.[49]

Some of the missionary efforts at converting Lobengula's subjects revealed the difficulties presented by the traditional religious beliefs. At least this was the experience of the Z.M. Jesuits. In 1887 Father Prestage, who was to be associated with the Catholic mission in Ndebeleland up to the beginning of the twentieth century, managed to extract permission from Lobengula to teach the Ndebele religious knowledge and trades and to found the Empandeni mission station. Empandeni was the headquarters of the Impande *buto* situated in the mixed population of the Leya and the Nanzwa, formerly from the Zambezi area, and the indigenous Kalanga. When Lobengula came to power, in his gratitude to the regiment for their support during the succession war, he permitted Induna Sindisa to go and settle with his people in the country from where most of his soldiers came. The regiment occupied the piece of land traversed by the Mgwizi stream and they were here when Prestage came to work among them. The population of their headquarters was estimated to be 3,000.[50]

Empandeni was thus a good example of mission work carried out among the Hole, whom the missionaries regarded as the slave class most likely to respond favourable to Christianity.[51] Yet, as things turned out, Empandeni was just as infertile to the Gospel as the rest of Ndebeleland. By January 1888 Fr Prestage had occupied his mission station and opened a school which he reported to have been regularly attended by sixty children.[52] But this initial favourable situation was short-lived, for in March of the same year the priest was reporting that there were no children attending school. He attributed this to the fact that the children were busy in the gardens as it was harvesting time. In 1889 the missionary was forced to abandon his station through fear of being massacred in a possible conflict between the Ndebele and the British South Africa Company.[53] When he left he could not show any tangible results of his labouring among the Impande.

The experience of the Catholics at Bulawayo was even more shattering than that at Empandeni. In early 1880 the mission station accumulated some property – thirty sheep, two cows, six oxen, one calf, and fifty hens.[54] Fr Croonenberghs, who was in charge of the station, soon became popular for his medical skill. The Superior reported with evident delight:

> Father Croonenberghs is doing very well, and has become the great Doctor of the country. Every day there are plenty of people who are here at our door asking for medicine or begging to be cured of their sores. Even the King sends his Queens and his children to be treated by him.[55]

He even had the privilege of treating the king himself for his gout.[56] There were also two preparing converts, but neither of them was Ndebele. One was a Bushman and the second was a Cape Coloured. Regarding the Ndebele the Catholics reported that they 'don't speak or ask about religion, and dread for their lives if they should openly join or profess any Christianity'.[57]

The Jesuits reported that it was also unwise to try to teach the Ndebele reading and writing, as the king would only suspect that the missionaries were engaged in a conspiracy to make his subjects wiser than himself. Further, it was almost impossible to set up a viable station because of the constant shifts of Ndebele towns.[58] In 1882, two years after the founding of the Bulawayo station, the people demonstrated their complete lack of appreciation of missionary efforts by moving away from the neighbourhood. Bulawayo, which had been the centre of population concentration, became a mere 'desert'.[59] This marked the end of the Catholic attempt to convert the Ndebele from Bulawayo.

The Jesuits seriously tried to discover the causes of their failure to convert the Ndebele. They declared that the king and his indunas set their faces firmly against any people relinquishing the traditional way of life.[60] Behind Lobengula and his administrative officials were 'in this dark country the engines of government', the superstitions, which were 'excuses for killing people and getting their cattle'.[61] This point was made even more clearly by Fr Prestage:

> Our failure at Empandeni was not owing to the unwillingness of the natives to learn, & even become Christians, but it was due to the overwhelming terror, engaged by the system of government, which seizes every native in the country, when it is a case of [casting?] off their pagan customs to [adopt the] new system.[62]

He said that any Ndebele who tried to turn away from his religion to adopt Christianity was immediately regarded by the rest of society as a traitor. Such a person became a 'marked man, and doomed to be knocked on the head as the cause of ill, should any misfortune attend his family or town where he is residing'. That, according to Prestage, was 'the barrier to missionary enterprise in Matabeleland'. He had foreseen this before going to that country, but he had hoped that 'some would have the grace' to break through the cocoon of the traditional religious system. 'There', he admitted with humility, 'I was mistaken.'[63] In short, the Catholics discovered that Ndebeleland was ruled by a government that was permeated through and through by a powerful traditional religion which set its face against the evangelisation of its adherents.

The experience of the L.M.S. during 1870–90 was not very different from that of the Catholics. The opening of the Hope Fountain station in 1870 was one of the two changes the missionaries had always called upon their Directors to effect. Another desired change was that of having two missionaries at each of the stations. This took some time to achieve.[64]

When Lobengula came to power, there were changes in the population settlement. He founded his own capital, Bulawayo, where the population became concentrated. There was also a temporary withdrawal of the people from around Inyati, the rebel area. These people were ordered to build their towns around Bulawayo. For a brief period Inyati became a desert: only three old men, four women, two girls and three boys remained there.[65] Lobengula perhaps took this measure to keep a watchful eye on the former rebels during Kanda's invasion of the country, as there was every possibility that the former rebel Mbiko's followers might attempt to join hands with the person in South Africa calling himself Nkulumane. As soon as this danger was averted, the king ordered the Inqobo regiment to go back to their homes and settle in the neighbourhood of Inyati. The Inqobo seemed to be much more amenable to missionary teachings than any people who had hitherto lived near the station. As soon as they were settled down, the Sabbath attendances rose from almost nothing to 200 and 250 people. Some of them were struggling to read and write.[66]

An interesting story is recorded by the trader Frank Mandy about the Inqobo people and their attitude to missionary work. Once the people were told by Sykes not to send annual gifts to Mwari. He said the so-called almighty deity was a swindler with no power whatever over rain. Only the white men's God controlled natural forces. The people obeyed him that year; but, curiously enough, rain fell everywhere in the kingdom except in the Inqobo region and around the mission station. As might have been expected, the people were furious with the missionary; they demanded that since he had hindered them from propitiating Mwari, he must pray to his European God to come to their rescue. Sykes prayed, and rain fell.[67]

The significance of this story lies not so much in the apparent coincidence that Sykes prayed and rain fell, but in the fact that the Inqobo people could obey a missionary to the point of defying the traditional religious institutions, which, as we have seen, exercised so much power over both the people and their king. The explanation lies in the meagreness of the loyalty of this regiment to Lobengula.[68] The king having come to power with some help from the Mwari institutions, the Inqobo had, so it seems, little faith in the deity.

Although these people as a group could defy the god, individuals found it impossible to be converted to Christianity. Those who desired to join the new faith told the missionaries: 'If it were known that we are believing what you teach us, we should not live long, at the same time we admit your words are finding their way to our hearts.'[69]

The missionaries at Hope Fountain discovered much to their sorrow that the people were dominated by the presence of the king and the witch-hunters.[70] The king strenuously denied that the people were afraid to learn because if they did so he would kill them. He insistently put it down to the laziness of his subjects.[71] But the people in turn persistently retorted that: 'we like to learn & to hear about God & His Word but if we say openly that we belong to King Jesus, then we shall be accused of disloyalty to Lobengula & of witchcraft & killed'.[72] They went on to show their predicament, saying that they were the king's subjects, they imitated him, where he went they went, what he did they did, and they looked up to him under all circumstances. 'It is no good hiding the fact', declared one young Ndebele, 'that as long as the king does not show the example by beginning to read himself we will never do it. Let the king show us the road first, then we will all follow him.'[73] Perhaps asking the king to attend any form of missionary education was too much for a person who was old and much of whose time was taken up by administrative business. In fact what the people wanted was that the king should show them an example by sending his own children to school. This, in spite of his wife's later claim to the contrary, he flatly refused to do.[74]

Nonetheless, there were people who continued to risk being killed as witches by showing some interest in the teachings of the missionaries. When Frederick William Sykes, the son of the earlier missionary, visited the country between December 1887 and May 1888, he found that about fifty to sixty people attended Sunday service at Inyati. At Hope Fountain twenty-five to thirty men and women came to church and always paid great attention to the words of the preacher.[75] Indeed, as Margaret Carnegie, after living under Lobengula's government, later pointed out, the king did not attempt to prohibit the people from going to church and attending school, but, as we have already seen, the diviners who dreaded to be undermined by the new faith frightened people from conversion.[76]

Moreover, to show any signs of being converted could bring about disastrous consequences even from one's own family. Shisho Moyo, who was to become the first L.M.S. ordained minister, presents a classic example of the dangers of being converted. Moyo was a Hole, and his adopted father was called Mbiza. The latter sent or allowed Moyo to go and work for Margaret Carnegie as a nurse boy. Then it soon became obvious that the young man was gradually accepting Christianity and throwing away the religion of his parents. In fact the zealous Moyo had quickly learned how to read and write and was praying regularly under the guidance of Carnegie. Mbiza got angry and went to demand that the boy must come home. Moyo refused to leave his teacher and employer, which was followed by a very unpleasant scene. The old man struck his son with a club in the face. Perhaps a more tragic event could have taken place had the missionary not persuaded Moyo to obey his father and go home. Even then the young man held tenaciously to his newly acquired faith: he gave everything he had earned to his father except his copy of St Matthew's Gospel over which he continued to pore and he also prayed. Eventually the other old people of the village exerted pressure on Mbiza to let him go back to his teacher.[77]

Mbiza may not have been a diehard anti-Christian. The fact was that a convert brought disaster not only upon himself, but also on the whole of his family. As the following incident illustrates, the old man might have dreaded being smelt out as a witch on account of the activities of his son. In the 1870s a girl became interested in reading. Her family was soon involved in the notorious witchcraft business and they were chased away from their village. The convert's clothes were savagely stripped away and her books confiscated by the accusers of her family. After much pleading from the missionaries, the king resettled the family. The Christian girl, who had taken refuge with the missionaries at Hope Fountain, wrote a letter to Lobengula, thanking him for his kindness. The letter was read for the king, especially to demonstrate that the Ndebele were capable of learning. The monarch confessed himself impressed, but took no steps to encourage his subjects to acquire literacy.[78] Yet it was also under such conditions that Thomas achieved some of the most interesting results of the period. In November 1874, Thomas returned to Ndebeleland after being dismissed from the L.M.S. for trading and involvement in Ndebele politics.[79] He negotiated for a place to set up a mission station from Lobengula, who gave him the Shiloh Fountain, 25 miles west of Inyati, in return for 'a case of . . . shirts and a box of knives and forks'.[80]

When Thomas first got to his new mission, the local people still looked upon Europeans as complete strangers. 'This neighbourhood being out of the way of all white people, everything European is looked upon with curiosity and every white person regarded with suspicion; while our religion is thought to be dangerous, guarded against and avoided.' But Thomas was by now a seasoned missionary; he knew the Ndebele language very well and above all he was now free to employ his own methods which previously had been frowned upon by the L.M.S. He began to link material benefits closely with the Gospel. He spelt out his methods:

We have, however, during the two months already gone by, employed, in various ways a large number of the neighbours. And hope, that by gaining their confidence and affection, their minds have been made somewhat softer and readier to receive the word.

He concentrated on the singing of hymns and reading the Scriptures and praying. And it was among these servants and labourers that he gathered his first fruits.[81]

After six years of toil at Shiloh, the patient missionary baptised his first convert, Lomaqele, on 3 July 1881. Lomaqele had been a servant of the Thomases for almost twelve years. She could read and write. In 1870 she had chosen to go for further studies at Kuruman but her mother had been unable to face the separation from her. Several others were baptised and received into church membership after Lomaqele. These were Baleni Gumbo on 5 November 1881, Sendika on 6 August (?), Tama on 1 October, Baleni Masibi on 3 December, all in 1882. In 1883 four more were added to the Church. Perhaps most gratifying for the veteran missionary was that on 24 April 1882, in the presence of twenty to thirty spectators, he 'united in holy wedlock' Baleni Gumbo, the first composer of an Ndebele hymn, and the steadfast Christian Lomaqele. Again on 7 August 1883, the same missionary married Moses and Sibongo, both Christian, according to Christian rites.[82]

Considering the difficulties in the way of Christianity in Ndebeleland, the results achieved by Thomas were by no means unspectacular. When he died in 1884, his mission station declined from lack of guidance and proper supervision. Baleni Gumbo, a very reserved but powerful preacher, however, did all he could to keep the mission going until it was taken over by the L.M.S. in the 1890s.[83] Although only a Hole, he was well respected by the king and people. Thomas had taught him how to grow European vegetables, for which Lobengula had developed a liking. By supplying him with vegetables, Gumbo received the protection and encouragement of the king.[84]

Although those who publicly professed to follow Christ were only twelve – six Hole, four Nhla and two Zansi – the missionaries maintained that there were many more secret believers.[85] 'Secret believers', reported Carnegie, 'there are in the land but hide in the caves and rocks, they fear the king, they dare not speak, they live secretly, they speak not of him in whom they have believed.'[86]

Whatever secret converts there may have been, it is obvious that the results achieved by the L.M.S. missionaries were not equal to the effort expended. J. S. Moffat, in a letter that has already been referred to, observed that the failure of the L.M.S. to realise significant results was due to their lack of appreciation of the problems involved and the shortage of manpower. They had, for instance, not done much to try to penetrate enkosini – the scene of the witch-doctors, the anti-missionary indunas and harem, and of the unscrupulous, degraded and irresponsible white residents whose way of life was a complete negation of Christian teachings. He recommended that an unmarried missionary be placed at the king's place to battle with these forces for influence over the king.[87] His recommendations, however, came rather late as it was becoming increasingly clear that the country was about to come under colonial rule.[88]

The missionaries to some extent agreed with J. S. Moffat but they tended to emphasise Lobengula as the chief obstacle against missionary enterprise. The king, they said, refused to compel the children to go to school arguing that, 'I am not the father of these children, and cannot say anything about it'. Moreover they erroneously maintained that he 'was the king, independent, great, mighty, and afraid of nobody or anything'.[89] According to the abafundisi, therefore, it was in Lobengula's power to order his people to assimilate Christianity or to prohibit them. This view came out clearly in Carnegie's prayer for the fall of Lobengula's regime in 1889:

> Oh! for liberty and freedom and a power to break the cords of this savage monarch! This done then our mission will begin. It was so in Zululand it is so here & will continue to be so until a new government is formed and just laws administered to the people.[90]

Of course the L.M.S. missionaries never for a moment discounted the evil activities of the traditional religious institutions.[91] But they were more inclined to think that the izinyanga, izangoma and the Mwari shrines were the instruments of the king rather than the reverse.

But as has already been pointed out, Lobengula's power over his people was much more limited than that of his father. Moreover, Lobengula was as much the pawn of the traditional religious authorities, as the latter were his. He could not act contrary to the interests of these sages without some serious loss of popularity and hence undermining his very position as king.

As J. S. Moffat declared, the missionaries were too few for the problem that was before them. Even as late as the 1880s there were Ndebele people who had never set their eyes on a missionary. But this point must not be exaggerated. It was as much a result as it was a cause of much of the failure to evangelise Ndebeleland.[92] From the very beginning the country did not show any promising prospects, so that the missionaries were loath to waste both manpower and financial resources on an unpromising field.

Thus the history of missionary enterprise in the Ndebele state proper between 1870 and 1890 had the following as its prominent features. The merging process of the Shona and the Nguni religious institutions and beliefs gathered unprecedented momentum during

the rule of Lobengula, whom they helped to power and continued
to form the mainstay of his power and prestige. The success of the
missionaries would have meant to some extent the weakening of
the very basis of Lobengula's power. Lobengula and the religious
institutions, which felt their very existence at stake, therefore,
combined to exert their influence against the new faith.

To complete the picture of missionary activity in Ndebeleland in
the nineteenth century, it is also necessary to make a brief survey
of the response of the tributary areas. It has already been mentioned that the Shona were interested in the missionaries only in so
far as the latter could provide material assistance towards their
struggle for independence from Ndebele domination; and it was
nearly impossible for the missionaries to establish any systematic
work because of the nature of the relationships of the Shona to the
Ndebele. Both these facts were borne out by the attempts of the
Paris Missionary Society and the Berlin Mission to penetrate the
south and south-eastern Ndebele tributary chiefdoms.[93]

What often baffled the missionaries and European travellers who
entered the Ndebele tributary areas in the nineteenth century was
the seeming absence of people and the lack of any central authority
among the Shona peoples. When these Europeans came across the
former Shona villages which had been abandoned, they simply
concluded that the Ndebele had massacred them. Perhaps typical
of what the Europeans often said is the following:

> [The Ndebele] began sweeping the country in all directions . . . with
> the result that the land, which when they entered was teeming with
> human beings, before many years had elapsed was reduced almost to
> a desert . . . Thousands of families were put to death by these blood
> thirsty warriors.
> At present [1897] the places where they used to have their gardens
> and the ruins of their old huts are still to be seen all over the country.
> At one time the country must have been inhabited by a dense and
> industrious population.[94]

There is no doubt at all that the Ndebele killed many of the Shona
during the establishment of their rule and also during their raids
for grain and cattle. However, the depopulated areas were not the
result of massacres. The three major causes of the depopulation
were, as has already been seen, the large numbers of the indigenes
who were either moved from their previous home areas to other

places – such as the Nanzwa and the Leya – or were incorporated into the Ndebele state. Secondly, there were the Shona who, like Tohochipi, chose to fly from their homeland to as far away from the Ndebele state as possible. Thirdly, and the most important cause of all, was the radical change in the settlement pattern of the Shona caused by their flight from the low lying areas to the mountains and hills.[95] In fact Beach says that even before the Nguni invasions the Shona displayed a marked preference to settle on or around the hills; but he adds that the incursions of migrants from the south greatly accentuated this Shona tendency.[96]

As might have been expected, the mountains on which the Shona took refuge were often separated from one another by vast distances. It was possible to travel considerable distances without meeting a soul. This is one of the problems that the Berlin Mission encountered. Between March and July 1887, the mission sent two of its evangelists, Samuel and Johannes, to go and work among the Pfumbi of Matibe and the Remba of Mpose. The catechists found that Matibe had two headquarters on two separate mountains – Rasha (Mabwene) and Marungudze. In other words the two evangelists were supposed to travel between the present Diti and Maranda African trust lands, just to reach nearly all the Pfumbi of Matibe alone. They had again to traverse half as much that distance to reach the Remba of Mpose, whose capital was on the Dumbwe hill, near the present Evangelical Lutheran Church centre of Chegato. Calculated in days, the distances were as follows: from the Limpopo to Marungudze one and a half days; from Marungudze to Mabwene three days; and from Mabwene to Dumbwe about one and a half days.[97]

Even more vexing than the sparse population distribution, was the apparently nomadic life of the people. Many of them had been forced to run away from the Ndebele into the low veld. The droughts of the low veld compelled them to practise transhumance in order to get water. For instance Johannes and Samuel, after working for four months at Mabwene, were suddenly told by Matibe that he was moving back to Marungudze. At the same time he informed the preachers: 'I am going to Marungudze and you shall build in my place there, as I want you there and my children (i.e. my people) and my own sons shall learn.'[98]

Moreover, the missionaries discovered that it was difficult to make initial contacts with the Shona. These people were suspicious of foreigners. This was to be understood, for if they allowed aliens into their mountain fortresses, their secret climbing routes and defence techniques might be exposed. C. Knothe of the Berlin Mission stated that it was difficult even to estimate the number of people in an area: 'If you wanted to be able to guess approximately the number of inhabitants in a region you would have to stay there and wander around for weeks.'[99]

Finally, there was the problem of the Ndebele discriminatory policy towards missionaries intending to start in the tributary chiefdoms. In 1887, the two catechists were told by an envoy from Lobengula that 'they have no objections if Black teachers spread the Word of God. They are only afraid of the Whites – afraid that they will come into their lands from this side too now.' As Knothe explained, this was particularly directed against the Boers, who were always reported to be planning to enter the country.[100]

Ndebele policy against the whites entering their country through the tributary parts was demonstrated when between 1877 and 1878 Francis Coillard tried to lead a group of evangelists into the Chibi region and was arrested by the Ndebele. Of course there were also other reasons why he was detained and finally deported with his whole mission. First it was said that he had entered the country without permission, and, secondly, the Ndebele professed to resent the fact that the Sotho had betrayed one of the Nguni chiefs, Langalibalele, to the British[101].

In spite of all these difficulties, the Shona exhibited a great desire to have missionaries working among them. Matibe, Chingoma of Imbahuru and Mpose, perhaps stand out among those who wanted missionaries. In 1886 the Pfumbi ruler had promised to welcome *vadzidzisi* (teachers) in his land. And when Johannes and Samuel finally came to Rasha, he said,

> You have come – my answer is the same now as it was last year; a great man does not change his mind, I tell you the same now: Teach, if you want to, build your houses here if you want. All my people who want to learn can do so. These are my words; I cannot speak with a double tongue, I only say one thing.

At Mpose it was the same thing. The chief told them that since the Ndebele did not mind the presence of black teachers, he would have them at his place. Both these chiefs supplied the evangelists with food and living quarters free of charge. Within the short period of four months the catechists were able to report that there were seven people at Matibe 'beginning to learn and read'.[102]

The results achieved by the evangelists were acknowledged by their superintendent:

> Our two catechists, Samuel and Johannes, have done some good preparatory work despite their very short stay amongst the people. They have countered objections against the Mission, have won the confidence of the chiefs and the people to a large extent and have already brought on several souls so far that they have asked for further lessons in religion. We found three catechumens at Mpose's and one at Matibe's whilst three others were away from home for the time being and one had moved to Bavenda with his father. So in all there are 8 beginners in the belief who have recognised the Lord.[103]

Such results were not spectacular except when compared with the Ndebele state proper, where only twelve converts were realised in almost half a century. From the missionaries' point of view, it was not the numbers of actual converts that were of interest. Rather they were mainly interested in the fact that these people were being brought to know something about the 'Living God'. When the time of full-scale missionary enterprise came, as it did following the introduction of colonial rule, it was not like breaking new ground. Rather the people were able to understand relatively easily the teachings of the missionaries.[104]

However, it was the almost amazing willingness of the Shona to have vadzidzisi which deserves further examination. This welcome for missionaries extended to the Mwari institution. The Berlin evangelists gave a report of the cult's change of attitude, which, at first sight, is almost incredible when considering its collaboration with the Ndebele king to resist change in the Ndebele state proper.

When the evangelists came to Matibe they found the local *nyusa* Musingavika present. He attended the classes with the other people. After some time he went back straight to the Mwari shrine, Mobvumela, about six days west of Mabwene, and apparently reported the presence of the teachers to the cult's chief priests. This was followed by a conference of all the chiefs – Matibe, Mpose, Chingoma Mapiravana, Cenda, Madindire, Chitawudze, and others – including their own manyusa, called by the high priests of Mwari. All these chiefs and manyusa received the following unbelievable instructions:

You shall listen to God's Words as they are taught to you by the two people 'abafundisi', you must throw away Zitongulo (armlets) and Tangu (wizard dice) and the teaching of the witch doctors (mafungo a valoi) and the gods of your fathers and mothers because you are using these in vain. Throwing magic dice and killing the witch-doctors is all for nothing; for if you kill the witch-doctors you will die too for the witch-doctors also die. If you do this I shall execute you for it if you do not like to hear the words of the two men and do not speak of God. I, too, must agree to them for these things grow – they are bigger than I am! When you get home say these things! Then come here, many of you, so that I can say goodbye to you and can go away from here and go into the roots of the grass.[105]

The catechists added that the report had come through Mpose's brothers who had come from the shrine, where they had also met Musingavika. This evidence is indeed corroborated by oral data collected at one of the active Mwari shrines that the high god welcomed the whites during the scramble for Zimbabwe. The god described the whites as 'the children of his sister'.[106] These pieces of evidence show, as already pointed out, the preoccupation of the Mwari priests with the extension of the responsibilities of the god to include the forthcoming rule on the eve of the establishment of colonial rule. It is also interesting to note that Mwari was urging the people to discard ancestral beliefs ('the gods of your forefathers and mothers') and the use of magic, diviners and witchcraft, and to place complete reliance on 'God'. The priests were advocating monotheism, so far not practised because of the power of local beliefs. It is possible that the priests were not satisfied with the Ndebele conversion to the Mwari cult, for they continued to carry out important annual sacrificial ceremonies to their amadlozi during the Inxwala and to use the izanusi and the izinyanga, instead of placing complete faith in the high god.

Notes

1. *The Diamond Fields Advertiser*, 26 Feb. 1887
2. *Letters and Notices*, xiv, p. 285; see also R.N.A. BO1/2/2, Alexander Boggie, 'Lobengula', unpublished article, 1905, pp. 3–4
3. For a full account of the succession dispute of 1868–77, see R. Brown, 'The Ndebele Succession Crisis 1868–1877' in *Historians in Tropical Africa*, Salisbury, 1962

4. This famous crisis resulted from the fact that the Ndebele had migrated to western Zimbabwe in two groups, one under Mzilikazi and the second under Gundwane Ndiweni. The Ndiweni group was first to enter the country and lived for a long time without its king; it finally decided to install Nkulumane, the heir-apparent, as king. When Mzilikazi arrived, he is reported to have massacred all the chiefs concerned at the hill known today as Thabayezinduna.

5. T. M. Thomas, *Eleven Years in Central South Africa*, London, 1873, p. 288; H. Kuper, A. J. B. Hughes, and J. van Velsen, *The Shona and Ndebele of Southern Rhodesia*, London, 1954, p. 105; H. Vaughan-Williams, *A Visit to Lobengula*, Pietermaritzburg, 1941, pp. 112–13; L.M.S. B1/F2/ JC, Sykes to For. Sec., 25 Dec. 1868

6. Richards, *The Mlimo Belief and Practice*; see also R.N.A. BE2/1/1, where Lobengula is referred to by the nickname throughout

7. Lobengula's position was presumably no higher than that of nyusa or *wosana*

8. G. Kingsley Garbett, 'Religious Aspects of Political Succession among the Valley Korekore (N. Shona)' in E. Stokes and R. Brown (eds.), *The Zambesian Past*, Manchester, 1966, pp. 137–70

9. Interview with Kakaka Tshabangu, 17 June 1971; L.M.S. B1/F2/JC, Sykes to For. Sec., 10 June 1870; B1/F2/JD, Thomson to For. Sec., 2 Dec. 1870; J. S. Moffat to For. Sec., 18 Aug. 1870

10. C.O. 417/27, Encl. C. in Encl. 3 in Desp. 71, Colenbrander to Maund, 29 Nov. 1888

11. L. H. Gann, *A History of Southern Rhodesia: Early Days to 1934*, London, 1965, p. 54; R. Summers and C. W. Pagden, *The Warriors*, Cape Town, 1970, p. 35; for how wealthy some of Lobengula's cousins and half-brothers were, see C.8130, pp. 9–11. We also hear that Lotshe Hlabangana and Magatshana, a cousin of Lobengula, were very rich in livestock

12. Thomas, p. 243

13. F. Mandy, 'Matabeleland: The Future Gold Fields of the World. Its People and Resources, 1891', *Rhodesia Pamphlets*, i, 1

14. C.4643, p. 114

15. D. Carnegie, *Among the Matabele*, London, 1894, p. 103; as a result of this close relationship with the missionaries there developed a myth among the Ndebele that Lobengula could read and write; see R.N.A. W18/1, statement by Nkungusi; *Cape Times*, 21 Jan. 1888

16. W18/1, statement by Nkungusi

17. *Cape Times*, 21 Jan. 1888

18. Brown, 'The Ndebele Succession Crisis', and R. Brown, 'The External Relations of the Ndebele Kingdom in the Pre-Partition Era' in L. Thompson (ed.), *African Societies in Southern Africa*, London, 1969

19. R.N.A. BA10/2/1, Bailie's Journal 1876–7, Bailie to Admin., 31 Oct. 1876

20. L.M.S. B2/F1/JB, Thomas to For. Sec., 17 Jan. 1870

21. Carnegie, pp. 103–4

22. R.N.A. TH2/1/1, Thomas's Journal, entry for 1 Dec. 1879; see also J. Cooper-Chadwick, *Three Years with Lobengula*, London, 1894, p. 109

23. *Letters and Notices*, xii, p. 151

24. J. P. R. Wallis (ed.), *The Northern Gold Fields Diaries of Thomas Baines*, 3 vols., London, 1946, ii, p. 322
25. *Ibid.*
26. R. Moffat, *Missionary Labours and Scenes in South Africa*, London, 1842, p. 5
27. *Ibid.*, p. 270
28. L.M.S. B1/F2/JD, Thomson to For. Sec., 2 Dec. 1870
29. *Letters and Notices*, xiii/xiv, p. 102
30. *Ibid.*, p. 260
31. S.J. U/1, A. de Wit to Fr Weld, 16 June 1880
32. *Letters and Notices*, xv, p. 151
33. L.M.S. B1/F3/JD, Cockin to For. Sec., May 1879
34. *Ibid.*
35. *Ibid.*; see also Ranger, *Revolt in Southern Rhodesia*, p. 145
36. Mandy, pp. 14–15; *Cape Times*, 21 Jan. 1888; *The Diamond Fields Advertiser*, 26 Feb. 1887, 28 June 1889; R.N.A. MISC/SY1/1/1, Sykes's Journal, p. 11; W1 6/2/1, Wilson's Journal, entry for 30 July 1888; BO 11/1/1, Borrow to Father, 20 May 1887
37. Vaughan-Williams, p. 126
38. Mhlagazanhlani, *My Friend Khumalo*, p. 34
39. M. L. Daneel, *The God of the Matopo*, pp. 49–50
40. L.M.S. B1/F3/JD, Cockin to For. Sec., May 1879
41. S.J.C.K., Depelchin to Weld, 18 April 1880; *Letters and Notices*, xii/xxiv, pp. 256–60; 'Matabeleland, Mashonaland and Territory Occupied by the British South Africa Company, 1891', p. 39; R.N.A. TH2/1/1, Thomas's Journal, entry for 12 April 1880
42. See Ch. 4
43. L. Decle, *Three Years in Savage Africa*, London, 1898, pp. 153–4
44. R.N.A. TH2/1/1, Thomas's Journal, entry for 20 Jan. 1880
45. For a fuller discussion of the Ndebele diviners and their methods, see J. R. Crawford, *Witchcraft and Sorcery in Rhodesia*, London, 1967, pp. 183–90; also see Ch. 1
46. Carnegie, p. 55
47. Crawford, p. 183
48. R.N.A. TH2/1/1, Thomas's Journal, entry for 18 Aug. 1879
49. L.M.S. B1/F4/JA, Moffat to For. Sec., 2 Feb. 1888
50. *Letters and Notices*, xiv, pp. 265–7; see also *The Zambesi Mission Record*, iv, 47, 1910, pp. 35–9
51. *The Chronicle of the L.M.S. for the Year 1875*, p. 15
52. *Letters and Notices*, xix, p. 578
53. *Ibid.*, p. 579
54. *Ibid.*, xii/xiv, pp. 263–70
55. S.J.C.K., Depelchin to Weld, 10 March 1880
56. *Ibid.*, 'Extracts from Law's Diary', entry for 22 March 1880
57. S.J. U/1, de Wit to Weld, 28 July 1880
58. *Ibid.*, de Wit to Weld, 1 Sept. 1880
59. S.J.C.K., Croonenbergs to Prestage, 31 March 1883
60. *Letters and Notices*, xiii/xiv, pp. 267–8

61. *Ibid.*, xv, p. 151
62. S.J. U/9, Prestage to Kerr, 1891
63. *Ibid.*
64. After the expulsion of Thomas, only one missionary, Sykes, remained at Inyati. J. B. Thomson, who later died in Central Africa, was appointed to Hope Fountain. In 1877 Sykes was joined by William A. Elliott, author of *Gold From the Quartz*; in 1875 Thomson had been joined by C. D. Helm, who later featured in the signing of the Rudd Concession. When Thomson left, his place was taken by Joseph Cockin, who left a valuable account of the Ndebele traditional religion just before he died at Shoshong in 1880. David Carnegie, son-in-law of Sykes, author of *Among the Matabele*, translator of a number of English works into Sindebele, and founder of the Centenary station, filled this gap in 1882. In 1887, Sykes, after nearly thirty years of missionary labour in the Ndebele kingdom, died and was succeeded at Inyati by Bowen Rees, popularly known among the Ndebele today as *Mnali* Rees, in March 1888. This remained the situation up to the fall of the Ndebele kingdom.
65. L.M.S. B2/F1/JD, Thomson to For. Sec., 16 Feb. 1871
66. L.M.S. B1/F3/JB, Sykes to For. Sec., 12 May 1876; also Sykes to For. Sec., 21 June 1878
67. Mandy, pp. 25–6
68. L.M.S. B1/F3/JC, Cockin to For. Sec., May 1879
69. L.M.S. B1/F3/JB, Sykes to For. Sec., 12 May 1876
70. A. W. Elliott, *Gold From the Quartz*, London, 1910, p. 148
71. L.M.S. B1/F2/JD, Carnegie to For. Sec., 4 May 1889
72. L.M.S. B2/Reports: 1881–97, Carnegie to For. Sec., 4 Dec. 1886
73. L.M.S. B1/F3/JD, Carnegie to For. Sec., 7 Aug. 1886
74. L.M.S. B2/Reports: 1881–97, Elliott to For. Sec., 28 Dec. 1887; R.N.A. W18/1, statement by Nkungusi
75. R.N.A. MISC/SY 1/1/1, Sykes's Journal, pp. 8–9
76. R.N.A. MISC/CA5, M.M. to Good, 1 Nov. 1937
77. R.N.A. MISC/SY 1/1/1, Sykes's Journal, p. 9; L.M.S. B2/Reports: 1881–97, Carnegie to For. Sec., 7 Dec. 1888
78. Carnegie, p. 148; L.M.S. B1/F3/JA, Thomson to For. Sec., 15 Jan. 1874
79. 'Papers respecting the Matabele Mission'
80. R.N.A. TH2/1/1, Thomas's Journal, pp. 6–7
81. *Ibid.*, pp. 40–1; cf. R. Oliver, *The Missionary Factor in East Africa*, London, 1952, pp. 71–3
82. R.N.A. TH2/1/1, Thomas's Journal, pp. 131, 133; Thomas, pp. 77–8
83. L.M.S. B2/Reports: 1881–97, Elliott to For. Sec., 9 Feb. 1885
84. *The Chronicle of the L.M.S.*, 1918
85. Elliott, *Gold From the Quartz*, p. 146
86. L.M.S. B1/F4/JB, Carnegie to For. Sec., 6 Sept. 1889
87. L.M.S. B1/F2/JA, Moffat to For. Sec., 2 Feb. 1888
88. L.M.S. 'South Out Africa 1890–1', For. Sec. to Moffat, 30 Jan. 1890
89. Carnegie, p. 102
90. L.M.S. B1/F4/JB, Carnegie to For. Sec., 6 Sept. 1889
91. Elliott, *Gold From the Quartz*, pp. 103–4

92. L.M.S. 'South Out Africa, 1887–8', For. Sec. to Moffat, 24 May 1888
93. R.N.A. BE2/1/1 HIST.MSS.; much of what is described below is based on this manuscript, which to my knowledge has only been used by D. N. Beach in this Ph.D. thesis, 'The Rising in South-Western Mashonaland, 1896–7', London, 1971, and H. von Sicard, who presented it to the Rhodesia National Archives in 1951
94. Boggie, *From Oxwagon to Railway*, pp. 7–8; see also Thomas, pp. 164–5
95. R.N.A. BE2/1/1, 'Short Report on the Journey to Bonyai . . . 1888', p. 5
96. Beach, thesis, p. 40
97. R.N.A. BE2/1/1, 'Short Report', p. 7
98. *Ibid.*, 'End of July 1887. Report from the two Native Helpers Johannes and Samuel from Mabwene, Matibe's land', pp. 2–3
99. *Ibid.*, 'Short Report', p. 6
100. *Ibid.*, 'End of July 1887', p. 2
101. For the P.M.S. see C. W. Mackintosh, *Coillard of the Zambezi*, London, 1907, pp. 211–65
102. BE2/1/1, 'End of July 1887'
103. *Ibid.*, 'Short Report', p. 6
104. This is also the view of H. von Sicard, the Swedish early missionary in the region in question; personal communication
105. BE2/1/1, 'End of July 1887'
106. R. Mwanza, 'Mwari. The God of the Karanga', Lusaka Conference, 1972, p. 7

4

Religious institutions and the fall of the Ndebele kingdom, 1888–97

The Rudd Concession, the Occupation of Shonaland, the Anglo-Ndebele war and the risings of 1896 – all political events leading to the saddling of the Ndebele and the Shona with colonial rule – do not concern us in this study, except in so far as they help to illustrate or shed some light on aspects of Ndebele religious behaviour. Undoubtedly resistance to or collaboration with the white invaders were the paramount issues among the Ndebele in the years 1888–97. Violent action against the Europeans and pacific ways of coming to terms with western economic and political intrusion were discussed as well as adopted by the Ndebele at different times in the crucial years of the scramble for their country. It was the resulting political vacillation of the Ndebele polity between acceptance and rejection of the western world that enabled both the traditional religious institutions and the missionaries to play significant and effective roles during the fall of the Ndebele kingdom. At the same time the Ndebele belief in Mwari afforded enough scope for the priests of the cult to continue playing an influential part in the political and religious life of the peoples of Ndebeleland even after the fall of Lobengula, who had formed the vital link between the public and the supernatural world. Above all, the troubled years 1888 to 1896 enable us to see the religious situation of the country as it had developed during the previous half a century.

In the last chapter we saw Lobengula's religious and intellectual development resulting from his association with both the missionaries and the Mwari priests – a process, indeed, enabling him to have sophisticated arguments with whites on religious matters. We also emphasised his crucial position as the vital intercessor between the

Mwari cult and the public. Perhaps his position as a priestly intellectual of the nation placed him in a better position than the ordinary people to deepen his understanding of the supernatural world. In fact his attitude towards the Mwari priests and other Shona religious authorities seemed to show that he had gone a long way towards making a distinction between Mwari and the priests, the intercessors of the deity and interpreters of his wishes and commands to his worshippers. As we shall see shortly, for a long time Mwari and the priests were identical in the minds of the ordinary people. On the other hand, Lobengula ordered the execution of the Venda Mwari priest Mbikwa Ncube (Malaba) in 1880 and Pasipamire, the spirit-medium of Chaminuka in Central Shonaland, in 1883.[1] The reasons for the executions are now difficult to establish; but one traditionalist suggested that the priests had begun to abuse their magical powers.[2] However that may be, Lobengula's killings did not in any way suggest his loss of faith in Mwari, as missionaries pointed out at the time. Rather it seems he had established in his mind the difference between Mwari's intermediaries and the god himself, so that he could punish the former without feeling that he was offending the latter.

It is also possible that Lobengula's understanding of the Mwari theology and its institutions derived from the activities of the Mwari priests themselves. For, as already suggested, in the latter part of the nineteenth century the priests of Mwari were universalising their god and identifying him with the Christian God. Perhaps the same process was being felt by the ordinary people. What evidence there is indeed points to a growing understanding of the Mwari religion among ordinary people in the late nineteenth century.

It is worthwhile examining this evidence in order to understand why the Mwari cult's influence outlived the high priest, Lobengula, among the Ndebele. By 1886, it appears, Ndebele religious leaders were only slightly above their followers in their knowledge of the local theology. In that year the L.M.S. missionary Thomas attended a sacrificial ceremony at the king's palace. He reported that for the first time the Ndebele 'prayed to one god and not to many, and that god was above and not below'. When after the prayer Thomas argued with the leaders on the question of offering meat to their god, they admitted that he was a Spirit who 'could not eat or require beef; that He was the owner and giver of all good; that they were all fed and kept alive by Him'. These qualities revealing a supernatural

being immune to basic human necessities of life were indeed new in
Ndebele religious thought. Even then the same prayer pointed to a
deity not yet completely divorced from human susceptibilities, because at the end of his prayer, the priest in charge 'came to the kraal
and reported that the god was thankful for the offerings, and said
that he [Mzilikazi] must do his part and all will be well'.[3]

Among the ordinary people the mixture of human and supernatural characteristics of the god took the form of close identification of the spirit-mediums and priests with the god. Joseph
Cockin, in the letter already quoted, described Ndebele beliefs and
how he tried to point out to the people their mistaken beliefs in
mere 'deified men'.

> To the north are a God also a Goddess. The name of the Goddess is
> Salugazani. The people say she has one eye, one ear, one nostril, one
> arm and one leg. When I ask how many mouths and stomachs she has
> they cannot answer, except with a laughter, for somehow or other these
> great Gods and Goddesses who can bring on or avert disease amongst
> the people cannot stay the cravings of their stomachs except with the
> carnal food of which ordinary mortals partake.

Cockin also said that he had managed to puzzle the Ndebele by
simply showing that the so-called gods were only men because they
'have come to white men to beg for blankets to cover themselves
against cold!'[4] This type of idea of Mwari was not confined to the
Zansi and the Nhla; it extended to his original worshippers, the
Kalanga, as well. As Thomas tells us, undoubtedly with the missionary bias against the deity: 'If the Amakalanga themselves are asked
concerning him [Mwari], they will say that Umlemo is a man with
only one foot, dwelling under one of their mountains in a cave –
that he knows all things, is almighty, and very greedy.'[5]

Perhaps popular theology could not be expected to draw a clear
distinction between Mwari, the god, and his priestly intercessors.
His attributes, although investing him with supernatural powers
and qualities, gave him names some of which were people's praise
names, as the following praises show:

> Lunji kusi fume ngubo belera fuma pasi
> [Needle which does not sew a blanket, it stitches the earth (raindrops
> pierce the earth which then sprouts)].
> Bimbani washongwe
> [Creator and piler-up of the rocks].
> Bambedzi nkulu bambani u si ne mako ka no tshidza sindi yanyala

[Big Bambedzi of the Mopani without holes, He went to help the tired squirrel (He helped the squirrels by putting holes in the mopani trees, so will he not help us?)]
Kukula unga Lutombo,
[hard like a rock].
Gumbo tandawara ibe muvumbi
[His stretched-out leg becomes a drizzle].
Tobela Ngwali Nkulu
[Lord! Big Mwari].
Shoko Dzangu mbereka.
Shoko, Bambedzi, Babambe.[6]

Thus Mwari's supernatural attributes, though couched in what were to his worshippers everyday metaphors and similes, presented him as the Provider of rain, Giver of fertility, Creator and Builder of mountains, Lover of creatures and therefore concerned with the welfare of the people, Almighty, Strong, Everlasting as rock, and Lord. At the same time the last two lines of Mwari's praise names closely identified him with ancestral spirits of what D. P. Abraham believes were the proto-Shona of Shoko-Mbereka, who entered Zimbabwe in the early part of the fourteenth century under the leadership of one Nembire and are supposed to have introduced the Mwari cult.[7] Even during inter-shrine feuds ordinary people sometimes could not make out that these were priestly quarrels over spheres of influence and operation as well as over succession.

Among the many stories of the origins of Mwari is one that says the deity originally came from the Transvaal and was a Venda. He established himself at Njelele in the Matopo Range on the Shashe River during the time of the Mambo rulers. His other name was Runji (Needle). When Mwari (Runji) had become well established and extended his influence over large areas, Shologulu (alias Zhendanengumba) also left the Transvaal to come and live in the Matopo Range. Although Runji was the son of Shologulu, traditionalists say that the former bitterly resented his father's encroachment upon his territory, saying: 'Why did my father Shologulu come and live near here?' But it is interesting to note that although these disputes gave the impression of human beings vying with each other for power, the divinity of the god was carefully preserved. 'Shologulu was never a man,' traditionalists maintain, 'we just knew his voice, the voice saying he was Shologulu. He had power over rain and dryness.'[8]

The priests of the Mwari cult sometimes did much to hinder the development of a clear understanding of Mwari by the ordinary people. Some of them, particularly the *amajukwa* (mediums possessed by the spirits residing at the shrines), apparently possessed powers to make miracles. A classic example was Siginya-matshe, alias Siminya, who, according to Professor Ranger, was a nyusa in the Bulawayo area and 'had a considerable reputation as a wonder worker'. Ranger quotes some evidence given during the trial of Siminya for the part he played in the rebellion of 1896, which said the nyusa 'would go down on his hands and knees and imitate animals. On one occasion he butted with his head a big stone on which they ground their corn and broke the stone in halves. The people on that occasion were quite convinced he was supernatural.'[9] Such priestly activities or alleged behaviour did not help to erode the ordinary people's close identification of the high god with his priests.

It appears, nevertheless, that frequent exposure to missionary attacks and influences as well as the priests' elaboration of their religion eventually enabled some people to get a fairly clear understanding of Mwari and the role of the priests and spirit-mediums. At least that is the impression got from Frederick Courteney Selous, a white hunter turned settler, who communicated freely with the Zansi, Nhla and Hole Ndebele just before the outbreak of the 1896 uprising. Selous learned from these people that there was a head priest living with his family in the Matopo hills,

> and is known as the Umlemo [Mwari], but as far as one can understand from the rather conflicting statements made concerning him by the ... [Africans], he is not actually the Umlemo, but a being possessed of all the ordinary attributes of man, – in fact a human being, with a spiritual nature superadded which enables him to commune with the unseen Deity that pervades space, and communicate the wishes or commands of the invisible spirit to the people.[10]

Thus, although sheer lack of evidence makes it impossible for us to understand the precise theological and religious changes and their exact causes in western Zimbabwe, we have an idea of the deepening of Ndebele beliefs in Mwari, giving his institutions the ability to play an influential role in the country's reactions and response to western penetration.

Apart from Ndebele growing faith in Mwari, their political divisions caused by white pressures, particularly the period leading to the 1893 Anglo-Ndebele war, afforded sufficient scope for both missionaries and the Mwari priests to assume advisory roles. A brief look at the nature of Ndebele politics at this time is necessary in order to understand the intervention of the religious institutions.

The Ndebele ruling elite seriously disagreed about the ways and means of meeting white threats to their independence. The king himself was well aware of British military superiority and was quite informed about how that power had overrun several African kingdoms in southern Africa. He also knew that the leaders of what are today Botswana, Lesotho and Swaziland had applied or were in the process of asking for the British Queen's protection – a mild political domination with an advantage of preserving the traditional way of life of the protected people. This knowledge to some extent persuaded him to favour peaceful means of coming to terms with the British. He was supported by a few chiefs, notably Gambo Sithole and Lotshe Hlabangana. Both chiefs had at different times travelled through Botswana and parts of South Africa. They had seen some of the concrete manifestations of European power and had further come in contact with Khama, who was working out peaceful compromises with the whites to avoid a violent overthrow of his power. Lotshe also wanted the material benefits, such as firearms and other western manufactures, that accrued through peaceful dealings with Europeans. In this respect he represented a number of old people with property, who appeared to welcome white presence for commercial purposes. Equally interesting in Lotshe's motives was that he may have wanted the establishment of colonial rule with its likely concomitant destruction of the system of smelling out witches. Again Lotshe was not alone in entertaining such a hope for there were people reported to be longing either for the destruction or for the modification of their society. These people were forced to such revolutionary or reformist sentiments by their desire for peace, by the wish to acquire property without falling victim to witchcraft suspicions, by disenchantment with Ndebele militarism, and by a yearning for stable family life. But the youths and a great many reactionary elders were violently against the European presence.[11]

Faced with such formidable opposition, Lobengula consulted the Mwari priests perhaps not only for advice, but also to obtain religious sanction for his peaceful policy towards the whites. Thus Hobasi, an Ndebele informant interviewed in 1937, said that he was a soldier before the white invasion of Shonaland in 1890. Soon after the Inxwala ceremony of the previous year the king fell ill, and, according to Hobasi, he sent some of his chiefs to consult a Mwari shrine about the cause of his sickness. The chiefs came back with the following message: 'You people must climb into the highest trees, and you will see my red boys are coming – Abafana bami ababomvana.' The following year the whites entered Shonaland.[12] To be sure, there are several versions of this oral tradition. Essentially, they all give the impression that Mwari priests advised the Ndebele king against military confrontation with the whites.[13] When Lobengula 'was fleeing', goes another tradition, 'he called on Molimo and bitterly repented of his wilfulness and craved mercy for his own head'.[14] The king wanted forgiveness for his cruel rule, so we are told. Recently, Mr Mwanza, one of the very few people who have collected oral data among the priests of Mwari, heard that Lobengula was advised against fighting the whites. 'The king told his warriors not to fight the Europeans and he passed on the word to his warriors who completely disobeyed him.'[15]

The tradition regarding Lobengula's consultations of the Mwari cult officials and other Shona religious officials on how to face European penetration was, to be sure, widely known. In 1892 the Nemakonde people of Central Shonaland described the type of communication that had taken place between the Ndebele king and Salugazana, the spirit-medium mentioned by Joseph Cockin. Salugazana was believed by both the Ndebele and the Shona of Nemakonde to have supernatural powers: 'They say she can make rain, govern the harvest, avert sickness or bring punishment. In her hand is the power of life and death and to destroy her voice means the destruction of the present and future'. The people also believed that both Lobengula and his father, the late Mzilikazi, were governed in their actions by Salugazana, and that the spirit-medium had averted a bloody confrontation of the Ndebele and the white pioneer column in 1890 by counselling Lobengula against attacking the white people. 'Had she spoken otherwise there is no doubt that a long and fierce struggle would have taken place between the English and the Matabele.'[16] The Nemakonde people may well have over-stated the influence of their spirit-medium over the Ndebele monarch. Yet it must be clear from this evidence and the above-mentioned similar traditions that there was apparently considerable communication between the Ndebele central political authority and the territorial religious institutions and that the latter's advice was for peace with the white people.

To be sure there were similar religious traditions elsewhere in Africa concerning the scramble for Africa. For instance, Marcia Wright, in her valuable study of missionaries and Christianity in the southern highlands of Tanzania, mentions a prophetess who was reputed to have foretold the coming of a people that would liberate the Safwa from king Merere's exacting domination. The Christians had later interpreted the prophecy to have meant the coming of the white men and their material benefits. Marcia Wright indeed comes to the same conclusion as ours though she states it differently that such 'prophetic traditions eased transition for a people under stress'.[17] The Ndebele rulers, though under no alien domination, were facing a critical situation in which their independence was being threatened and in which there was much violent disagreement as to what policies should be adopted towards the white invaders. It was a situation in which the Ndebele ruling elite felt the need for an over-arching authority, commanding the respect of all the people, irrespective of their factional and ethnic differences, to sanction their peaceful policy towards the whites.

Besides seeking the advice of the traditional religious institutions, Lobengula, perhaps conscious of the religious pluralism of his people, but definitely aware of the missionaries' superior knowledge of the economic and political forces now pressing on his country and probably seeking some positive confirmation of his peaceful policy, also turned to these white teachers for advice.

Because of their failure to make converts under Lobengula's regime, the missionaries had by the 1880s come to the conclusion that the Ndebele political system must be overthrown to pave the way for Christianity. Indeed, when Carnegie, alarmed at the imminent closing-in upon Lobengula's kingdom of Boers, Portuguese, Germans and British concession seekers, anxiously wrote to his Directors, the latter welcomed the advent of white rule as a factor that would either destroy Lobengula and dispose his people to accept the Gospel, or drive the raiders out of the country leaving the peaceful Shona to receive the blessings of Christianity. Moreover, a violent destruction of the Ndebele kingdom, the Directors reminded their missionary, would be God's punishment of the Ndebele for their past atrocities upon other black people. In short, the L.M.S. remained convinced of the salutary effects of the overthrow of the kingdom on the evangelisation of its people; they were not going to use their influence with their fellow whites to mitigate the violence that might be called for to dismantle the kingdom: in fact, they would be interested spectators in the whole affair.[18] It is also clear that the missionaries knew that their future success lay in the existence of gold in Zimbabwe. Long before the mounting of western economic and political pressures, the veteran L.M.S. missionary Sykes had repeatedly warned Lobengula 'that the white men will go into his country for gold and that if he won't allow them, force will be used. Should the chief allow prospecting matters will go smoothly, but if not, there will be war.'[19] Thus unlike the Mwari priests who supported the advent of white settlement apparently as part of their efforts to evolve a universalistic theology, the missionaries hoped for a factor likely to create a congenial situation for evangelical work.

It may well have been in that context that Helm agreed to participate in the negotiations for the Rudd Concession between 20 September and 30 October 1888. Helm himself reported in October 1888 that the Ndebele kingdom was in a state of turmoil because of a large number of concession seekers infesting enkosini. The situation, in his opinion, could only be saved by Lobengula entering into some agreement with Cecil John Rhodes, who would exploit the Shona gold fields and keep out other gold seekers.[20] Both Lobengula and his chiefs agreed that Helm played an important role in advising them to sign the Rudd concession.[21] Even Carnegie later stressed the part played by his colleague 'in bringing about that change in the country's government and in adding this large country to the British Empire'.[22] In the light of Lobengula's attitude towards European expansion, however, it is likely that he viewed Helm's advice in the same way as he may have done that of the traditional religious institutions: as an encouragement to do what he had in fact wanted to do.

The political controversy that later arose over the Rudd Concession is not important for this study. But it is relevant to point out that it seems both the missionaries, and Helm in particular, on the one hand and Lobengula as well as his chiefly advisers such as Lotshe on the other were in the dark regarding Rhodes's intentions to use the agreement as a basis for the extension of the British Empire to Zimbabwe. Most likely Helm believed that Ndebeleland would be opened up to British mining enterprise and that the Ndebele would be involved in this as labourers, thus making them amenable to missionary influences. When Rhodes's opponents revealed to the

Ndebele that by signing the Rudd Concession they had jeopardised their political independence, Helm consistently and adamantly rejected the idea as a malicious misconstruction of the concession document. Moreover, when Francis Thompson, one of the grantees and representative of Rhodes in Ndebeleland, submitted to Lobengula an addendum refuting any intention on the part of the grantees to endanger Ndebele sovereignty, a move supported by W. A. Elliott, Helm's missionary colleague, Helm publicly turned down the suggestion as being unnecessary and redundant. Probably then Helm was not deliberately playing the villain in the Rudd Concession affair,[23] even though Professor Samkange has pointed out that this missionary was secretly in the employ of Rhodes.[24]

However, this did not mean that the missionaries were opposed to the destruction of the Ndebele kingdom. They did not want to be directly involved at this stage. As the Foreign Secretary of the L.M.S. put it:

> whatever you do, be sure to keep out of every suspicion of connection with the gold hunters and land grabbers. If the missionaries keep a strict neutrality, and if their hands are seen to be clean of any speculation, they will have an influence among the natives and Europeans.[25]

But once Rhodes's people entered the country, missionaries were just as involved in land-grabbing as the white settlers.[26]

In the event the missionaries had failed to maintain a neutral position. Soon everyone in the L.M.S. interested in the Ndebele country felt like Carnegie that 'Mr Helm before connecting himself with Mr Rudd and Part should have talked the matter over with us in the first instance and this unfortunate business might have been prevented'.[27] The fact was that even the ordinary people in the country were furious with what they now regarded as the double-faced missionaries; and it had become quite dangerous for the latter to go preaching in the villages. Helm himself became a marked man among the Ndebele, and some L.M.S. officials strongly advised him to remain outside the country until the situation had improved.[28] Carnegie also indignantly reported how he had narrowly escaped a beating at a village:

> why just two Sabbaths ago while preaching at a town four miles away my pocket knife was stolen, [and on my] accusing them of it – they threatened to beat me, I however, got on my horse and off. The last words I heard were these, 'You – you little white slave – if you come

back here to preach again we will see to it that you don't escape without a thrashing.' Can anything be more disheartening, more cruel, more humiliating than this.[29]

It was becoming apparent that the king himself had become so disillusioned with the missionaries that for a while he valued the missionaries' 'presence not one jot'.

While the missionaries and the Mwari cult were for different reasons supporting the advent of white settlement, and while Lobengula and some of his chiefly advisers were vacillating between acceptance and rejection of European intrusion, the izinyanga and the izangoma remained implacably opposed to the whites and their religion. Perhaps the most virulent and outspoken representative of this class of traditionalists was Hlegisane, the army doctor. Hlegisane, like most of his class, had everything to lose from the establishment of colonial rule. Lobengula frequently paid him handsomely for protecting the soldiers before a raid and for cleansing them after it. He knew full well that a white colonial regime would not only destroy the very basis of his income – the Ndebele army – but it would also legislate against the whole system of smelling out people as witches. His own father Mbulali had been a victim of such white colonial action, when he was forced to flee the Cape to Waterboer's territory to escape a charge of witchcraft.[30]

Hlegisane found the opportunity to attack the whites and their religion during the several meetings that were held at enkosini from early 1889 to the time of the Anglo-Ndebele war in 1893. At one such meeting which had been called to discuss the Rudd Concession a missionary pointed out that the Ndebele were being deceived to sign documents selling their country to the whites because of their refusal to learn 'English, reading and writing so as to be independent of white men in such matters'. While Lobengula appeared to agree with the statement, one man, well acquainted with the work of the missionaries at Inyati, bitterly disapproved of the suggestion, shouting '[the missionaries] don't give us any meat, or any present, but only words when we do go [to their services]'. This was corroborated in a much more vicious way by Hlegisane: 'True quite true, O Malibamba! . . . ay they tinkle tinkle the bell to tell us child's tales but they don't tinkle it to tell us bad news like this [the deceitfulness contained in the Rudd Concession].' The missionary added in his report that the caustic remarks of the doctor did not surprise them as Hlegisane was a long standing 'hater of missionaries'.[31] On another occasion the doctor apparently tried to incite the Ndebele nation against white people, launching a bitter attack on one of the grantees of the Rudd Concession, and exposing to the Ndebele listeners some cunning deceitfulness of Europeans in their dealings with Africans. He said he knew the whites and their activities, having observed them in the south.[32]

Although most of these things were said after the Ndebele discovery of how they had been cheated into jeopardising their independence by signing the Rudd Concession, it seems clear that the izinyanga and izangoma were firmly opposed to the coming of the whites. In 1890 when the missionaries abandoned their mission stations and lived in Botswana for fear of being caught up in a possible military confrontation of the Ndebele with the white pioneer column, it appears pressures were applied on the few converts to return to traditional religion. Several executions for witchcraft were carried out under the very nose of the former missionary and then British representative, J. S. Moffat. The missionaries also claimed that the izinyanga and izangoma actively undermined them in the face of their converts by telling the latter that the abafundisi had abandoned mission work for ever.[33]

To appreciate the power and authority of these men in Ndebele society, it is important to note that their decision was final and the people they accused were nearly always executed. As the missionary Thomas put it:

> That which astounds one in such cases [of witchcraft] is the complete success attending the isanusi's work invariably. The people seem to be entirely at his command because they never seem to doubt his infallibility. Everyone seems to believe that he never can make a mistake and thus is entirely in his hand and at his mercy.[34]

The reason indeed why people did not protest against the decisions of the isanusi was that he was an excellent judge of public opinion. The man he singled out as a witch was frequently the one everybody thought of as having an odd type of behaviour or as possessed of evil intentions. This was why Christian converts were such easy victims of dangerous suspicions. They were ostracised by the rest of society for their refusal to conform to the traditional ways. In the event of people recoursing to an isanusi the Christian would turn out to be the odd man and would invariably be picked out as the practitioner of evil magic.

It is easy to see how the Christians placed themselves in a suspicious position from the example of a female convert reported by Mrs Mary Carnegie, the wife of the Rev. Carnegie:

> A young girl who had been converted was wondering what she would do when the yearly feast dance [the Inxwala] took place at the king's kraal. It was her duty with a number of other girls to carry beer to where the feast and dance were held. She was determined to take no part in the heathen festivities but was obliged to carry her portion of the beer. So she got out of her difficulty by going alone at night the 10 miles with the beer and leaving it at the appointed place and returning home before anyone was about.[35]

We cannot doubt the strong faith of this girl in her new religion. But to move about at night and to refuse to attend the Inxwala were among the things that caused one to be suspected of witchcraft.

Apart from having a good sense of public opinion, the diviners might also be used to smell out one's enemies as witches so as to have them killed. A report on how the Shona izinyanga or bone-throwers were employed by the Ndebele reveals this possibility of their being misused. A white man observed:

> When such an accusation [of witchcraft] is made by one Matabele against another, the case is tried before the king, both parties in the meantime having used their utmost endeavours by backstairs influence to secure a decision in their favour . . . the trial usually takes place at night. The witchdoctor is summoned and he comes with his hands full of charms, such as small bones, snake heads, a bit of crocodile's liver, etc. These he throws on the ground and having attentively examined them and perhaps altered the position of one or two of them slightly with his fingers, he will say, for example – 'The bones say there is a hill'. The king and his surrounding indunas exclaim in deep, guttural accents – [*aya kuluma amatambo*] – the bones are right.

The diviner would go on along those lines until he arrived at a decision which was unanimously supported by both the king and his indunas.[36]

These then are the izinyanga, izanusi, and izangoma, who in the 1890s were setting their faces against the missionaries and their converts. We can only imagine the amount of persecution the converts went through from the general attitudes of the people towards them and their own refusal to conform to the traditional norms. In April 1890 the Rev. David Carnegie was rejoicing over the progress that was being made by Shisho Moyo, Mbiza's adopted Hole, and another girl. Both converts were faithfully participating in the weekly private prayer meeting, held in Carnegie's study. In their 'short, broken and sincere prayers' they prayed for themselves and 'those dark deluded people' living around them. Shisho Moyo had lived with the Carnegies for years. During that whole period he had

> never once expressed a desire to return to his old companions and habits of life and there [is] no reason to doubt that Christ has formed in him the hope of Glory. He knows something about Jesus, but best of all knows Him to be his Saviour, and feels the power of His dying love for him in his heart.

Although the female convert was still somewhat immature in the new religion, she too had become 'deeply conscious of her need of a Saviour and set about finding him in dead earnest'. 'Her life, walk and conversation' had begun to change showing how she was finding peace in believing in Jesus Christ. Both of these converts had become outcasts in the Ndebele society. 'I am told', Carnegie reported on their social plight, 'that these two souls no more belong to the nation – that they belong to me.'[37]

In fact most of the Christians during the troubled years of 1890 to 1896 survived being forced back into the traditional fold or being actually executed simply because, like their missionary teachers, they were either in the south or protected in the white laager in Bulawayo. The Ndebele Christian and moderniser, Mika Nxobe, who wrote a letter to Lobengula urging him to establish an administrative bureaucracy consisting of missionary-educated Ndebele and advising the king against military confrontation with the whites, was himself holding tenaciously to his new way of worship in the safety of the Transvaal. Nxobe also told Lobengula that there were many more Ndebele Christians living in Transvaal.[38] No doubt Nxobe was referring to such Christians as Baleni Masibi, one of the early converts of Thomas at Shiloh, who left for the Transvaal with the missionary's widow and children soon after 1884. Masibi remained in the south until after the complete subjugation of the Ndebele in 1896, when he returned to take up an appointment as one of the black preachers of the L.M.S. The famous Shisho Moyo's sojourn in the south was even much more fruitful than that of the others. The Rev. Carnegie took him to Lovedale, where he underwent some training as a preacher and also received his baptism. He did not return home until 1896 when he found the country in a state of war.

He was afforded protection at Bulawayo and after the rebellion became the first black teacher at Hope Fountain.[39]

At this point we can now look at the salient features of the religious situation in Ndebeleland during the scramble era. First, the territorial Mwari cult appeared to be broadening its interests and responsibilities beyond the Shona and Ndebele parochial limits so as to include the coming white rulers. The priests of the cult were apparently also universalising their high god to the extent of identifying him with the missionary God. These efforts may well have caused the attitude of the priests towards the advent of colonial rule to coincide with that of the missionaries, who saw white rule as a factor that would destroy the Ndebele system and thereby pave the way for the Gospel. Naturally, the converts went along with their white teachers in supporting colonial rule, apparently hoping that such a change would bring in its train freedom of worship. But the izinyanga, izangoma and other medicine men foresaw their doom as influential and respected authorities in the coming white rule. They were able to assess correctly their imminent destruction because the missionaries had always preached against them. As we have seen in the preceding chapters their tradition as upholders of the traditional beliefs and institutions and their resistance to missionary work were long standing. These diehard traditionalists seem to have made the life of the converts, particularly during the scramble period, uncomfortable to the extent that the Christians had to seek refuge outside the country or among the whites. At the same time we have noted how apparently the universalising of the Mwari cult system together with the presence of the Christian religion was helping the Ndebele to deepen their faith in Mwari as well as to formulate a fairly sophisticated theology, in which the priests were being distinguished from the god.

These features remained essentially true up to the fall of the Ndebele kingdom in 1893 and the subsequent white occupation of the country. First, the fall of Lobengula, the vital link between the Ndebele and Mwari cult as well as the rest of the supernatural world, called for some adjustment in the functional relationship of the people with the fertility cult and the royal amadlozi. As we shall see this led to increased Mwari priestly activity in Ndebele villages and to the growth of the prestige of some of the Ndebele high priests. The white settlers, hailed by Mwari as his special sons, disregarded the deity on their occupation of the country, a serious omission causing some of the cult's shrines and individual priests to take an active part in the Ndebele-Shona uprisings of 1896–7.

To understand these religious changes it is necessary to take a brief look at the risings of 1896–7, on which three interesting studies have been carried out by Professor T. O. Ranger, Drs D. N. Beach and Julian Cobbing.[40] The first two scholars slightly disagree on the causes of the rebellions. Ranger, for instance, believes that the natural desire to preserve and defend their way of life as well as onerous economic and administrative pressure drove the Ndebele and Shona societies into rebellion against the British South Africa Company regime. Beach, on the other hand, sees no simple relationship between these causes and the rebellions because European pressure – such as the demand for labour in the mines, land alienation, seizure of livestock both in lieu of Hut Tax payments and as 'loot', and interference with autochthonous judicial systems – were unevenly distributed throughout the country. Moreover, Beach shows that in some cases societies greatly affected by European economic and political activities either remained neutral or collaborated with the whites in suppressing the rebels.

It is this lack of a 'correlation between [European] pressure and resistance' that has led Beach to disagree fundamentally with Ranger on the organisation and co-ordination of the risings. Examining the revolt on a national scale, Ranger came to the conclusion that the Ndebele military system, that had survived the previous war in 1893, formed the basic means of organisation in Ndebeleland, with the former indunas and doctors furnishing the local and divisional leadership. But the co-ordination of the insurgent groups in the whole of Zimbabwe was carried out by the religious institutions. The Mwari cult officials harmonised the different fighting units in Ndebeleland and western Shonaland, and the spirit-mediums those in central and eastern Shonaland. Concentrating on a much smaller region, an advantage enabling him to pay adequate attention even to the collaborators overlooked by Ranger, Beach has come up with a different theory. Thus after a thorough examination of the historical background of several chiefdoms in south-western Shonaland as well as their former political interrelations and their positions in relation to the Ndebele state, Beach argued that chiefdoms formerly dominated by the Ndebele rebelled in sympathy with their erstwhile rulers; those that had a tradition of resisting the raiders either remained neutral or collaborated with the new white rulers. As for central Shonaland, the recent Portuguese activities involving the distribution of guns and flags had not only infused the Shona with a common feeling of confidence in their resistance against the perennial Ndebele menace, but had also led 'to a certain amount of unity'. In short, the Shona's past internal and external political relations determined their decisions to collaborate, to resist or to remain neutral. The religious factor, to which Ranger attached decisive importance, was not universally important in the whole country. Indeed, to those who would contend that you cannot understand Shona politics without a sound knowledge of the religion of these people, Beach says the very opposite. So if the religious institutions participated in the 1896–7 upheavals, they were only a reflection of the political aspirations of the people. However Beach acknowledges the crucial role played by the religious sector in certain parts of the country – particularly by Mkwati, a senior official of the Mwari cult in Ndebeleland and the Rozvi districts of Gwelo and Somabula and by Kagubi and Nehanda, both *masvikizo* (spirit-mediums) in central Shonaland.

Cobbing, on the other hand, takes the opposite view to Ranger. He maintains that the 1893 Anglo-Ndebele war had left the Ndebele state largely intact and therefore capable of organising itself militarily to fight a second war with the whites. 'In sum', Cobbing tells us, 'the Ndebele state had not expired in 1893 and lived to fight again.' The Ndebele were apparently so united and well organised that they were able to elect as their king Nyamanda, who 'both in respect of his birth and martial talents . . . was the only possible claimant in that rising year'. It was Nyamanda and the 'great families' or 'royalized caste' of the Ndebele state 'who, together with the lesser chiefs, instigated the first murders, arranged for the distribution of ammunition, organized the supply routes, and sent the women and children into the hills at the time of the outbreak'. The Mwari cult played no role whatsoever in the Ndebele uprising. For none of the Ndebele chiefs, including their priest Unlugulu, were in touch with the cult caves'. Furthermore, the Shona chiefs that rose with the Ndebele did not do so at the instigation of Mwari priests. They did so because 'They all belonged to what may be loosely termed the Ndebele tributary state, a series of firm alliances which Mzilikazi and Lobengula had forged during the previous half century'.

To be sure, Cobbing goes on, the Mwari cult was not in a position to play a role in the uprisings of 1896. Ethnically it was a Venda cult and as such could not command the obedience of the Ndebele and the Shona. Its history was a recent one in western Zimbabwe, probably dating as late as the 1820s and 1830s. Moreover, in 1896 the cult was in terrible disarray organisationally. The priests of the four important shrines were either dead or in exile. As for Mkwati who is supposed by Ranger to have played a leading role in the co-ordination of the Ndebele and Rozvi in the north and east, Cobbing dismisses him as simply a Mwari messenger, who probably never founded a shrine in Manyanga. Finally, Cobbing boldly declares: 'The Ndebele did not succumb to cult influence, not even between March and July 1896, but maintained their previous coolness towards the priests.'

To try to argue with Cobbing at length would be tantamount to reproducing some of my arguments already stated in this book. For instance, I have already argued that the Ndebele were culturally influenced by the Shona and that one of the cultural traits assimilated by the Ndebele was the Mwari cult. To maintain that the Ndebele held their own culturally throughout the nineteenth century is to miss the point. Cultural assimilation of the conquerors by the conquered was indeed not unique to the Ndebele state. P. L. Bonner, who has studied the Swazi kingdom, shows how the Ngwane, who conquered and subjugated the Sotho, the original inhabitants of present-day Swaziland, were so culturally assimilated by the latter that it is surprising that conventional historiography classifies them among the Nguni.[41] In fact, instead of postulating a pure Ndebele state that 'maintained . . . coolness towards' the culture and institutions of its subjects, research should begin to be seriously directed towards the traits that differentiated the Ndebele kingdom from other Nguni states, most of which characteristics emanated from influences of the peoples they absorbed.

The weakest point in Cobbing's radical interpretation of the Ndebele–Mwari cult relations is the dating of the cult's instrusion into western Zimbabwe to the mid-1830s, which is only slightly earlier than the establishment of the Ndebele kingdom in the country. Cobbing accepts Thomas's observation that the cult's influence and power were incompatible with those of the Ndebele king so much so that Mzilikazi was forced to suppress the activities of its priests. The question is, if the Mwari priests had entered the country so recently why did they for half a century hold on to the

Matopo Hills and western Zimbabwe in particular, areas which were dominated by their inveterate enemies? Moreover, when Thomas says Mwari's 'fame and influence are of such recent date' he is not referring to western Zimbabwe, as Cobbing would like us to believe. Thomas is talking about Mwari's influence among the Ndebele themselves and not among their Shona subjects. If anything, Thomas gives an impression of a long-established institution in the country – an institution with a thorough knowledge of its country's geography and societies. Thomas tells us:

> On arriving in their land, about forty years ago, Umzilikazi found several Amakalanga [and not Venda] doctors and wizards there, and for a time, on account of their influence over the chiefs of their own tribes, and knowledge of the country, they were of much use to him as newsmongers, and leaders of his troops on their raids into different parts of the interior.[42]

Even more curious is the fact that the Venda were able to infuse the beliefs and practices of their cult among the Kalanga in the teeth of Ndebele opposition so much so that by the turn of the present century the Mwari beliefs had become an inseparable part of Kalanga culture. Recently collected oral data says that:

> As the Bakalanga moved into Botswana [after the establishment of the Botswana-Rhodesia boundary] they were establishing at various places shrines and some Daka where they gathered once every year, after harvesting, to either celebrate their harvest or pray for the rain if it failed to come on time for them to plough.[43]

The Daka are the Mwari cult's centres of workship where the *wosana* or manyusa come together to hold dances. Clearly the cult was part and parcel of the Kalanga way of life.

Cobbing also doubts that Mkwati established a Mwari cult centre in Ntabazikamambo and dismisses him as a mere wosana who sought refuge in those hills. When problems of communication arose between outlying chiefdoms and the cult's centres in the Matopo hills, as they must have during the uprisings, a wosana could found a centre where Mwari oracularly manifested himself. Evidence from northern Botswana again shows that the first person to found a Mwari shrine there was Naka Pasi, who had all along been simply a wosana. 'Tradition states', Mtutuki says, 'that during Kgosietsile Habangana's reign as chief, Naka Pasi was instructed by "Mwali" when she was in a trance, to build him a hut where his voice could be heard. She obeyed.'[44] Mtutuki further gives the example of Ntogwa, the successor of Naka Pasi, who started off as a *lombe*, a popular traditional dancer, became a wosana and ended up founding his own Mwari shrine. These people were forced to establish new shrines apparently by the communication difficulties between Botswana and the central shrines in Zimbabwe. In short, there is nothing unreasonable about assuming that Mkwati may have been forced to establish a Mwari centre in the north-east, thereby becoming the dominant religious figure in the area. Above all, indications are that the Mwari cult had a long history in western Zimbabwe, probably recruited its priests from as far afield as Vendaland and participated in the uprisings in the manner that Ranger portrays.

Indeed, the evidence adduced by Ranger of the part played by the religious factor in Ndebeleland is impressive. From the standpoint of the present study, the manner in which the Mwari cult officials commanded the obedience of the Ndebele and co-ordinated the various fighting units was a remarkable indication of how the Shona religious system had penetrated the former conquerors' way of life. It was undoubtedly the most spectacular manifestation of the Zansi and Nhla acceptance of the religion of the vanquished, a process, which, as we have seen in the previous chapters, had been going on for almost half a century.

It is to this evidence of the religious participation in the rising that we must now turn.[45] As noted in the previous chapters the Ndebele were adopting Shona religion at the same time as they were retaining their own beliefs and practices. This pattern was clear during the uprisings. After the removal of Lobengula, the national priest and chief intercessor between the guardians of the state, the amadlozi, and the people, Ranger tells us, the only religious authority left to fulfil these functions was Mulugulu. Mulugulu was the successor of Mtamjana, who was responsible for organising the annual worship of the amadlozi (Inxwala) and for conducting the burial and installation rites of kings. In fact, just before his death, Lobengula had commissioned Mulugulu to continue the Inxwala ceremonies. This commission coupled with the absence of a nationally recognised regent made Mulugulu the central figure in the Ndebele efforts to revive the kingdom in 1894–5. He was in the forefront of a group of indunas planning rebellion against the new regime and preparing to hold the Inxwala on 26 March 1895, during which he would proclaim Mfezela, a member of the royal family, king, in spite of the B.S.A. Company administration. The decision to install Mfezela king was opposed by the young generation led by the militant Mpotswana in favour of Lobengula's eldest son, Nyamanda. This split was never resolved throughout the rebellion – causing the Ndebele to fight in two major divisions which we can call the Nyamanda and the Mulugulu divisions.[46] The most important point to be established, however, is the persistance of the Zansi religious beliefs and institutions as represented by Mulugulu and by the unsuccessful efforts to hold the Inxwala.

The Zansi beliefs and practices were not universally respected by the Ndebele and the Shona in the former tributary areas; only the Mwari cult, worshipped throughout Ndebeleland, could and did offer the co-ordinating machinery among the various ethnic groups.[47]

We have already noted the way in which the Mwari cult in 1890 and 1893 welcomed the white settlers and how the officials of the latter had ignored the cult. This as well as the disappearance of the Ndebele king, who had regulated the relations of the institution with the people apparently forced 'the Mwari officials greatly [to extend] their activities between 1893 and 1896'. We get an impression of this development from Nyanganyoni Mhlope's account of the risings:

> The wosana were rain bringers . . . they used to come in a group and say that they were sent by Mlimo to make rain. They would dance at the kraal and the people would give them presents. In the time of Lobengula they were not allowed to go round the kraals and dance. Lobengula used to send a few men to Njelele with black oxen and they would find wosana there and the wosana would dance to make rain. When the white people came into the country then the wosana started to go round kraal to kraal.

At the same time the Mwari officers achieved tremendous prestige to the extent that they were viewed as kings.[48]

The natural disasters from 1894 to 1896, like those of the early 1860s, gave added influence to the religious institutions. The rinderpest that mercilessly slew cattle, the drought and the locusts and the resulting famine, moreover, could all be blamed on the presence of Europeans, who were disregarding the established beliefs and institutions of the country. The whites were not only ignorant of the art of making rain, it was claimed, but they seemed

totally unconcerned about the disastrous plight of the people resulting from the natural misfortunes.[49] Indeed, as Ranger puts it:

> alone among the conquerors of Rhodesia the whites had, in African eyes,
> neglected the necessity of making peace with the land; no accommo-
> dation had been made with Mwari; Mwari in his wrath was punishing
> all. As people turned to Mwari's officers for advice in early 1896, and
> as they consulted with the Ndebele leaders and with each other, most
> of the senior Mwari priests came to the conclusion that the whites
> must be driven out. Only then could rain fall, the cattle recover, the
> locusts pass on.

In early 1896 some of Mwari's priests proclaimed war on the
whites:

> These white men are your enemies. They killed your fathers, sent the
> locusts, this disease among the cattle, and bewitched the clouds so that
> we have no rain. Now you go and kill these white people and drive them
> out of our fathers' land and I will take away the cattle disease and the
> locusts and send you rain.[50]

Further on Ranger quotes Father Prestage of the Z.M. as saying in
April 1896:

> [Mpotswana] went at the beginning of the last [month] hoping to consult
> Usalugazana (mother of Molimo). She advised him that the Amandebele
> should kill the white man in the country outside Bulawayo, undertaking
> to send a bolt of fire to destroy Bulawayo with its inhabitants at the
> time of rain.

Indeed, more evidence has been put forward by Ranger to show
that Mwari officials such as Mkwati, operating from Thabazika-
mambo or Manyanga and Siuminya or Siginyamatshe not only
mobilised men and women who were not responsive to the surviving
Ndebele military machinery, but also played an important part in
'directing the first murders of whites by the Ndebele and in bringing
the Ndebele regiments together around Bulawayo'. The cult
officials further maintained high morale among the soldiers once
the war broke out by promising them supernatural aid.[51]

Impressive though the evidence is of the Mwari cult's inspiring
of the rising as well as of maintaining the morale of the soldiers, not
all shrines and priests of the cult supported the rebellion. Apparently
by 1896 there were about six important shrines – Dula (alias reZhou,
Mazwawe, Maswabe, Nambeni, Matonjeni); Magubu (Majubu,
Maguhu, Daba, Manyengwe, Matonjeni); Mangwe (Umkombo,

Manyembe); Njelele (Matonjeni) all situated in various parts of the Matopo Range; and Ntabazikamambo or Manyanga. Of these Mangwe remained neutral during the rebellion; Magubu, Manyanga and Dula were actively involved; though Njelele was closely related to Manyanga, its position during the rising is obscure.[52]

The non-involvement of the Mangwe shrine coinciding with the neutrality of the Kalanga of the Plumtree area led Ranger to think that these people were persuaded to stay out of the rebellion by the officials of the shrine. An additional reason for the neutrality of the Kalanga and many others may well have been the religious plurality of the peoples of Ndebeleland, leading them to respect not only the Shona and Zansi religious authorities and institutions, but the Christian ones as well. In previous pages we saw how the missionaries were able to play an influential role in the signing of the Rudd Concession in 1888. We also suggested that though the Ndebele were generally against actual conversion to the new faith, their religious systems and particularly their theological understanding were evolving through assimilation of certain Christian concepts. Though the evidence relating to the Christian factor during the uprisings is very scanty, it appears that some parts of the country did not join the rebels on account of such special relationships with the Christian institutions and missionaries.

Indeed at the end of the Anglo-Ndebele war in 1893 there were noticeable signs of people living around the few mission stations beginning to be affected by the Christian teachings. At the oldest Christian centre, Inyati, many people were attending the services and for the first time were coming to church as well. As an outward visible sign of the changing attitudes of the women they were 'taking to wear dresses'. On one Sunday in 1894 'there were fifteen women very nicely dressed in the Church' and their numbers were reported to be growing every Sunday. But the shining star among the Inyati congregation was Matambo. He had been Sykes's faithful servant, taken over upon the death of his master in 1887 by Bowen Rees. By 1897 he 'could read and write nicely'. In 1894 he had become fully committed to the new faith, going to the out-station of Inyati, Msindo 'to deliver the Good News with a face beaming with gladness and delight'. He was calling upon his fellow blacks as well as appealing to their hearts to embrace Christianity in the idiom they could understand. One Sunday he delivered a sermon in which he said:

I am very glad to see so many of you dressed with such fine garments; but do you know it will help you nothing unless your hearts are clothed with Christ. You must not think that you are good people because you have clothes on. It means quite a different thing to have Christ as your dress. One is for the body, the other is for the spirit. One for time, the other for eternity.[53]

Matambo and many others around Inyati, groping earnestly for the Christian light by going to Bible classes every Wednesday afternoon, by attending the daily school conducted by Rees, and the sewing classes run by Mrs Rees, refrained from participating in the *impi yamahloka* (the war of the axe or rebellion of 1896).

The most remarkable Christian pacifist was Makaza Nkala, who died for his Christian beliefs. The story of Makaza, son of Tinyani and also Matambo's close friend, was given to me in 1971 by Fipa Nyoni, the daughter of Makaza's brother Dedani. On the outbreak of the war in early 1896, Fipa recalled, Kongwani, Matambo's father, and Tinyani, both living near Inyati, were gravely concerned about the safety of Mnali (teacher) Rees, because the Ndebele had suddenly turned wild, killing every European they came across. During consultations between the old men and their Christian sons on the best means of protecting the missionary, Makaza volunteered to take the missionary and his family to Bulawayo at night, while Matambo remained guarding the mission house and property. At Manxeleni, just a few miles out of Bulawayo, the fugitive missionary party was surprised by an impi of rebels, which apparently would have massacred it had the leader Kabu Bebebe not calmed the soldiers, reminding them that Rees was *imbiza kayibulawa* (sacred pot), admitted into the country by the late Lobengula. Having accomplished his wish to see the missionary safe in the Bulawayo laager, Makaza felt the urge to return to Inyati to go and face the dangers of the war with the rest of the black Christian community. Rees also gave Makaza a letter in which he apparently appealed to the Inyati Christians to continue to meet together in the church for prayers and to place their trust in God, and on his part promised to pray for them during the troubled months. Back at Inyati, however, Makaza was immediately branded a dangerous traitor, working hand in hand with the missionaries to win all the black youths over to the white enemy by means of the Gospel. A meeting was soon called at Kongwani's village to discuss the activities of Makaza, the 'sell out', and apparently when Makaza stood up at the *Indaba* to explain his position, a furious and disgusted man called Mafule Moyo suddenly lodged a spear in the Christian's chest. With the lethal weapon fixed in his body the veritable martyr, Makaza, is said to have sung a hymn and prayed for his killer's forgiveness as well as for himself. After this Makaza requested his killer to pull out the spear, which was done, and he fell down and died.[54] After the war Rees exhumed Makaza's bones where his family had buried him and interred them in the mission graveyard where all the missionaries that died at Inyati were buried.

Dispassionately though Fipa Nyoni told her uncle's story, we should suspect it of being naturally biased in favour of a relative. Nevertheless, Makaza's fate dramatises the fact that Christianity had begun to affect some people's lives in Ndebeleland to the extent of making them opponents of the struggle against whites in 1896.

Equally illustrative of this point, though not as spectacular, was the situation at other mission stations. At Solusi, the Seventh Day Adventist mission, the local Kalanga chief of the Mazwanyana community had by 1896 struck a fast friendship with the missionaries, and throughout the rebellion he and his people remained loyal to the abafundisi, guarding their property against raiders. At Dombodema, the L.M.S. missionary Cullen Reed was advised to escape to Bulawayo by the local people, who did not join the uprising; at the Z.M. Empandeni mission people did not rise either. Hope Fountain was unfortunately located too near the strongholds of the rebels. But since the 1893 war the people living near the mission had become noted for their loyalty to the new white regime and for sending their children to school. Among these children was Mtompe Khumalo, who was to be one of the first black ordained preachers of the L.M.S. In 1944 he recalled his plight with his family, when he told the missionary Neville Jones how he and his people had been driven by the rebels out of their homes into the Matopo caves where they eked out a precarious existence, sometimes being forced to eat hides to avoid starving to death.

Thus the political upheavals of 1888–96 brought out clearly the religious situation of Ndebeleland as it had developed over the last half a century. It was indeed a religious spectrum made up of elements ranging from diehard traditionalists, through mixers of the new ideas with old ones, to pure Christians. The class of the izinyanga, izangoma and izanusi represented the 'bitter enders', rejecting outright the white men's world with its religion, and using their witch-hunting privileges to frighten would-be or actual Christians from the new faith. The national 'intellectuals', or shall we call them philosophers, such as Lobengula and the various priests of the Mwari cult, were the mixers, apparently ceaselessly seeking to elaborate their beliefs and practices by borrowing from Christianity in order to accommodate their religious systems to the changes wrought by the European presence. Matambo, Makaza, Shisho, Nxobe, Baleni and many other converts of the time stood out as pure Christians, already shouldering the task of bringing the Gospel to their own people. Their sincerity found testimony in their preparedness to die for their faith, their willingness to leave their country and go to South Africa for studies in order to improve their preaching techniques, or to live in exile in order to worship their new God freely. These pure Christians of Ndebeleland give an interesting, if not a classic, example of the 'quarantine' phase postulated by Humphrey J. Fisher in his reply to Robin Horton.[55] As Fisher defines the quarantine phase, the converts are few and they tend to 'pass into the separate world of their new brothers-in faith'. Indeed we have seen how these Ndebele converts managed to retain their faith by associating themselves closely with the missionaries or seeking the protection of the white settlers.

The variegated religious pattern we have now seen was by 1896 poised for change; the western economic and political factors that were causing traumatic experiences among the traditional societies of Ndebeleland were largely working in favour of Christianity. The remaining chapters will therefore analyse the struggle between Christianity and the traditional beliefs.

Notes

1. F. C. Selous, *Travel and Adventure in South-East Africa*, London, 1893, pp. 113–16; I. G. Cockroft, 'The Molimo (Mwari) Cult', *Nada*, 1972, p. 84; D. N. Beach, 'The Rising in South-Western Mashonaland, 1896–7', unpublished Ph.D. thesis, London, 1971, p. 157; *Letters and Notices*, xiii/xiv, p. 260
2. Interview with Khumalo, 26 June 1971
3. See N. M. B. Bhebe, 'The Ndebele and Mwari before 1893', Lusaka Conference, 1972, p. 7
4. L.M.S. B1/F3/JD, Cockin to For. Sec., May 1879
5. Thomas, *Eleven Years*, p. 288
6. Interviews in 1971, document in African Languages Department, University of Rhodesia
7. D. P. Abraham, 'The Roles of "Chaminuka" and the Mhondoro-cults in Shona Political History' in E. Stokes and R. Brown (eds.), *The Zambesian Past*, Manchester, 1966, pp. 32–3
8. Interview in 1971
9. T. O. Ranger, *Revolt in Southern Rhodesia*, London, 1967, p. 153
10. F. C. Selous, *Sunshine and Storm in Rhodesia*, London, 1896, p. 15
11. See N. M. B. Bhebe, 'Ndebele Politics During the Scramble', *Mohlomi* (National University of Lesotho), 1977; Bhebe, 'Ndebele Trade in the Nineteenth Century', *Journal of African Studies*, i, 1974; W18/1, statement by Siatcha with Stambe, daughter of Lobengula, and Lubane, son of Mkubane, present.
12. R.N.A. WI8/1, statement by Hobasi
13. Interviews with Tshabangu, and Khumalo; see also Ranger, *Revolt*, p. 144
14. J. P. Richards, 'The Molimo', *Nada*, 1942, p. 54
15. R. Mwanza, 'Mwari, The God of the Karanga', Lusaka Conference, 1972, p. 7
16. W.M.M.S. C. Mashonaland, 'The Mashonaland Mission-Journey to Lomagundi's' by Isaac Shimmin
17. M. Wright, *German Missions in Tanganyika*, Oxford, 1971, p. 86
18. L.M.S. B1/F3/JD, Carnegie to For. Sec., 17 Aug. 1886; B2/F3/JC, Carnegie to For. Sec., 17 June 1887; B1/F4/JA, Carnegie to For. Sec., 12 Aug. 1887; 'South Out Africa 1886–7', For. Sec. to Carnegie, 11 Nov. 1886; For. Sec. to Carnegie, 24 Nov. 1887
19. R.N.A. MISC/SY 1/1/1, Sykes's Journal, p. 10
20. L.M.S. B1/F4/JB, Helm to For. Sec., 11 Oct. 1888
21. *Ibid.*, Carnegie to For. Sec., 26 March 1889
22. L.M.S. B3/Reports: 1898–1903, Carnegie to For. Sec., 6 Dec. 1900
23. The following is some of the evidence relating to the controversy over the Concession and the part played by Helm: L.M.S. B1/F4/JB, Helm to For. Sec., 11 Oct. 1888; F. Thompson to Helm, 9 Nov. 1888; Elliott to For. Sec., 29 March 1889; Carnegie to For. Sec., 26 March 1889; Helm to For. Sec., 29 March 1889; B1/F4/JC, Ashton to For. Sec., 19 Feb. 1889; 'South Out Africa 1888–90', For. Sec. to Helm, 13 June 1889; R.N.A. USI/1,

Usher's Correspondence and other Papers, Usher to Fry, 16 Feb. 1889; 'The Matabele Travel Letters', p. 29; *The Diamond Fields Advertiser*, 27 March 1889

24. S. Samkange, *Origins of Rhodesia*, London, 1968, p. 67
25. L.M.S. 'South Out Africa 1888–90', For. Sec. to Elliott, 18 Jan. 1889
26. R. Palmer, *Land and Racial Domination in Rhodesia*, Berkeley and Los Angeles, 1977, p. 367
27. L.M.S. B1/F4/JB, Carnegie to For. Sec., 26 March 1889; see also B1/F4/JC, Ashton to For. Sec., 19 Feb. 1889; 'South Out Africa 1888–90', For. Sec. to Helm, 13 June 1889.
28. L.M.S. B1/F4/JC, Ashton to For. Sec., 21 June 1890
29. L.M.S. B1/F4/JB, Carnegie to For. Sec., 26 March 1889
30. R.N.A. BA10/2/1, Journal, Bailie to Administrator, 31 Oct. 1896
31. L.M.S. B1/F4/JB, Elliott to For. Sec., 29 March 1889
32. R.N.A. WI 6/2/1, Wilson's Journals, entry for 12 March 1889
33. L.M.S. B1/F4/JD, Carnegie to For. Sec., 13 June 1890; B1/F4/JC, Elliott to For. Sec., 12 June 1890
34. R.N.A. TH2/1/1, Thomas's Journal, entry for 18 Aug. 1879
35. R.N.A. MISC/CA5, Mrs Carnegie to Good, 1 Nov. 1937
36. *The Diamond Fields Advertiser*, 28 June 1889
37. L.M.S. B1/F4/JD, Carnegie to For. Sec., 16 April 1890
38. L. H. Gann, *A History of Southern Rhodesia: Early Days to 1934*, London, 1965, p. 109
39. *The Chronicle of the London Missionary Society*, 1913, p. 76, and 1918, p. 101
40. Ranger, *Revolt*; Beach, thesis; J. Cobbing, 'The Absent Priesthood: Another Look at the Rhodesian Risings of 1896–1897', *Journal of African History*, xviii, pp. 61–84
41. P. L. Bonner, 'Early State Formation Among the Nguni: The Relevance of the Swazi Case', unpublished and undated paper, Department of History, University College of Swaziland, pp. 15–16
42. Thomas, p. 290
43. M. J. Mtutuki, 'The Mwali Cult in Northern Botswana – Some Oral Traditions c. 1893–1976', unpublished B.A. thesis, University College of Botswana, 1977
44. *Ibid.*
45. Note the emerging two schools of thought represented by Ranger and Beach; see their works for detailed accounts of the causes and course of the risings
46. Ranger, *Revolt*, pp. 136–9
47. *Ibid.*, pp. 140–2
48. *Ibid.*, p. 144
49. *Ibid.*, p. 147
50. *Ibid.*, pp. 147–8
51. *Ibid.*, p. 147ff
52. Schoffeleers; see also Mwanza
53. L.M.S. B3/Reports: 1898–1905, Rees, 'Annual Report Inyati Station Matabeleland 1894'
54. Interview with Miss Fipa Nyoni, 16 June 1971; other informants inter-

viewed at Inyati, such as Kakaka Tshabangu, Dube and Mambambo, were unwilling to talk about Makaza and I was unable to discover the reason for this.

55. H. J. Fisher, 'Conversion Reconsidered: Some Historical Aspects of Religious Conversion in Black Africa', *Africa*, xliii, 1973, pp. 27–40

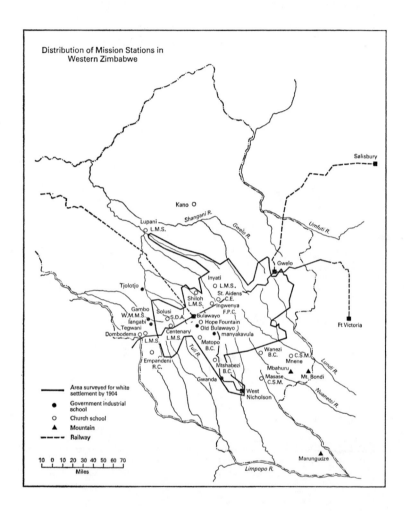

Distribution of Mission Stations in
Western Zimbabwe

Salisbury

Kano O

Shangani R.

Gwelo R.

Umfuli R.

Lupani
O L.M.S.

Gwelo

Inyati
O L.M.S.
Tjolotjo ●   St. Aidens
                         Shiloh   O C.E.
                         L.M.S,   Ingwenya
Gambo   Solusi   F.P.C.
W.M.M.S.   O S.D.A.
Iangabi   ● Bulawayo
Tegwani   Centenary O Hope Fountain
Dombodema O O   O Old Bulawayo)
          L.M.S.   L.M.S.   manyakavula

                         Matopo
                         B.C.   Wanezi
                                            B.C.   O C.S.M.
          Empandeni   Mnene
          R.C.   Mtshabezi   Mbahuru
                            B.C.   Masase   ▲
              Gwanda   C.S.M. Mt. Bondi

                         West
                         Nicholson

Ft Victoria

Tuli R.

Lundi R.

Nuanetsi R.

Marungudze ▲

Limpopo R.

——— Area surveyed for white
      settlement by 1904
●   Government industrial
      school
O   Church school
▲   Mountain
- - - Railway

10 0 10 20 30 40 50 60 70
|__|_|__|__|__|__|__|__|
        Miles

5

Missions and the traditional societies, 1897–1923

The fall of the Ndebele kingdom in 1893, the suppression of the 1896–7 risings, as well as the subsequent rapid development of a capitalist economy, created a congenial atmosphere for the growth of Christianity among the Ndebele. These cataclysmic events not only stimulated fresh interest among the missionaries already labouring in the Ndebele dominions, but they also lured new evangelical societies and organisations from Shonaland, South Africa and overseas. The avidity with which missionaries availed themselves of the new opportunity was shown by the fact that by 1900 no fewer than eight powerful societies had carved out for themselves spheres of operation in Ndebeleland.

The L.M.S., though chronically vexed by shortages of finance and personnel because of its extensive commitments in the world, responded to the new prospects by extending its mission field. Instead of having two missionaries at each station, at Hope Fountain and Inyati, the Society decided to have only one. Consequently the Rev. C. D. Helm, an active participant in the Rudd Concession negotiations in 1888, remained at Hope Fountain while David Carnegie, who had translated John Bunyan's *The Pilgrim's Progress* into Sindebele, went to open Centenary in October 1897. Bowen Rees, a strong believer in the ethnic superiority of the Ndebele Zansi over other black groups, was left superintendent of Inyati, while Cullen Reed, a recent arrival, was asked to start the Dombodema station near Plumtree in 1895. Each of these stations dominated a vast district of out-stations run by African evangelists, and all of them were situated in the Kalanga-Ndebele homelands.

In contrast to the L.M.S., the Jesuit Zambezi Mission, which had acquired Empandeni under Lobengula, and had temporarily abandoned it in 1889, did not spread itself over a large area. Rather it concentrated its efforts on the Empandeni farm and strove to make it self-sufficient. The farm was re-occupied in 1895 by Fr Peter Prestage and Fr Andrew Hartmann, former chaplains to the pioneer column. In 1892 the Jesuits opened another station at Embakwe, only eight miles south-west of Empandeni. Similarly their out-stations – with only one exception – were within the farm and within easy reach of the Empandeni central station. Silima was seven to eight miles north-west of Empandeni, Kitwe six to seven miles north-east, and Mkaya five to six miles north. This concentration of effort within a limited area resulted in Empandeni becoming the best developed mission station in the country and enabled the Jesuits to build up an almost completely Christian community in the area. Only in 1921 was this concentrated pattern broken by the establishment of St Joseph in the Semokwe district.

At the same time as the Jesuits were resettling Empandeni, the Seventh Day Adventists, an American sect notorious for its lack of respect for other denominations' spheres of operation as well as for producing evangelists whose teaching verged on Ethiopianism, obtained the Solusi farm, about thirty-eight miles west of Bulawayo. Although work at this farm started in 1895, it was interrupted briefly by the 1896–7 rebellion, when the missionaries abandoned their station and went to seek refuge at Bulawayo. But the starvation that followed the suppression of the uprising enabled the S.D.A. to harvest their first converts from the hungry children.

The Wesleyan-Methodist Missionary Society was attracted not so much by evangelical possibilities among the Ndebele as by the desire to minister to the spiritual needs of the white settlers. As a result the first service to be held for Africans was among servants and other black labourers living in the Location – an event that marked the beginning of the Methodist Church in Bulawayo in 1895.

In the same year Isaac Shimmin, the Chairman of the Rhodesian W.M.M.S. District, successfuly applied for a mission farm to Dr L. S. Jameson. The restoration of peace in 1897 enabled the missionary, C. H. Temple, to mark out the Tegwani Mission farm of approximately 12,000 acres, situated in a mixed Ndebele-Kalanga area, about seventy miles west of Bulawayo.

In 1908 John White, the famous third Chairman of the Rhodesian District, founded the Zuzumba station, forty miles north of Tegwani and located in an almost wholly Kalanga-speaking area. Moses M'fazi was put in charge of the new station. He was a black South African, who had migrated to Zimbabwe as a Methodist preacher and was ordained by John White in 1911.

Meanwhile the expansion of the Methodist District to eastern Ndebeleland, where vigorous mining enterprise was attracting peoples from different parts of southern Africa, assumed a slightly different picture. There Methodist African preachers shouldered the onerous task of laying the foundations of mission work. They erected preaching places, conducted regular services, and catechised candidates for baptism. In 1903 when White undertook one of his extensive tours and visited Selukwe, he was met by a number of people waiting to be baptised who had been prepared for the sacrament by a black preacher. It was upon such beginnings that H. J. Baker, detailed to the area in the wake of the Chairman's tour, built up the Selukwe circuit.

The propitious Ndebele situation further attracted the attention of the Church of Sweden, then labouring in Zululand. The Belingwe and Selukwe districts were found to be devoid of missions, so they were immediately earmarked for occupation. Although the Swedish Mission arrived almost at the end of the British South Africa Company's spree of land grants to religious bodies, it ultimately managed by purchase to set up a powerful mission centre at Mnene and, with time, to build up a network of out-stations around Belingwe. The Church of Sweden was, moreover, among the first to break the tendency of missions to locate themselves on the Ndebele high-veld, which was rapidly developing into a white area. By going into the middle and low-veld the Swedish missionaries plunged into the malarial parts of Ndebeleland, a lethal health hazard exacerbated by distance from the burgeoning centres of western civilisation and medical facilities. The deadly danger was eventually overcome by building mission stations on elevated places away from swampy ground.

Other missions at this time included the Brethren in Christ and the Church of England. The Brethren in Christ concentrated on Matopo and Insiza, setting up the Matopo, Mtshabezi and Wanezi missions.[1] The Church of England opened up two centres, St Colomba in Bulawayo and St Aidan in the Mfengu Location, with a whole host of minor stations scattered between the Bulawayo-Wankie and the Salisbury-Bulawayo railway lines. The Anglican

Church's heavy commitments in Shonaland as well as among the white settlers, who were thinly distributed over much of the colony, seriously reduced their strength and severely limited their impact on the Ndebele before 1923. Moreover the outbreak of the First World War further strained their resources for several missionaries went as chaplains to the fighting forces.

The general picture of evangelical work being initiated by whites was varied by the arrival of John Boyan Radasi in Bulawayo on 21 December 1904. Radasi was a Mfengu of the Cape Colony who was converted to missionary work whilst in America with a group of musicians. Upon completing theological training in Scotland, he was charged with the task of extending the Free Church of Scotland's southern African mission field to the Ndebele.

After some difficulty with pass regulations, Radasi succeeded in 1905 in building a station at Ingwenya, thirty-eight miles from Bulawayo. This was near the home of Chief Ngege who, though refusing to be converted personally to the new faith, was well disposed towards missionary enterprise. In 1908 Radasi extended his work to the Mfengu location on the lower Bembesi river and to Koce. But the white regime's discriminatory regulations against black missionaries frustrated Radasi's efforts to extend his field into western Shonaland.

The coming of Radasi concludes our survey of missionary occupation. It is important to note that, with the exception of the Church of Sweden, nearly all missionary organisations were concentrated in the Ndebele-Kalanga-speaking areas. However, it is also necessary to say a few words about the attempt of the Christian Catholic Apostolic Church in Zion to penetrate Ndebeleland at this time.[2] In 1919 the Rev. P. M. Mabiletsa of the A.C.A.C.Z. made an application to the High Commissioner to be allowed to extend his work into Zimbabwe. The Chief Native Commissioner, who was requested by the Administrator's Office to comment on the application, recommended that Mabiletsa be informed that the white regime only extended recognition 'to organizations which are under European control'. The High Commissioner objected to this suggestion as 'it might possibly give rise to a protest against discrimination on the grounds of colour in religious matters', and instead thought that 'it would be sufficient to state that the facilities asked for could not be granted'.[3] Actually, the officials of this sect wanted to station their representative, the Rev. T. M. Mwelane, at Chief Sendla in the Insiza district.[4] In 1924, just after our period, the movement informed the Administrator that they now had a large following in western Zimbabwe, and 'Therefore your Petitioners Humbly Beg your allowance as to whether you can allow or late [sic] Our Teachers of Gospel to Teach and preach [to] their own Native Race'.[5] The Chief Native Commissioner saw no reason to change the policy of not granting recognition to sects not supervised by whites. The Minister of Native Affairs agreed with the Chief Native Commissioner and the petitioners were refused permission to come into Zimbabwe.[6]

Indeed, the A.C.A.C.Z. had a large following in western Zimbabwe if the claims of its ministers are correct. A number of people had over the years gone to Johannesburg and had there become converted to this faith. In August 1921 the Rev. Jonathan D. Mgoma, President of the sect, came into Zimbabwe and travelled through the Mzingwane and Filabusi districts, ordaining preachers and baptising members who had already been prepared for the sacrament by local preachers. Among the ordained and confirmed were Joyi, a temporary labourer in Johannesburg for three years, and a preacher for three years in Zimbabwe; Zachariah, with the same amount of time spent in South Africa; Mhlatshwa, baptised Petros, under Chief Maduna of Filabusi; Ndungu, son of Chief Maduna; and Makubila, the brother of Mhlatshwa. All these teachers were doing good work for their faith, but Petros seemed to have the largest congregation in Filabusi – estimated at about 500; and the President baptised a record number of fifty converts during his brief sojourn there in 1921.[7] Because of the apparent popularity of this faith in some parts of western Zimbabwe, the white officials refused to accept it in the country.

Nevertheless, it is those societies that received the administration's recognition and their relationship with the traditional societies of western Zimbabwe to which attention must now be directed. In order to understand the reactions of the traditional societies, it is necessary to know the missionaries' views about them. Before embarking on their important task of evangelising a people, the Christians asked themselves a basic question: 'Have they any spiritual consciousness?' Perhaps nearly all the Protestant missionaries, with varying degrees of assertiveness, would have agreed with the Methodist C. H. Temple that: 'The Matabele's spiritual sense is in a very underdeveloped condition, and their belief in spiritual things is very vague.' As far as he could see, 'the only worship they have is the worship of their ancestors, and the only creed they possess may be embraced in the word Fatalism'. He conceded that the Ndebele believed in life after death, but this was 'a very poor belief'. Even then to Temple, and probably to all the non-Catholics, these crude beliefs were positive signs of undeveloped spiritual consciousness to be improved by Christianity.[8] W. C. Willoughby, once Professor of Missions in Africa in the Kennedy School in America, and later teacher and principal of the L.M.S. Tigerkloof School, viewed the Bantu as a 'child race', whose belief 'in the spirits of things and its consequent magic' was only a 'childish notion', which the Europeans had no right to 'scoff at'. To him, like Temple, there were 'points of contact with Christianity', or 'much in Bantu religion which looks like groping after truths, rather than finding them'.[9]

It was this conception that the African people had some glimmering of spiritual life that distinguished the Protestants from the Catholics in Ndebeleland. From the Catholic missionaries' point of view, the Ndebele and the Kalanga were so grossly sensual and selfish and preoccupied with the materialistic aspects of life that they could never develop any meaningful spiritual consciousness, let alone understand the profound truths revealed in the Holy Scriptures.[10] The point was illustrated by one Jesuit priest at Empandeni. The carnal things, 'and those only, are what they appreciate and seek after', he declared. He said that they did not believe in the immortality of the soul. All they were concerned about was to make the most of their earthly life. Moreover, it was useless and futile to speak to them about Heaven and Hell, as their general reaction would only be, 'Who has seen Heaven? Who has seen Hell?'

> And if the word of God Himself is quoted, they laugh at it. *Amanga kodwa* – 'It is all lies'. How often has one heard this! If they were to see some great material benefit following upon Baptism a number would ask to be baptized . . . but they have no intention of giving up their pagan habits and submitting to the law of God and His Church for the sake of future happiness, or to escape from punishment which they disbelieve.[11]

Even such a priest as J. O'Neil, Superintendent of the Embakwe station, who made remarkable investigations into the way of life of the Kalanga and Ndebele of Mangwe, did not credit their traditional religious systems with anything except that they were the products of 'senseless people'.[12]

However, the differences between the Catholic and Protestant missionaries should not be overemphasised. In their day-to-day work of evangelising the people of western Zimbabwe, all the missionaries saw themselves as fighting Satan in his own kingdom. J. R. Mackay, of the P.C.S., after preaching in Ngege's village, had this to say:

> I was met with a specimen of almost pure heathenism, and I had the feeling, . . . that one had there to fight Satan on his own ground. Not that they are fierce; but especially the women and children have a very poor, degraded look, and their minds . . . enveloped in such mists of darkness and ignorance that if the Gospel were merely an agency of human power, one would be apt altogether to lose heart in setting to address them.[13]

Confronted by such a mass of degraded and depraved people, as it were, the missionaries' duty was obviously to spread the Gospel. It was a task of raising these people, as one missionary indicated, 'from unbridled lust, and all pernicious influence of heathen life' to 'the purity and moral earnestness of Christians'. The missionaries believed that this could be achieved through a thorough knowledge of the Bible, and 'a deeper grasp of the Christian Graces'.[14] Although they were convinced of the uplifting power of the Scriptures, they also emphasised the role of western civilisation in ensuring the permanence of the Church. Civilisation, of course, in its simplest form, meant adopting European ideas, culture and customs by the Africans. In the circumstances, the missionaries found themselves condemning almost every aspect of traditional culture as the outward and visible manifestations of the pagan inner person. This total condemnation of the traditional ways of life not only baffled the peoples of Ndebeleland, but also drove some of them into becoming stubborn enemies of the missionaries. The missionaries, perhaps not surprisingly, expected the white administration to assist them in the formidable task of civilising the Africans.

The question of African marriage customs demonstrates clearly not only how the missionaries expected the assistance of the British secular power, but also the unwillingness of the administration to engage in ventures that might arouse African opposition. The missionaries bundled together polygamy, *lobola*, and the *kuzwarira* practice (which was equated with infant marriage) and condemned them as inhuman institutions and practices which a civilised country like Britain had no justification in tolerating among its subjects. Perhaps the most powerful plea for the abolition of these customs was the one made by Fr Prestage, who claimed to draw for his arguments heavily on his long experience in the country. He denounced lobola as a practice that was indistinguishable

> from the purchase of a wife by a man for the purpose of begetting children, among whom the girls, when marriageable are disposed to obtain lobola, which is used again to purchase other wives, the final object being to acquire position and substance through possession of women and children.

He argued that African marriages were devoid of love and that polygamous families were always infected through and through with jealousy, quarrels and dislike. Perhaps the gravest evil of these unions, he thought, was the kuzwarira practice, which denied the girls their natural right and freedom to choose their own future husbands. Finally, he corrected the misconception of the gold syndicates in Zimbabwe that lobola was an incentive to labour. Lobola encouraged polygamy and cultivated laziness among the Africans – the more wives a man had the less he was inclined to work as his wives supplied him with all the food he required. Fr Prestage called on Britain to stamp out this evil.[15]

The allusion to, and the sometimes apparent concern about, labour problems, must not obscure the aim of the missionaries to persuade the Government to reform African marriages by law. But the Administration did not go anywhere near to satisfying the missionaries. The Native Marriages Ordinance, 1901 and the Native Tax Ordinance, 1904 only discouraged the kuzwarira practice, fixed the amount of lobola and imposed a tax on polygamous marriages to stimulate labour. The taxing of polygamists was a concession to the mining interests, rather than to the missionaries.

In fact during the years following the uprising, however much the missionaries might try to demonstrate the evil effects of polygamy on women, the Administration was unlikely to pay any significant attention. In western Zimbabwe the policy was to try to conciliate the Ndebele chiefs.[16] At the second Indaba of 23 June 1897, which was attended by nearly all the leading Ndebele chiefs, Rhodes, the Acting Chief Native Commissioner and the Deputy Administrator, the indunas heard that the Government would recognise and legalise lobola, and would also 'respect their native laws and customs' which were compatible with equity and justice.[17] In 1898 a commission was appointed to frame and draft a Code of Native Law. All the principal Ndebele indunas were invited to participate.[18] Obviously, the missionaries, who sought a radical and complete alteration of the African way of life, stood very little chance, if any, of persuading the Administration, which was concerned with preserving as much of the African way of life as possible in the interest of peace and order.

The white secular opinion, which for a long time dominated the Native Department, was that if polygamy was abolished there would be an immediate increase in the number of unmarried girls with consequent immorality. To this was added the optimism that the institution was doomed to a natural death. The ever increasing cost of living would make it impossible for a man to marry more than one wife, while with the gradual enlightenment of women, yet another thin end of the wedge would be driven into the institution.[19] Firmly holding such ideas, the Native Department became almost hostile to the activities of the missionaries and their suggestions to alter by law African matrimonial customs.

The question of African marriages, therefore, demonstrated to the missionaries that the establishment of colonial rule did not mean the coming of short-cut methods of inculcating Christian principles upon the Africans. The secular power would not attack apparently harmless African practices, simply because they did not conform to the requirements of Christian life. Nor was what was administratively or economically expedient necessarily Christian. Peace and labour were the special concerns of the Administration. The measures adopted to ensure them, and some of the criticisms of the Native Department against the Churches, only made the Administration appear indifferent to the work of the missionaries.

Indeed, the missionaries soon began to admit their initial folly and to adopt their own measures of fighting polygamy. In 1902 Fr Richard Sykes, the Superior of the Zambesi Mission and founder of the *Zambesi Mission Record*, warned his fellow missionaries to stop counting on the Administration as an ally in their struggle. The Government, he said, believed that to abolish lobola and polygamy would be striking a blow at the whole African social and economic order, which was bound to provoke universal disaffection and dangerous unrest. Left alone, as it were, Sykes said that the missionary could only turn to 'the instincts of the moral law and the precepts of Christianity'. With regard to the moral law, unfortunately, the 'degraded' African neither thought it immoral to practise polygamous marriages, nor did he perceive any moral superiority in monogamy to polygamy. It was further useless and futile for the Christian teacher to turn to the 'sublime doctrines of the author of his religion', as the African was 'apt to think that it was all very useless self-abnegation'.[20] Under the circumstances, the Zambesi Mission augmented its teaching at Empandeni mission with the law that 'no young man is to have more than one wife' and remain on the farm.[21]

However, the response of the African societies to missionary enterprise was largely determined on the one hand by the incidental effects of the establishment of colonial rule and its concomitant measures of pacification as well as by the pressure of white settlement,[22] and on the other by the tenacious hold of the traditional way of life. The traumatic experience engendered by the loss of their king and the clear demonstration of the white men's technological superiority during the military clashes of 1893 and 1896 produced a strong feeling among the Ndebele of coming to terms with the white man's world. Indeed, the Ndebele themselves admitted in 1898 the ineffectiveness of their old ways in the face of white advance:

> the people were delighted to see me [Carnegie], many of them I knew and our talks round the camp fire reverted to those olden days compared with the present regime. The impression I received from the old men was that if power were ever to come back to their scattered and conquered race it was not by way of guns or spears or shields but through the channels of teaching and educating their children.[23]

There was also the rapid development of economic enterprise, which was accompanied by some measure of urbanisation. It soon became clear to the people that it was those who acquired something of the white man's mysteries of reading and writing, and especially those who had picked up at least some smattering of the English language, who went about with relative ease in the changing environment. Before 1923, it was only through the mission schools that the Ndebele could ever hope to thus try to come to terms with western culture. In what appeared to be a hostile environment, especially in the early days, the missionary remained the only friend of the black men. When they starved, they turned to the nearest white teacher and he mediated with the Government for relief.[24]

At the same time the ability to read and write soon conferred upon a person distinction in society, causing him to have an air of arrogance. Perhaps white settlers were not far from the truth when they complained that a missionary-educated African was a bad labourer because he lacked docility and was so proud that he shunned manual labour as dirty. As Elija Dube, an old Christian at Inyati, pointed out in an interview with the writer in 1971, a person with the mere equivalent of the present Zimbabwean Grade II would go about in his village with haughty deportment and was in turn regarded with envy by the people. Indeed the people thought of such a person as one who shared in the white men's wisdom and cleverness.

But the dilemma of the peoples of western Zimbabwe was very real. In spite of all these powerful forces acting upon them and compelling them to throw themselves into western life, including its religion, they found it almost impossible to break away from their traditions. They were secure in their own traditional practices and institutions, so much so that to abandon them was to make a leap in the dark where anything could happen. Moreover, the missionaries demanded that their converts make a clean break with traditional beliefs and practices.

This predicament caused individuals and societies in Ndebeleland to react to Christianity in a variety of ways, ranging from genuine fear of totally abandoning old traditions mixed with deep conviction in the efficacy and salutary effects of Christianity on the one hand to stubborn resistance to missionary work on the other. This produced several pluralists who at once held fast to their old way of life and encouraged their children to embrace the new faith and to come to terms with western culture and technology. So before looking at the diehard opponents of Christianity, we should examine the pluralists' solutions. Tshoko, one of the widows of Mzilikazi, presents a classic case of the fear of the Ndebele to be committed to the Christian way of life. Until she died in 1915 she refused to be baptised, saying either the sacrament would kill her or she would never fulfil the obligations of a Christian.[25]

Chief Ngege, on the other hand, presents a case of the Ndebele after the fall of their king. The king had been the spiritual link with the supernatural world. In times of drought they had turned to him either to propitiate his amadlozi or to send gifts to Mwari. But this time, when confronted by such hazards, the only alternative seemed to be the missionaries. In 1905 western Zimbabwe was hard hit by a drought which threatened the lives of the people and their livestock. A number of the Ndebele chiefs went to Bulawayo where they demanded that the recently erected statue of Rhodes be pulled down. They told the Chief Native Commissioner that since that monument was built rain had never fallen properly in the country. What is remarkable, however, was that Ngege, a traditional induna, in that he owed his position to the Ndebele king and not to the new administration, refrained from joining the protesting chiefs. Instead he asserted that only Nkulunkulu (God) had power over nature. He requested his teacher, Radasi, to conduct a special service for rain. The chief summoned a large congregation to attend it, and, in spite of his old age and feebleness, he trudged the seven miles from his home to Ingwenya to attend the service himself. Fortunately, Radasi's prayers were answered by a downpour. Ngege was not an isolated case. Another chief called Mhlahle informed Ngege that 'a missionary in his own district prayed for rain and they got it'.[26]

However, although Ngege was convinced of the beneficial aspects of western civilisation, he could not commit himself to it. The rain service was indeed the last chance for Radasi ever to see the old chief in church. He died illiterate and a heathen. But his conviction in the worthiness of the white man's culture was only too well demonstrated in his resolution that his children must not die in the old ways, but must acquire the mysteries of the West under the tutelage of Radasi. Perhaps the decisive event which made the chief adopt such a view was when he saw the 'magic' power of literate people. When Radasi first met the chief in 1904 the latter had letters from his son working in Kimberley, which had never been opened since their arrival. When Radasi read them, Ngege 'was surprised when I mentioned his son's name and some of the people his son mentioned in his letters. He could not make out how I could mention people's names that I had never known or even seen simply by looking at the letter.' Indeed, the old man was reported to be 'anxious that I should teach the children to read as well'.[27]

The most remarkable example of Ndebele chiefly behaviour is that of Gambo. He was briefly exiled to Botswana and the Transvaal in the 1880s and he came back imbued with Khama's ideas. He remained an admirer of Khama until he died. When he received the missionaries for the first time he suggested that he be taught reading and writing in order to be like his friend Khama.[28] During the war of 1893 Gambo also witnessed the gallant battle put up by Major Wilson at Shangani, and from that day 'he never doubted that the whites are brave people, and how hopeless it is for his nation ever to think of conquest'.[29] After the fall of the Ndebele kingdom the chief made up his mind to accept the advent of the British philosophically. He saw the futility 'of attempting to arrest the march of civilization'.[30] But what is even more striking was how he exploited the new political situation, although his fellow black men might condemn him as profiting through the methods of a traitor. During the uprising he collaborated with the whites to suppress it.[31] The B.S.A. Company Administration rewarded him well for his loyalty. He was among the first to be chosen as a salaried Ndebele induna. Not only that, but he owned an immense herd of cattle representing more than £2,000, indicating that a large number of Ndebele cattle had passed into his hands through the agency of the new regime. Thus Gambo had managed to exploit a situation from which the majority of his people emerged impoverished.

If there was anything that added much to Gambo's awe and reverence of British power and civilisation, it was his visit to Sir Alfred Milner in Cape Town. The High Commissioner, it appears, did everything he could to impress the Ndebele chief. In the first place Gambo was astonished to see the railway engine. But the British armed ship which he boarded in Cape Town was something he was convinced was not man-made. Stanlake asked Gambo what he thought of it:

> making series of sounds expressing his utter astonishment, he said, 'It is a great and wonderful thing . . . It could not have been made by man – it made itself.' I was greatly amused at the description of a steam pinnace, which 'swam like a fish'. He was very much afraid, but was all right again when he reached the white men's kraal (i.e. the ship) . . . This visit has done much to impress him with the power of the men.[32]

But how did people like Gambo respond to missionary enterprise, as opposed to white secular power? Clearly they were fully aware that the old ways stood no chance of saving them from the overwhelming forces of western culture. Yet participation which they so successfully pursued in politics was ill-suited to Christianity as the missionaries demanded total commitment as well as a complete break with the past. The solution adopted by Ngege was the one to which Gambo turned with impressive success.

As soon as the Tegwani mission station was set up Gambo went in person to Stanlake and applied for a teacher to be stationed in his home. He said his nation was in the dark and he wanted his children to learn. Nevertheless, the chief had no illusions about the power of the old life especially on the old generation. In his own richly metaphorical language he described to his missionary how he saw the whole situation:

> The conversation turned upon the subject of his son and heir Sibindi ... Gambo said he would like his son to be well educated and that *he would place him entirely in our hands* to be educated, where and how we thought best. He then went on to say that as for himself he was getting old and could not change his ways – 'can you,' he asked, 'change the growth of the horns of an ox when he is already old – can the horns which have already grown backwards for many years be suddenly changed to grow forward?'[33]

Like Ngege, Gambo displayed religious heterodoxy because the traditional religion after the disappearance of the monarchical institution seemed inadequate to meet natural disasters. In 1914 he tried to pray for rain in the old way and failed. He therefore turned to his minister M'fazi and requested him to 'pray to the living God for rain'. The chief informed the congregation gathered for this service that: 'I have called you that you must ask for rain Up above for we are all his people. We have failed to find the rain by our own ways; our cattle and children will die for [sic] starvation, if God does not give us the rain.'[34]

Before concluding the story of the career of Gambo, it is worth observing the consequences of this transitional period in the history of missionary enterprise in western Zimbabwe, in which the old section of the society refused to break away from the old order, but took special interest to encourage their youths to embrace western culture under the guidance of the missionaries as well as to patronise mission stations. By the First World War the results were clearly marked at the Gambo station. C. W. Harpur of Tegwani, who addressed the congregation there, said that he was struck by 'the vivid and startling contrast ... between "Heathen" and "Christian" South Africa'. He went on:

> There in front of me was Old Africa – ages old. And what faces those heathen had! Faces that were cunning; faces that were merely stupid, with a fearful ignorance stamped all over them; faces that were branded with lust: faces that were drink-sodden and vicious.

And at my side was New Africa – and a new face. For the most part New Africa is composed of young people, and these were clean, alert, and on their faces was written faith, hope and love. How eagerly they entered into worship! With what new light of dawning hope their faces shone! Reverent and responsive, they showed in their faces and whole demeanour a glowing contrast to the old heathen men before me.[35]

Whatever criticisms may be marshalled against Harpur's sense of values it cannot be doubted that contrasts were beginning to emerge between Gambo's world and that of his son, Sidindi, who was studying at Lovedale in Cape Colony. Indeed, Gambo, perhaps beginning to feel the difference between himself and his heir declared that 'when this young man marries he must marry a Christian girl!' In 1917 Gambo died a heathen. Although he had 'clung to the customs of his fathers to the last', he had shown a tremendous grasp of the rapidly altering environment as well as a great deal of foresight especially with respect to the future of the young generation of Ndebeleland. His skill in combining the new and the old, both of which meant a great deal to him, was appreciated by his headmen, who made it a point that they buried him according to the traditional rites, but at the same time invited a Methodist missionary to speak to the people after the burial.[36]

Let us now turn to the former subject people of the Ndebele. As has already been seen, missionary enterprise before 1923 was much more effective with the Kalanga than any other single Shona group in western Zimbabwe. For this reason, discussion on the Shona of western Zimbabwe will centre on the Kalanga.

Kalanga culture had for more than half a century withstood Ndebele domination with remarkable resilience. At the turn of the present century it was still possible to speak of a distinctive Kalanga culture. The impressions of Ndebele domination were particularly marked in the field of language. The Kalanga males and young women spoke both Ndebele and Kalanga. But what distinguished the Kalanga from their rulers were the local religious beliefs and practices.

The Kalanga responded to missionary enterprise in a complicated way. First of all they showed stubborn resistance to Christian influences. They even went so far as to exercise violent coercion on converts and to accuse them of witchcraft. Yet it was among the Kalanga that some startling conversions were made, startling in that they involved such staunch traditionalists as bone-throwers. But, as in the case of the Ndebele, the old section of the Kalanga tended to remain aloof from Christian influences, while at the same time they encouraged their youths to learn from the missionaries. The outstanding examples of the latter group were Mpini, who though a Zansi was chief over a predominantly Kalanga area, and Majila, both of the Tegwani circuit, and Tjingababili and Malaba, of Dombodema. These chiefs invited missionaries to open up educational institutions in their own areas. They built churches and houses for teachers and sometimes cultivated school gardens asking no remuneration whatever. They urged their people to listen to the words of the missionaries and to refrain from working in their gardens on Sundays. Nevertheless, they told the missionaries to direct their efforts towards the children because the 'adults . . . were too old to alter'.[37]

But Chief Tshitshi of the reserve adjoining the Empandeni farm represented the side of the Kalanga which shrewdly dreaded the revolutionary effects of Christianity.[38] In later years Fr O'Neil recalled the chief as 'a jovial old chap, but an awful savage'. He could not forget that one morning he had found Tshitshi 'engaged in the brutal work of banging the head of one of his wives (he had seven) against the ground'. Nevertheless, he 'was the most influential and important [chief] on the Reserve' and the Jesuits could not hope to open a school there without his support and approval.[39]

The catechist Inja Mhlope was charged with the responsibility of running the first school in the area of this redoubtable authority in 1906. The two personalities were bound to clash, for Mhlope, himself a former bone-thrower, who had sacrificed all the popularity of his profession to become a Christian, was a remarkably strong believer in the new faith. His burning enthusiasm to spread the Gospel among his fellow black men sometimes overpowered his sense of discretion. He had some experience as a teacher and a catechist. Before undertaking the onerous task of extending the Catholic faith into the Reserve, he had taught a class of fifty children in the three R's, hymns, and catechism under Fr Charles Bick, the founder of the Embakwe station in 1902.[40]

When Mhlope first came to the school, the chief was against mission work, and this was reflected in the children who did not come to learn. Mhlope even suggested that the school be closed down. But Fr O'Neil went personally to speak to Tshitshi, whom he found in a high state of drunkenness. The chief promised his visitor that he would not stand in the way of the Gospel, but on condition that the girls, some of whom had already been given to husbands according to kuzwarira, were not taught. The result was that within three months thirty-one children were baptised and many more were being prepared for the ceremony.[41]

At this point Mhlope's enthusiasm and industry shone brilliantly. He opened a night class to meet the burning desire of the boys for reading and writing. On Sunday he visited villages and preached in the open air. The upshot of Mhlope's efforts was that the Embakwe chapel was filled to overflowing.[42] Indeed it seemed as though the mass movement towards Christianity which was already taking place at Empandeni might be experienced at this out-station. O'Neil even appealed for funds to extend the chapel which was becoming too small.[43]

Yet this was only short-lived. Within about three months of the first signs of this phenomenal upsurge towards the new faith, no boys were coming forward to ask to be baptised. The fact was that the traditionalists had suddenly turned hostile, when Christianity seemed to be sweeping over their area. They attacked the chief, and 'taxed him with deserting the people and their traditions, and going over to the enemy'.[44] Of course the chief was only too willing to admit his error, for he had already become dissatisfied with the teacher's activities. Mhlope was continually flouting Tshitshi's agreement with O'Neil not to teach the girls. The chief therefore decided to stop the children from going to school, and the out-station was closed down in 1908.

It was reopened in 1909, because Tshitshi had fallen ill and the people insisted that he had been bewitched by the priest for breaking his promise to allow children to go to school. At the same time there was a great deal of pressure brought to bear on the chief by the children and the parents who wanted their children to be educated. Even then the school had to be reopened on Tshitshi's terms. Mhlope, the indiscreet teacher, was replaced with a local man who understood the wishes of the parents,[45] and was more likely to respect their customs.

Tshitshi, therefore, stands out as a Kalanga traditionalist who dreaded the effects of Christianity, both on his authority over the people and on the authority of the parents over their children. It is most doubtful whether this chief ever appreciated the benefits of education. What seems to have influenced him to allow the missionaries to come into his area was the pressure of the young generation which wanted to learn to read and write. The chief hoped rather naïvely to check the objectionable effects of Christianity through personal understanding with O'Neil. However, the fact that this check did not work was as much the result of Mhlope's undoubtedly powerful appeal to the people as it was of a powerful local movement of both female and male youth towards the new teaching.

But opposition to mission work was not always expressed through traditional authority; even individuals might decide to take matters into their own hands and put up a fight with the missionary. In 1914 M'fazi reported some outrageous incidents that took place at Zuzumba. He said that children were being prevented from attending school. One woman had been shamefully 'made to pull off the dresses given to her by the Christian women, and four girls were also taken away by force from school and given to men to marry, who had their own wives'. Again some people had invaded the school with sticks and axes and had literally dragged away two girls who were learning there. Chief Mate's wife had shown some interest in the Gospel only to find herself summoned to the chief's court, on charges of witchcraft.[46] In other words she became a victim of that loss of respect, friends and security which the Chief Native Commissioner said attended those who were smelt out for witchcraft.[47]

Perhaps the most pathetic victim of individual opposition to mission work was the one reported by Rev. Radasi of Ingwenya mission in 1909. A Christian wife had been so badly treated by her pagan husband that she had been forced to separate from him and return to her parents. 'Her husband used to beat her very cruelly for going to church, but the woman would say: "I should obey you in everything, but not in this." ' The man would order her to violate the Christian sacred day, telling her to go to work in the fields on the Sabbath day; but she would go to church with her little girl. When she returned she would receive a brutal and savage beating from the husband. 'The last time she was at Church', the minister said, 'she had her front teeth knocked out by her cruel husband. Her parents heard about her ill-treatment and came and fetched her'.[48]

Stubborn resistance to Christianity was also put up by the *Shumba* system. This was a form of Kalanga traditional ancestral belief which the missionaries admitted to be difficult to uproot.[49] The

Kalanga believed that there was a class of ancestral spirits 'styled *izishumba*, who wandered about in the air seeking to enter into or take possession of some female member of the clan or family to which they belonged while on earth'. If a boy happened to be a victim of such a spirit, it was immediately transferred to a girl. When a spirit wanted to go into a girl for the first time, she became ill. A diviner was consulted and he usually diagnosed that the Shumba was troubling her, and that to save her life the spirit must be inducted into the girl. Then an old Shumba woman was called in to perform the inducting ritual, at the end of which the girl was said to be a Shumba. J. O'Neil described it:[50]

> She is henceforth under the tutelage of the hag who 'raised' the spirit in her: she must marry into the family of this woman, and is obliged to take part in all the dances performed at the old creature's kraal in honour of the Shumba spirits. Consequently the more Shumba girls the old creatures can make, the more important their standing, and hence they try to make as many proselytes as they can.[50]

This cult exercised tremendous influence and control over its individual members and hence it was almost impossible to convert a Shumba to Christianity. This influence was extended to the husbands, and the latter were 'often unable to send their children to school'. In 1909 the catechist teacher of Mkanya complained that only forty to fifty youths in his area came to school, and that about seventy were hindered by the Shumba cult.[51]

The Jesuits met the challenge of the Shumba cult in many ways. First of all they tried to show the people that their belief in the spirits was unfounded, and even attempted to put to ridicule the Shumba mediums. They also used the same punishment they were meting out to polygamists, which was expulsion from the farm.[52] Apparently it was soon found out that expulsion was wasteful of potential converts, and violence was used instead to terrorise the Shumba women. Fr Biehler, the Superintendent of the Empandeni out-stations, was particularly notorious for his violent means of fighting the cult. One day in 1911 he invaded a village where people were holding the cult's ceremony, and with a 'substantial *shambock* of the donkey-cut' lashed mercilessly the old women who were dancing. After this brutal punishment, the Shumba were warned that if they held their ritual dances again they would be sent to jail.[53] Fr O'Neil also once dispersed a group of worshippers, using a dog. Again he tells us that after his exciting exploits of chasing old women up and down in the middle of the night, he suitably punished the 'principal delinquents', which means he either lashed them with a whip or expelled them from the farm.[54]

The Jesuits held that Africans were children who only responded well to 'firmness and justice' rather than to 'weakness and indulgence'.[55] Such thinking, coupled with the notions that the native was sensual, materialistic in outlook and typically lazy, made them most unsympathetic towards and impatient of the religious beliefs and practices of the people they sought to convert at Empandeni. In other words, what a critical and sensitive observer might consider as brutal and savage treatment of innocent people was in fact regarded by the Jesuits as corrective measures meted out to misbehaving 'children' – the Kalanga who were pursuing wrong beliefs.

But how did the Kalanga see the role of the missionary? They could never be persuaded to understand that the missionary had left his 'kith and kin for their sakes', and that he had come among them for their good. They always detected selfish and material motives behind the missionary. If the missionary said that he was sacrificing everything that was dear to him overseas in order to come and uplift them from darkness, they simply replied, 'Ah, but you are well paid for doing it . . . By the king of England.' Some even went so far as to conclude: 'No wonder you want to baptise us, when you get a box of gold for every baptism you administer.' When questioned whether any of them had seen the gold payments, they replied, 'No, but we know you get it: all the old people say so'. The commonest argument was: 'All white people come into our country to get rich. You are a white man. *Ergo.*'[56] Moreover, the Kalanga saw themselves as being at the mercy of the white people, who appeared to be bent on destroying all that was precious to them.

> As might have been expected the old people listened to the missionary with incredulity and contempt; in fact from the very start they distrusted the missionary, whom they regarded as an emissary sent by their white rulers to divorce them from their customs and traditions. To the grown ups he spoke in vain and he knew it.[57]

To complete the picture of the reactions of the Ndebeleland societies to missionary enterprise, it is convenient to turn to the Mwari institution, as this was the supra-tribal cult. There is very little evidence from which to draw a sound impression of the attitude of this system towards the missionaries. This can only be attributed to the fact that Mwari must have interfered very little. Indeed, the institution had no cause to engage in religious confrontations with the missionaries since the old people refused to abandon their ways and continued to worship him. As we have seen, even classic admirers of western civilisation, such as Gambo, turned to the missionaries in times of drought after first trying their traditional rainmaking ceremonies.

Nevertheless, the Jesuits' intensive methods of transforming the Empandeni community must have looked like a real threat to the god, for in 1906 one of his mediums displayed a somewhat aggressive attitude towards the Catholics. In the spring of that year, Nina kaPansi, 'Mother of the Ground', an influential priestess of Mwari, came and stayed in a hut a few miles outside Empandeni. She was an awe-inspiring creature, and one Jesuit priest who went to chase her from her temporary shrine told his colleague that 'the very sight of the old hag gave him the creeps, and he added that when he began to chaff her, the language she used far surpassed in violence and abusiveness anything he had ever heard from a native'.[58]

Before being driven away by the Catholics, however, Nina kaPansi accused the people of ploughing before propitiating Mwari. She threatened to punish them with locusts that would devour all their crops. A little later she changed her mind and called upon the people to bring offerings to her, to stop working on Saturdays and work on Sundays instead, and to bring seeds to her to be fructified. All these commands were obeyed.[59]

In 1912–13 Empandeni was unfortunate to have no rain when the rest of the country had it. The traditionalists took this to be a clear demonstration of the impotence of the missionary God and of the power of Mwari. Nina kaPansi reappeared and called on the Empandeni people to return to their old ways. She gave similar orders to the previous time, this time promising them rain. The people obeyed her but no rain fell. A group of men who considered themselves deceived by the priestess went to where she was staying and thrashed her. She disappeared from the neighbourhood of Empandeni.[60]

But there is a piece of evidence pointing to the fact that at least by the First World War the territorial cults were beginning to accommodate themselves to the changes wrought by Christianity.

In 1914 Bowen Rees went to Sihalihali, the traditional praying place of the Rozvi, to dedicate an L.M.S. church. The Sihalihali priest attended the dedication service, contributed money to the collection, and then went to pray at his traditional and sacred shrine to his god 'to remember the missionaries and their work'.[61]

Thus we have seen the missionary occupation of western Zimbabwe, missionary attitudes towards traditional societies and the reluctance of the administration to 'civilise' the Africans by legislation. Finally, we have examined some of the ways in which the traditionalists reacted to missionary intrusion. It is clear that, although some efforts were made to keep away Christianity, the general tendency was for the old people to remain aloof while they encouraged their young people to adopt the ways of the missionary. Therefore, in the next chapter, we shall try to see how New Africa was being created.

Notes

1. For a full treatment of this organisation, see J. N. Hostetter, 'Mission Education in a Changing Society', unpublished D.Ed. thesis, State University of New York, 1967
2. For a fuller and more competent account of the early history of Independency, see T. O. Ranger, 'The Early History of Independency in Southern Rhodesia' in W. M. Watt (ed.), *Religion in Africa*, Edinburgh, 1964, pp. 52–74
3. R.N.A. A3/6/1, H.C. to Administrator (Rhodesia), 25 July 1919; C.N.C. to Department of Administrator, 2 Aug. 1919; H.C. to Administrator, 8 Sept. 1919
4. *Ibid.*, Mabiletsa to H.C., 23 July 1919
5. *Ibid.*, Mgoma and Mabelle to Administrator, 19 Jan. 1924
6. *Ibid.*, C.N.C. to Secretary to Premier, 1 Feb. 1924; Minister of Native Affairs to Ag. Colonial Secretary, 5 Feb. 1924
7. *Ibid.*, S.N. (Bulawayo) to N.C. (Umzingwane), 3 Aug. 1921; N.C. to S.N., 8 Aug. 1921; N.C. to S.N., 1 Aug. 1921; Thomas to S.N., 17 Aug. 1921; Thomas to S.N., 21 Sept. 1921; C.N.C. to Administrator, 1 Oct. 1921; Mgoma and Mabelle to Administrator, 19 Jan. 1924
8. C. H. Temple, 'Some Matabele Notes', *Worker and Workers*, Sept. 1896, pp. 387–90; *Worker and Workers*, Oct. 1896, pp. 426–9, and Nov. 1896, pp. 478–82
9. W. C. Willoughby, *Race Problems in New Africa*, Oxford, 1923, pp. 61–3, 80–1
10. *The Zambesi Mission Record*, v, 73, July 1916, pp. 374–7
11. *Ibid.*, iii, 45, 1909, p. 582

12. For O'Neil's interesting articles see *The Zambesi Mission Record*, iii, 33, Jan. 1907, pp. 185–8; iv, 47, Jan. 1910, pp. 35–9; iv, 48, April 1910, pp. 77–9; iv, 58, Oct. 1912, pp. 467–71; iv, 60, April 1913, pp. 539–43

13. Mackay to Cameron, Rec'd., 18 Oct. 1909; Free Presbyterian Church Correspondence regarding early work in Zimbabwe is published in J. V. Taylor, *Life and Labours of the Reverend J. B. Radasi*, Gisbone, 1966

14. W.M.M.S. S/M South Africa 1906–11, Stanlake's Report of the Bulawayo and Tegwani Circuits, 31 Dec. 1907

15. *The Zambesi Mission Record*, i, 13, July 1901, pp. 443–5; see also Hostetter, pp. 31–2

16. Ranger, 'Early History', p. 315

17. *The British South Africa Company Report* 1889–92, pp. 91–2

18. *Report of the Chief Native Commissioner (Matabeleland)*, 30 Sept. 1898, p. 219

19. *Report of the Native Affairs Committee*, 17 April 1911, p. 4

20. *The Zambesi Mission Record*, ii, 15, Jan. 1902, pp. 53–7

21. *Ibid.*, iii, 42, Oct. 1908, p. 451

22. One of the measures of pacification was the 'Witchcraft Suppression Ordinance, 1899'. But the Chief Native Commissioner admitted that legal measures would not effectively destroy the superstitious practices of the Africans. See *Report of the Chief Native Commissioner (Matabeleland)*, 31 March 1898, p. 20

23. L.M.S. B2/F2/JB, Carnegie to For. Sec., Nov. 1898

24. *Letters and Notices*, xxiii, pp. 85–6; L.M.S. B2/F5/JB, Carnegie to For. Sec., 2 Feb. 1895

25. *The Zambesi Mission Record*, v, 69, July 1915, pp. 227–8

26. Radasi to Cameron, Rec'd., 15 Jan. 1906; for the statistical illustration of the drought in western Zimbabwe, see *The Zambesi Mission Record*, iii, 34, Jan. 1907, pp. 63–5

27. Radasi to Cameron, 19 May 1905

28. W.M.M.S. C. Mashona, 1891 9, Shimmin to Hartley, 26 Aug. 1897

29. *Worker and Workers*, Nov. 1899, pp. 478–9

30. *Ibid.*, Sept. 1897, p. 385

31. W. H. Anderson, *On Trail of Livingstone*, Mount View, 1919, p. 91; *Rhodesia Herald*, 30 Sept. 1897

32. *Worker and Workers*, Nov. 1899, p. 479

33. *Ibid.*, p. 480; see also W.M.M.S. BG1/1, Bulletins, 63

34. W.M.M.S. S/M Rhodesia, 1912–22, Report of Tegwani Circuit, 1914; M'fazi's Report of Zuzumba Mission, 3 March 1914

35. *The Foreign Field*, xii, 1915–16, pp. 116–17

36. *The 103rd Report of the W.M.M.S.*, 1917, p. 108

37. *Worker and Workers*, Sept. 1899, pp. 394–9, Oct. 1899, p. 457; L.M.S. B58, Bechuana and Matabele, 1900, Reed to For. Sec., 12 July 1900

38. *The Zambesi Mission Record*, iii, 42, Oct. 1908, p. 457

39. *Ibid.*, v, 77, July 1917, p. 507

40. *Ibid.*, ii, 24, April 1904, pp. 380, 390

41. *Ibid.*, iii, 39, Jan. 1908, p. 344

42. *Ibid.*, iii, 42, Oct. 1908, p. 456

43. *Ibid.*, iii, 39, Jan. 1908, pp. 344–8
44. *Ibid.*, iii, 40, April 1908, p. 369
45. *Ibid.*, v, 77, July 1917, pp. 506–7
46. W.M.M.S. S/M Rhodesia, 1912–22, M'fazi Report of the Zuzumba Mission, Dec. 1913
47. *Report of the Chief Native Commissioner (Matabeleland)*, 31 March 1898, p. 220
48. Radasi to Cameron, Rec'd., 1 Oct. 1909
49. *The Zambesi Mission Record*, v, 78, Oct. 1917, p. 527; iv, 60, April 1913, pp. 539–41
50. *Ibid.*, v, 70, Oct. 1915, p. 267
51. *Ibid.*, iii, 45, July 1909, p. 588
52. *Ibid.*, v, 78, Oct. 1917, pp. 527–8
53. *Ibid.*, iv, 52, April 1911, pp. 229–30
54. *Ibid.*, v, 76, April 1917, pp. 476–8
55. *Ibid.*, pp. 457–60; cf. L. Vambe, *An Ill-fated People*, London, 1972, pp. 7–10, 14–15. Vambe shows how the Jesuits at Chishawasha exercised iron rule on the tenants and apparently eventually forced the Vashawash to realise 'that the best way to get along with the missionaries, and white people generally, is by cultivating the "virtue" of cunning'.
56. *The Zambesi Mission Record*, iii, 45, July 1909, pp. 581–2
57. *Ibid.*, v, 73, July 1916, p. 375
58. *Ibid.*, iv, 58, Oct. 1912, p. 470
59. *Ibid.*, iii, 36, April 1907, pp. 210–11
60. *Ibid.*, iv, 58, Oct. 1912, p. 471; iv, 60, April 1913, pp. 515–16
61. L.M.S. B5/Reports: S.A. 1913–19, Rees's Annual Report of Inyati, 31 Dec. 1915

6

Christianity and education in western Zimbabwe before 1923

It is to the aims and aspirations of the missionaries as well as to what they actually did in western Zimbabwe that attention must now be directed. The paramount aim of the missionaries was of course to instil Christian moral principles into the minds of the Africans. In order to establish Christianity on a firm and permanent basis, the missions combined their evangelical activities with programmes of transforming the physical and intellectual life of their converts. Because of this comprehensive approach it is difficult to separate their spiritual from their secular education in the early twentieth century. Indeed the two aspects were so intertwined that their institutions often performed dual functions: the church was at the same time the school; the Sunday congregation and Bible classes were also the weekly class of pupils; the missionary was at the same time the agricultural and health demonstrator; the evangelist served as the schoolmaster.[1]

There were other reasons which led them to adopt this broad approach. Nearly all the missions labouring in western Zimbabwe had the difficulty of securing a sufficient supply of European personnel from overseas. This class of mission staff was also expensive to maintain. To alleviate this problem, the missionary societies from the very beginning evolved literary education to produce local workers. Besides it was soon discovered that the missionary's efforts met with more success among the youth than among the old people. The young generation was attracted to the mission station more by literary education than by the Gospel. Nevertheless, this at least made it possible for the missionaries to use literary lessons as a bait to the children in order ultimately to convert them to Christianity.

Moreover, it was easier to bring the new faith to the homes of a literate society than to illiterate people. Those who were able to read bought scriptural literature which they studied at home in the presence of their families. In this way the Christian religion spread from the stations to the farthest points where the missionary staff might never hope to reach. The points that suggest themselves for closer examination are missionary education, the production of evangelist teachers as well as catechists, and the African response to these activities.

The crucial factor in the spread of the Gospel was the African agency, which often carried the faith to places sometimes inaccessible on account of health reasons to European missionaries. The black agents were also cheap to maintain; their basic needs were simple: they lived in pole and daga huts, ate the same food as the people, needed no furloughs, and above all lived with people without being inconvenienced by their way of life. Monthly stipends ranged between 10s. and £6 only.[2]

Moreover, the African workers were said to have the singular knack of appealing to the hearts of their fellow men, which a European, however versed in the vernacular language and indigenous customs, could not acquire. For this reason all the missions in western Zimbabwe stressed the importance of employing black evangelist-teachers.[3]

The problem that beset the various Churches with respect to African agents was one of recruiting and training them. The W.M.M.S. and the Church of Sweden Mission, which already had prosperous districts in South Africa, brought their first evangelists from there. The Methodists secured the services of such people as the steady Sotho preacher and later minister Josiah Ramhushu, who worked for them for twenty-six years before dying of influenza in 1918.[4] The advantages of bringing African workers from South Africa were quite obvious. They were better educated than the Zimbabwean blacks; Christianity was no longer a novelty to be adopted out of curiosity or as a matter of fashion, as the Ndebele and the Shona were just beginning to do.

The best example of such South Africans was Rachel Masinga, the Zulu girl who with the L.M.S. missionary Neville Jones founded the Hope Fountain Girls' Boarding School in 1916. Masinga, born of Christian parents in Natal in 1895, was both highly educated and spiritually advanced by Ndebele standards. With missionary financial support she had obtained a teacher's diploma after standard six. She was also brought up in a Christian home, and, according to her, she could not remember any other form of worship. Furthermore, she had grown up in a society in which any young person aspiring to lead a successful and comfortable life was anxious to be educated. Above all, she professed that her one ambition throughout her school days had been to become a missionary among heathen people.[5]

There were, however, many limitations, problems and dangers associated with recruiting South Africans. The obvious limitation was that facing the S.D.A., the L.M.S. and the Brethren in Christ, which did not have flourishing evangelical work among the Nguni. Coupled with this was the aversion of the missions to employ agents from other denominations. Moreover, black South Africans were beginning to be involved in a nationalist protest movement. When these nationalists were by mistake brought to Ndebeleland where people were dissatisfied with the land distribution between whites and blacks, they offered the Ndebele their sophisticated leadership and organisational skills. Even the Company Administration had as early as 1904 come to the conclusion that Africans from the South and Mfengu in particular constituted a dangerous element in the country. The Chief Native Commissioner was already urging that the Mfengu be prevented from contaminating the local Africans.[6]

Such a dangerous case to the L.M.S. was J. L. September, a Coloured certificated teacher from Colesberg in the Cape Colony. He joined the staff at Hope Fountain in 1912. At first he threw himself 'heartily into the work of the station' and it was hoped that he would soon raise the standard of education. But in 1915 he 'constituted himself a leader of the tenants in stirring up sedition and disaffection among the people'. When the L.M.S. summarily dismissed him from his post, he protested that they were treating him unfairly because of his dark skin and threatened them with a court action. He also demanded damages for what he called a breach of contract. In the end the missionaries dealt with him cautiously and also tried to meet his claims generously.[7]

Apart from the fear of being party to the expansion of protest movements from South Africa to Ndebeleland, the whole system of relying on foreign Africans did not solve the problem of the missionaries. Africans did not volunteer in large numbers to come to Zimbabwe – they were still communalistic and wanted to work near their homes.[8] Some missionaries were sceptical about both the quality of those who volunteered and their ability to reach the hearts of the Ndebele. Bowen Rees argued that, 'The Matabele do not take kindly to [Africans] from the South', and that 'the best colonial [Africans] stay at home'.[9] In fact the people in the South demanded higher wages than the L.M.S. could afford to pay.[10] All these factors forced the missionaries to start training local Africans. There was no uniform system of training, so each mission will be considered separately.

The Adventist missionaries took advantage of the starvation of the local inhabitants soon after the risings of 1896–7. They either bought or accepted into their care children offered by parents who were unable to feed them. These adopted youths formed the first pupils of the Solusi Boarding School where, under the direction of the missionaries, they cultivated the farmland and looked after cattle to produce both their own food and other products, such as butter, which were sold in Bulawayo. Apart from this industrial work, as it was called, the boarders received literary instruction at the same time as they were infused with the fundamentalist doctrines of the sect. At the end of their training the boys went to open sub-stations and some of the girls married the evangelists.[11] In addition to the area already mentioned, this mission expanded to Mkupuvula, Gwai and Wankie. W. H. Anderson explained:

> In these outstations, the [African] teachers carry the pupils through the first two or three grades. Then we select from those finishing these grades, capable, consecrated young men, bring them to the central station, and place them in the training school to be educated for God's service.[12]

By 1916 the sect had at its command twenty-six preachers and teachers. The primary object of the S.D.A., therefore, was not to educate the people for their own benefit but for the Church's sake.

But it was the Adventists' fundamentalist interpretation of the Bible and their lack of respect for other societies' sphere of operation which not only irritated their neighbours, but also caused the Native Department to keep a close watch on the African preachers. In 1922 this sect's powerful and well organised team of black preachers was pushing forward its work in the Gwelo, Selukwe and Somabula districts, where it was continually clashing with the W.M.M.S. In that year Holman Brown recorded a number of reports from his teachers and evangelists, all of them being complaints against the S.D.A. The first was from P. Juba, an evangelist trained at Nengubo, who said that the S.D.A. teachers were persistently breaking into the Methodist area and telling the people that the Methodists were preaching lies and 'were in league with the white people to deceive the Natives, lest they should learn too much. The white missionaries have a plot against the black people'. Another, John Ngono, also a Methodist teacher, alleged that the S.D.A. preachers were informing his converts that, 'Your religion and your preaching is not respected by God who hates your falsehood. Your Ministers and teachers are liars.' J. Mgugu, another Methodist teacher, called the Adventists 'snakes'. They urged people to keep away from the Methodists, whom they called liars and unbelievers. 'They rebaptized our children and people', Mgugu said. 'They cause very much anguish and sorrow and our people are beginning to get restless. I am afraid there will be fighting'.[13] But it must have been Mafa Sibindwana's report which frightened the Native Department into action:

> These people take pleasure in always troubling us, they threaten us with punishments, bad crops, no rain, and personal dangers, because we listen to our white missionaries who, they say, are in league with all the white people to bring disaster and destruction to the black people. The white people desire more than to simply lead astray the black people from the good way. It is all on this day – Saturday. They say we only have the proper way, all other Missionaries and teachers are plotting against the happiness and safety of the Natives.[14]

The Native Commissioner of Selukwe, when forwarding these reports to the Superintendent of Natives (Bulawayo), commented that these preachers were not properly supervised by their European missionaries. The Chief Native Commissioner, who had already received a similar complaint from N. Jones of the L.M.S., advised that a careful investigation be made into the substance of some of the reports with a view to taking court action for sedition against some of the S.D.A. teachers.[15] No direct evidence, however, could be obtained to enable any court action.[16] In the meantime, the Chief Native Commissioner advised the Administrator to empower the Native Commissioners to make regular checks on the teachings and activities of the Native preachers.[17] The result was that a circular of instructions was issued to the Native Commissioners requiring them to visit regularly all the preaching places to check against the spread of Ethiopianism. The Native Commissioners were now duty bound to 'keep themselves constantly informed on this subject, and to acquaint themselves at first-hand with the persons engaged in teaching and preaching and the nature of the propaganda and doctrines inculcated'. These officials were especially to direct their attention to the 'political teachings and tendencies'.[18] Thus the failure of the S.D.A. to remain within the limits of their own circuits and their peculiar interpretation of the Bible, which in African hands verged on Ethiopianism and political sedition, had ultimately dragged the Native Department to infringe upon the people's religious freedom. At the same time, however, the S.D.A. preachers demonstrated how the Africans were enthusiastically bringing the Gospel to their own people.

The W.M.M.S., like the S.D.A., grasped the need to train local manpower for evangelical service at a very early stage. In 1898 the Rhodesian Synod deputed John White to collect funds in England during his furlough in order to set up a training centre in Ndebeleland.[19] The following year the Synod asked for financial assistance from the Committee to meet part of the cost of the projected school. At the end of the same year, even before a definite reply from the Missionary Committee could come, the Methodists in Zimbabwe reported that three students had already been registered.[20]

But the efforts of this mission to educate the Shona and the Ndebele were mainly successful because of White's personal forceful character, determination, initiative, as well as his simple but decisive knack of dealing with his slow superiors in England. There were times when he so committed the Committee to a scheme in Zimbabwe that his superiors had no alternative but to see it through. He believed that the society was not spending as much money on African development in Zimbabwe as it was supposed to. The moment he was put in charge of opening the Nengubo training institution he began to visualise it through its first year by exploiting local resources. He would produce a large quantity of grain on the mission farm for selling in order to meet the expenses of the school. The first students would be the ill-qualified evangelists who would give up their salaries which would be added to the income of the institution.[21] Thus by 1901 four students were already studying religion, reading, writing, arithmetic, spelling, and translation from Zulu to Shona, besides doing manual labour in the school gardens, which was part of industrial training.[22]

The Nengubo training school expanded very rapidly. Already in 1906 it had twenty-two students, of whom eight were Ndebele, nine Shona, four Mfengu, and one Tswana; only four were girls. One Ndebele was expelled before the end of the year for grave misconduct.[23] In 1911 the number of pupils increased to thirty-one, in 1912 to forty-seven, in 1913 to forty-eight, and in 1914 to fifty-five. The total expenditure of the institution in 1906 was £263; the chief source of income was the W.M.M.S. grant of £175, and the money earned by students through repairing harness, shoes, footballs and other leather equipment of the white farmers and town dwellers, as well as by selling the crop and animal produce of the mission farm. It had also been hoped that much of the money would be raised by charging a fee of £8 per year for each pupil not studying for mission work. But this was soon found out to be too high for the Africans, who after all had not yet started to appreciate the value of schooling. Of the twenty-two students, in 1906 only four paid fees. But as the school expanded its curricula to include systematic industrial training, so did the government grant increase; in 1911 it was £86; in 1912 it rose to £104; and between 1913 and 1914 it went up from £164 to £198. Meanwhile the W.M.M.S. Committee also stepped up its annual assistance from £175 to £250 in 1914.[24]

In designing the curricula for the school, the Wesleyans took a number of factors into consideration. In the first place, they strove to satisfy the general desire for education among the youths.[25] Secondly, they tried to meet the needs of non-evangelist teachers who paid fees. Thirdly, they could not ignore the general opinion of the whites that the Africans were lazy and therefore must be taught the habits of manual labour. Moreover, they had their own ideal of the African they wanted to produce. Such a person they said should go and work in the villages and be able not only to raise the spiritual and intellectual thought of the people, but also, through his comprehensive training, be capable of being instrumental to changes in the way of life of the villagers and their environment. He should teach the people elementary reading and writing, religion, carpentry, building, hygiene, and modern agriculture.[26]

In addition to this task of creating an African class charged with the light of civilisation and Christianity, the Methodists felt the need and responsibility to alter the life of the women as well. They were particularly concerned about the lack of 'civilised' girls to marry their educated agents. The women who were 'ignorant of all except heathen family life' were a burden rather than a help to the teachers. In view of this, the Rhodesian Synod recommended that two boarding schools – one at Epworth and another at Tegwani – be started for females.[27]

However, after considering the expense involved in conducting three boarding schools, and after much discussion and consultation with the experienced missionaries in the Cape Colony, who in fact told him that 'the influence of the girls tended to the reinforcement of the boys', White decided to expand the Nengubo institution into a fully equipped co-educational school. During his 1914 furlough in England he had also campaigned for funds and had received a donation of £1,500 from J. K. Waddilove of Southport, after whom the school was later named. At this juncture White laid his plans for 'one central strong school for boys and girls at Nengubo' before the W.M.M.S. Committee, estimating the total cost of building at £3,000.[28]

White committed many blunders in his redevelopment scheme for Nengubo in 1914–17, but they all proved to be of little consequence. The upshot, however, of his activities was the great expansion of the school into a boarding institution of learning with living and teaching facilities for 200 students – 100 boys and 100 girls – in 1917. This extension was accompanied by an increase of students from 55 in 1915 to 131 in 1921. Whereas there were always sufficient males to use the facilities provided for them, the girls were too few. In 1917 the female dormitory was almost empty. In fact, in 1913 there were thirteen girls and by 1921 they had slightly increased to twenty-five.[29]

The reasons for this disparity between the sexes cannot be established with any certainty. First, some boys attended school free of charge, since they were training to be evangelists; but all the girls paid a fee of £4 each. Secondly, the social restrictions were more severe on the young women than on the boys. On account of this, it would appear that there was much truth in what the missionaries often said. They thought that the Ndebele and the Shona considered their females only slightly above things of commercial value, that the role of the women in society was to act as beasts of burden, to breed children and to satisfy men's sexual desires. This was demonstrated in the deprivation of the women's right to choose their own future husbands.[30] Naturally, when the missionaries attempted to house the girls at the mission stations their parents protested that the teachers would indoctrinate them to rebel against such customs as the kuzwarira. The lobola practice had in fact caused even the white authorities to recognise the fact that an African woman did not outgrow the guardianship of her parents until she was married. Consequently even girls of twenty-one years of age had to seek their parents' consent before entering into a marriage contract. In addition to this was the African's view about education, that it was a key to a good job and a good salary. Since it was regarded to be a man's duty to fend for his family, while the wife remained at home looking after the children and the gardens, the Shona and the Ndebele saw no reason for sending females to school. Perhaps the other reason was that Nengubo was in the Shona country. As we shall see in the case of Hope Fountain which seemed to be quite popular with the girls, it seems there were differences in attitudes towards unmarried women between the Ndebele and the Shona, the former being less restrictive than the latter.

In any case, the new Nengubo-Waddilove school offered as scholastic subjects: religion, English, Chiswina (Shona), history, geography, writing, singing, hygiene, arithmetic; as industrial sub-jects: farming, brick-making, carpentry, building, leather-work, tree-planting, and gardening. The girls did gardening, laundry, sewing, cooking and general housework. Only four hours of the school day of nine hours were devoted to industrial subjects. Because of the generally low educational standards in the country which caused many intending teachers to come to the school only after standard two, it was at first felt necessary not to separate the normal training from ordinary classes. But by 1921 it was becoming quite apparent that many of the students were not intending to be evangelists or go into mission service but to follow secular vocations. As a result in 1922 the department of teacher training was begun.[31]

From the point of view of Ndebeleland, the greatest defect of Nengubo was that it was remote: it was 500 miles from Tegwani and 360 miles from Bulawayo. Although the boys could go and live at such a distant place, parents were reluctant to see girls going there. The result was that in 1929, for instance, there were 1,600 girls in village schools and only twenty of them could manage to go higher than standard two. Indeed educated Ndebele boys were said to be clamouring 'for girls as wives who will be able to bring that culture which makes them real companions, with common interests'. With such a situation, Christian homes could not develop.[32] It is also obvious from the discussion that before 1923 the institution was still developing, so that its products did not begin to make an impact on the Shona and the Ndebele until after our period. In fact in 1921 H. Carter, the Superintendent of the Bulawayo circuit, was complaining that he did not have properly trained and qualified evangelists. In other words, the responsibility for spreading the Gospel was still largely in the hands of semi-literate preachers.[33] Nevertheless, the Wesleyans during this period had clearly made a splendid start in the field of African education.

Before taking a closer look at the work of the evangelists we must survey the efforts of the L.M.S. as well. The L.M.S. schemes lacked continuity during the early years, mainly due to the poverty of the society. Their first attempts were carried out by the lay industrialist George J. Wilkerson between 1898 and 1910. Wilkerson apprenticed boys for a minimum period of three years, and taught them brick-laying, carpentry, and agriculture. He also gave them a few lessons in the three R's.[34] Between 1903 and 1910 his boys almost transformed the buildings at the central stations from pole and mud huts to modern structures. He also set up churches at Hope Fountain and Inyati. The most important point to be emphasised is that nearly all the actual brick-laying, roofing, and the making of furniture and other woodwork were done by the students. Therefore, it is vital to try to evaluate these structures, to relate Wilkerson's efforts to the current settler thinking, and also to discover the reaction of the students themselves and how they benefited.

Taking the Hope Fountain church building, for instance, there is no doubt that it had deficiencies. But a Mr Scott, an architect from Bulawayo, 'spoke very highly of the work'. Wilkerson himself observed that, 'Everybody speaks in such glowing terms, really I feel a little puffed up'.[35] Perhaps the best summation was given by a local newspaper correspondent who attended the inauguration ceremony at Hope Fountain. To him the most significant fact to bear in mind when judging the building was 'that the whole of the labour was supplied from a native training institution'. Considered in that light, the church was 'the finest of its kind' in Zimbabwe; in fact, it bore 'signs of careful workmanship' everywhere. All the whites who saw it 'expressed their astonishment that the natives of this country could be trained to execute such excellent work'.[36] There can be no doubt then from these few observations that Wilkerson's pupils were making tremendous strides in acquiring western skills.

In spite of all this, the L.M.S. teacher explained that he was not aiming at producing skilled workers. He was unwilling to go against the white wishes. The Europeans said 'before they [the Africans] are taught theology they must be taught work', or 'muscular Christianity'. The settlers complained that institutions, such as Lovedale, which laid much emphasis on literary education, only managed to 'turn out a good many "ne'er-do-wells" '.[37] At the same time the spectre of black skilled workers scared them very much. Wilkerson himself was fully alive to this racial problem, and solved it not by producing carpenters and builders, but by turning out 'Christian lads, tidy, clean, sharp & useful'. He achieved this 'by labour, which may be building or gardening, etc. mixed with a fair education'.[38] Wilkerson therefore is an illustration of the way the missionaries in Zimbabwe found themselves having to satisfy the white demand for alert semi-skilled servants.

From the point of view of the students the whole programme was of qualified benefit. When the institution was finally closed down in 1910, twenty boys, the majority of whom were Hole or Zansi and the rest Kalanga, had been trained. After the completion of their apprenticeship, most of these pupils ended up as daga boys for the building contractors as well as foremen of the farms, earning something like £3 a month. In 1907 Wilkerson reported that the demands by the whites for his boys was exceeding the number of those that offered themselves for training. In spite of this apparent benefit, the students were not satisfied with the scheme. They wanted more time devoted to academic subjects than to manual labour. They demanded specialisation in some trades instead of doing everything without acquiring much skill in anything. One boy went so far as to demand a certificate to show that he had served a three years' apprenticeship at the institute. In other words the boys were asking for exactly what the whites did not want, skill.[39] The complaints further show that the young Ndebele and Kalanga were struggling to break through the limits of advancement set down for them by their white rulers.

The other L.M.S. educational experiment was that conducted by Richard C. Williams, also a lay missionary at Hope Fountain. It was a response to the Matabeleland District Committee's call upon their authorities to provide an advanced form of education for the Ndebele. In 1906 Williams was charged with the task of instituting a training school at Hope Fountain. Financial problems and the illness of the teacher himself forced the postponement of the whole project until 1909. At the end of the same year the whole thing was stopped again for financial reasons.[40]

Williams, however, was a hard-working and able European edu-cationist, but too single-minded to work properly with his col-leagues. As an indication of their dissatisfaction with Williams, when the Directors called for retrenchment in western Zimbabwe, the old missionaries voted for the closure of the institute first.[41] He was also criticised for trying to impart to the Ndebele a system of learning that was out of touch with their stage of civilisation. To this he replied that the old L.M.S. workers were to blame for neglecting elementary schools for a long time.[42] In any case, his training institute was found by the Inspector J. B. Brady to be efficient, up-to-date and impressive.[43] The students also liked it and the teachers who were trained by him were quite able. Some pupils even returned to school long before the holidays were over. When it was stopped many boys were said to be very upset, even though the L.M.S. had made provision for their transference to Tiger-kloof.[44]

But the students had complaints about the school. Two boys from Dombodema came with the sole aim of studying English in order to have 'the opportunity of earning more money' in town; when the principal refused them this chance they left. All the stu-dents were against doing manual labour as it made their clothes dirty and caused them to wear out. Those who were preparing to become evangelists told the headmaster that they were busy setting up modern houses at their homes yet when they left the institute they would not work in their own villages. So they requested the Society to provide good accommodation for them at all the village schools and preaching places. At the end of September all the pupils wanted to go home in order to dig their gardens.[45] All these requests represented a need for an educational system that was adapted to traditional economic activities, that could solve employment prob-lems, and would take into account the inability of the people to secure clothes easily. A school that produced teachers only was too narrow for the needs of the people.

After the closure of the training institute in 1909 the L.M.S. went into girls' education with more success. With the case of September and the farm tenants over, Neville Jones decided to provide schooling for females at as little cost to the Society as possible.[46] We have already seen the coming of Masinga. The way she and Jones began the Hope Fountain Girls' Boarding School had a somewhat fortuitous touch. When she first arrived she taught in the school, which was then very backward. In a very short time, however, she raised the standard of the children's literacy. She further visited regularly the surrounding out-schools, which were just as bad: classrooms were invariably unfurnished, ill-ventilated, without teaching aids and equipment, and the irregular attendance of the pupils was appalling.

But soon something happened that would attract Masinga's energies away from the village schools. A girl by the name of Fute Dlamini came to the mission, running away from the persecution of her father who wanted her to marry a polygamist. Later two more young women arrived seeking to live with Masinga. It was at this point that the schoolmistress and the superintendent started the boarding school for girls who could pay their own fees, orphans, or women suffering persecution in their own pagan homes.

The rapidity with which the school grew is amazing, considering that these were girls and not boys. In 1916 only six were studying at the school. They increased to seventeen in 1917 and to thirty-three in 1918. But two of them, including a granddaughter of the late Lobengula, Mirriam Khumalo, died during the influenza epidemic. Nevertheless, between 1919 and 1923 the figure went up from thirty-two to sixty-four, more than double the number of female students at Nengubo, which was much older than Hope Fountain. Again the composition of the staff affords another contrast with Nengubo, where foreigners remained in control throughout our period. For the first four years at Hope Fountain the teachers were all foreigners: Masinga, the headmistress, and Letta Mazibuko, the assistant mistress, also a Zulu with standard five and a teacher's certificate. The matrons of course were local. But in 1902 an Ndebele, Hobile Hlabangana, was appointed to the staff. By 1923 only the lady principal, Jessie Simmonite, was an immigrant. Hilda Matambo, the head assistant, Priscilla Ncube, the industrial assistant, and Adelaide Ntuli were all local girls who had trained at the school before going to finish their studies at Tigerkloof. Masinga left in 1923 to be married.[47] Moreover, most of the students were paying their own fees. In 1918, for example, twenty-one were maintained by their own parents, ten by European friends, and one by what was called the Native Charitable Fund.[48] Thus the number of those using the institution as an asylum was far outnumbered by those who solely wanted to learn.

The reasons for this favourable response of women in western Zimbabwe can only be guessed. Even in the nineteenth century Ndebele women had enjoyed a certain amount of freedom to associate with the white traders. Their behaviour led Ivon Fry to declare that they were all prostitutes.[49] Then the starvation after the 1896-7 rebellion forced many Ndebele females to go into Bulawayo to sell 'themselves for food to be the mistresses or concubines of young men or to Native boys who are in good work'.[50] Perhaps when these girls ultimately returned to their homes in smart dresses and brought goods for their parents and other relatives, people saw how it was possible even for women to make a successful living in town. Of course everybody disapproved of *amahule* (women living by prostitution). On top of that, Europeans were demanding girls who could speak some English and who had some rudiments of domestic service. Probably it was this combination of the parents' fear that if their daughters were uneducated they would end up as prostitutes and the European demand for domestic servants that made the Ndebele send their daughters to school.

Just as interesting as the response of the Ndebele women to western ideas were the very ideas behind the education of females and its type. As already shown, the Methodists as well as other missions in general were preoccupied with producing the future wives of their educated staff and Christian boys, as well as with liberating the girls from the bondage of their restrictive traditional societies. To these, the L.M.S. added the ideal of equality between the sexes, especially in what was regarded as 'The New Age in Africa' or simply the 'New Africa'. Christian education was viewed as a means of preparing 'stalwart young Christian leaders'; and this elite would have to consist of both males and females.[51]

As to the type of education, Masinga said that she was not imparting a revolutionary set of ideas that would make the girls avoid their own backward social environment. Rather she wished 'to show them that it was possible to live in a native way and yet be clean and tidy'. When they first arrived at the school she drilled them into the habit of having a bath every day; she taught them the use of western cooking utensils and eating manners; they slept on mats because beds were still a luxury afforded by only a few. The whole day was fully occupied with industrial and academic learning.

The staff was very strict on morals. Indeed the girls' behaviour, outlook and appearance were completely changed at Hope Fountain. On Sundays they epitomised the power of western ideas to change a people: they were smart and clean; their choir, which sometimes went into Bulawayo to sing there, led the congregation splendidly. There is no doubt that their example led many parents to send their daughters to Masinga. Besides, all the village shyness of the girls did not take long to vanish. Soon they would throw themselves heartily into the games, such as netball and swimming. Furthermore, they learned the use of the clock instead of the sun and became accustomed to a new type of discipline – that of the prefects of their own choice.[52] Unfortunately, most of the products of Hope Fountain begin to show up after our period. Nevertheless the few that completed their training during this time became domestic servants in Bulawayo and, as we have already seen, school teachers.

Since the Brethren in Christ's work is very well treated by Hostetter, a few remarks will suffice. Like the rest of the Protestants, this sect also experimented with boarding schools. Its Mtshabezi station began as a refuge for girls escaping traditional marriage customs and eventually developed into a flourishing institution where female industrial subjects, together with literary education, were taught. The station further catered for the local population's needs, by providing 'medical care and agricultural aids, such as grinding and the dipping of cattle'.[53] Matopo on the other hand grew from being an industrial school for boys into a teacher training centre.[54]

Equally involved in African education were the Catholics at Empandeni. The Catholics rejected the two extreme views held by the secular whites and some Protestants – too much or no education at all for the natives. They declared that for the foreseeable future the black man would remain inferior to and a servant of the white race. The duty of the Jesuits was then to uplift him to a state of being civilised and a Christian, and to train him 'to submit cheerfully to the destiny so long ago foretold, a servant of servants shall he be unto his brethren'.[55] A strict adherence to this doctrine of creating docile, subservient and Christian black drawers of water and hewers of wood for the white superior and master race in Zimbabwe, and the compactness of their Empandeni field – which required few catechists – caused them to be less interested in, if not opposed to, the schemes of higher literary learning carried out by the

Protestants. Moreover, Fr E. Biehler, who was responsible for the out-schools, argued in 1922 that he had lost faith in scholastic learning, for it only produced 'court and Police interpreters and money earners', but did not alter African village life.[56] Thus the emphasis of the Catholics was on manual teaching and a little literary education that would enable the Christians to read their religious books.

Indeed judged in this context, Fr Biehler's work was impressive. His aim was that people should improve their homes and means of livelihood. So he taught them carpentry, the seasoning of local timber and the production of planks out of it, the making of doors, benches, chairs, tables, shelves, beds, and many other pieces of furniture. The students also learned how to make *pisé* homes, to sink wells and maintain them, to clear fields of stumps, manuring them, gardening, tailoring, mending of roads and many other useful trades. He was not intending to manufacture skilled workers who would run away from their homes to the towns, but to produce intelligent and well equipped men and women to transform their own homes.[57] Even though Fr Biehler's intention was to train Africans for a subordinate status, he, more than any other missionary, was making an immediate impact on the local population. The people around the village schools were for instance beginning to fertilise their fields regularly. In short, the scheme fell within the framework of European attitudes that the African must be taught to improve his own areas so as to keep him out of the so-called European places.[58]

All these schemes we have surveyed so far had several common characteristics. Except for Fr Biehler's work, all the missionaries were evolving a higher system of education for a few Africans who would be the leaders of their own people. In other words they were endeavouring to produce a small class which was equipped with western ideas and which would bring civilisation and Christianity to the pagan and traditional societies both by example and by direct instruction. The combining of handwork instruction with literary education, however, was an outcome both of the missionaries' conviction that the Gospel could only flourish in a western cultural setting and of the need to meet the settlers' demands. Furthermore, the Government gave higher grants to schools teaching some industrial trades. The missions, being poor, naturally taught these things in order to get financial support. Besides, the Churches were playing the important role of bringing the African to terms with the western world. Most of the vital concepts of a successful life in a modern society were permeating the African societies through the medium of the missionary: the blacks were learning punctuality, control by the bell, self-discipline, figures, the use of money, English, and many other things. In other words, the missionaries were trying to reduce that misunderstanding of habits and customs that was causing a great deal of disharmony between white and black. An educated African might be more acceptable to his white countryman than the village man, who was found to be dirty, lazy and good-for-nothing. The village man also looked upon 'the white man as the plunderer of his country and would-be slave-driver'. The only solution, and that which the missionaries were effecting, was to raise the African to the stage of development of the ruling race.[59]

Paradoxically, although the settlers and the businessmen did not take kindly to the efforts of the missionary, it was the mission-educated boys they found useful. The demand for Wilkerson's boys clearly showed this. The Resident Commissioner in 1919 also reported that these students were finding employment very easily in town.[60] The very thirst for better education displayed by the girls and boys demonstrated that it was the thing that was a sure passport to making money. If this had not been the case few would have chosen to pay for their fees, and many would have behaved as the Dombodema boys who returned home after being told that Williams was only producing mission workers. The fact was that the traders wanted literate storekeepers and salesmen, the miners and farmers wanted the *mabalani* (clerks and foremen) who could count cattle and workers, write reports and take stock of the tools and implements, and above all, a man they could easily converse with in English. Not all the settlers, especially those coming from England and South Africa, knew the *Silapalapa* (the bastard language of the mines).

But the missionaries were not only interested in bridging the cultural gap between white and black; they were above all pre-occupied with the spiritual advancement of the local people. Indeed the various schemes which served to civilise the Ndebele and the Shona were in fact designed to produce mission workers. The expansion of Christianity in western Zimbabwe can, however, be divided into two periods – the first ten years of rapid growth, and the second decade of steady expansion tending towards stagnation.

In the last chapter it was shown how the traumatic experience of the Ndebele at the hands of the whites was causing them to want to come to terms with western culture through the medium of the missions, and also how this same spirit was infecting the Kalanga. The various Churches on their part responded by releasing bands upon bands of semi-literate evangelists to the villages. These two developments combined to make the years before 1910 a period of unmatched quest for the new faith in western Zimbabwe.

Although statistics are hard to come by in missionary records, it is clear that the number of evangelist-teachers was enormous during this period. The L.M.S. and the Methodists alone were employing sixty-eight preachers in western Zimbabwe before 1910. The way the missionaries went about expanding their mission fields was perhaps best described by the Chief Native Commissioner in 1912. The practice was that

> the Mission Society establishes an evangelist at a kraal to give religious instruction: that evangelist has a smattering of two out of the three R's: and that advantage is taken of this claim that a school has been established, and that education is being given to the natives.[61]

These men who were given such enormous responsibility of taking the Gospel to their fellow men were certainly barely trained. One missionary described a typical evangelist as a convert of some ten to twelve years' standing, 'placed at the head of station because he showed a desire to preach endowed with sufficient ability to read, to write fairly legibly, to speak a certain amount of English and with sufficient self-sacrifice to accept a small wage of a teacher'. This man would at first work diligently, but after some time his meagre training would begin to show up.

> Either he gets 'dried up' or he quarrels with the new congregation. 'Dried up' his preaching becomes mere scolding: or quarrels arise over temporalities, his position, church building, lands to plough, or over such things as to who is to take classes under him, who to preach in the neighbouring kraals etc. Then the underlying superstition breaks out at first misfortune to himself, his family, or some of those involved in the quarrel.[62]

We can also get an impression of the bare intellectual achievements of these teacher-preachers, their financial problems as well as their zeal to bring the Gospel to their fellow blacks from the two letters written by Weary Nyoni, one of the first products of Nengubo, who was stationed at Lalapantsi Siding. The letters are reproduced exactly as they were written.

Wesleyan Church
Lalapantsi Siding
District of Gwelo.

My Dear Sir I come to see you Minister the boys here in Lalapantsi they dont liked to pay me an month Because they stay on farm them work only to ploughs they have not got any some money to pay me they only give me food they said why your Minister don't give you little wages and month I am very sorry I have not got any some money to buy trousers to dress

Faithfully
I am dear Sir
Yours servant Weary
Nyoni Teacher
Lalapantsi.

The same teacher wrote from a different station in April 1913 urging his missionary supervisor to go with him to establish a new school on a farm where a new Ndebele-speaking group had recently settled. These Ndebele, as the letter shows, were appealing to him for an educational institution.

Wesleyan Mission Station
Guruguru April 25/4/13

My Dear Sir,
On 19 April I was went to Hogohill I met the chief his man is Ngungu Dlodlo he said he want school very badly. I think you & I awe go both & you see the place but the people they are in the farm but the Chief he himself will come to Selukwe you will see him I was want to come to see you about this but I am sick. When I was there I met a grait number of people they craying for school these people I tell you about they were under the London missionary at Insiza now they removed from Insiza they now in Selukwe District.

Yet no missionary could ever ignore the crucial importance of the evangelist in expanding the circuit, catechising the converts and teaching literacy.

The results of this decade of missionary aggressiveness and the people's favourable disposition towards the mission can be seen from statistical information. Between 1900 and 1910 the Inyati adherents increased from 300 to 2,000 and the church members from seven to 265; at Hope Fountain in 1901 there were 300 adherents, while there were five church members; by 1911 the former had multiplied to 2,000 and the latter to 125. The W.M.M.S. also in 1901 claimed 482 on trial and 186 full members, and in 1911 their records showed 911 on trial and 385 in full membership.[63] By 1910 the Jesuits had administered 1,400 baptisms at Empandeni.[64]

This growth was accompanied by a spectacular interest in scriptural literature, which further showed the success of the evangelist-teachers in spreading literacy. Old women were surprising their missionaries, asking them to explain certain passages in the Bible which they read very well but could not comprehend.[65] Moreover the questions asked at the Bible classes indicated beyond doubt that the Bibles were being read.[66] The demand for Bibles, hymn-books, catechisms, and the Gospels was also phenomenal. In 1903 a thousand copies of the New Testament were sold at Inyati alone and more people were still coming forward looking for them.[67] Interest in the church was also demonstrated by the people setting up teachers' houses, preaching places, and schools without payment.

Even more edifying were the confessions made, as well as the Christian behaviour of the converts. In 1901 the villagers around Centenary started to hold weekly prayer meetings, where they prayed for the success of the Gospel throughout the country, for themselves and their neighbours. Many were coming forward to Carnegie renouncing their traditional beliefs and professing their trust in the Christian God. They professed to feel the burden of their sins and were looking for ways and means of being saved from eternal condemnation. There was also a clear search for 'the truth'.[68]

Accompanying all these confessions of faith in the new religion were some very interesting cases of conversion. We have already mentioned the fervent Christian catechist and former bone-thrower Inja Mhlope at Empandeni. He was certainly not the only member of the bulwark of the traditional religion who turned to the missions. At Inyati one Sitjumi came forward to Rees to renounce his traditional divining trade. He was accompanied by his son who had already been initiated into the profession. They with the missionary prayed 'to God to give them something more durable & profitable than the wretched bones'.[69] Nor did the former Ndebele ruling class lag behind. Lobengula's son Tshakalisa, who was a chief in the Shangani Reserve, offered his son to be brought up by Rees. Lobengula's cousin and daughter of the famous Mncumbata, Muyengwa Khumalo, who was already very old, also became a staunch Christian at Tegwani. The superintendent at this circuit said 'She is the pillar of our Church, and we trust she may be spared for years yet to carry on her quiet but effective work'. She was gathering young women around her and teaching them to pray.[70]

The permeation of Christianity in the way of life of the people was further evident in the Christian marriages taking place. Both Mrs Machina Ndiweni and Miss Fipa Nyoni, interviewed in 1971, emphasised how anxious young women were to get married according to Christian rites. At Hope Fountain, Ndiweni said, it was a mark of disgrace to be refused a Christian marriage on grounds of premarital pregnancy. The strict moralist Mrs Helm would, just before the marriage took place, take the bride to a private room and examine her to find out whether she was pregnant or not. If she was she would be denied a Christian marriage. To pass this test, so it seems, was one of the greatest aspirations of the young ladies.

Indeed these young folks had every reason to aspire to be married in church; for even during these early days African wedding feasts in Zimbabwe had already acquired their spectacularly joyful quality. Fipa Nyoni recalled with apparent nostalgia the early weddings at Inyati, when Mnali Rees was still the superintendent. With the marriage rites over, the bride and bridegroom, the best man, maids of honour, the train-bearers and nearest relatives marched in a procession out of the church. At the door they were met by a choir of young Christians singing merrily the Ndebele song given here with tonic-solfa and translation:

O Kalaqiye	O she has no headgear
O Kalaqiye	O she has no headgear
(d. r. d. t. l.)	
Ha Mtshadiseni	Ha wed her
Ha Mtshadiseni	Ha wed her
Um tshadiseni	Wed her
(S. S. f. m. d. r.	
r. r. m. f. r. m. d.)	
O Kalaqiye	O she has no headgear
O Kalaqiye	O she has no headgear
(d. r. d. t. l.)	

Ha Kelizeni	Ha she invites you
Ha Kelizeni	Ha she invites you.

The song accompanied the marching of the procession until it reached the home of the bride, where a huge crowd of pagan men and women met the Christians dancing and singing their *mtshikitsha* (Ndebele traditional songs). The climax of the event came at some time between midday and evening, when the wedding party sat in the shade to receive presents (*ukukunga*). The master of ceremony, standing on a raised platform, announced each gift and the crowd showed its appreciation with an explosion of mixed clapping of hands and feminine whoops of joy. It was a day on which people rejoiced and consumed enormous quantities of meat and *amahewu* (a mild traditional beverage). We can expect that the young couples involved must have thought such days the brightest moments of their lives. At the same time it is interesting to note that the participation of the pagans meant that Christian celebrations, feasts and ceremonies were in a measure becoming substitutes for such traditional ceremonies as the annual Inxwala.

The thirst for intellectual and religious learning inspired among the societies of western Zimbabwe were observed in several villages where the teacher-preachers were stationed. H. Jackson, the Native Commissioner of Matopo District, complained in 1902 that the L.M.S. evangelist-teachers had brought literacy to his district so that he had 'been already the recipient of many somewhat ill-written scrawls in the native language from pupils' of these teachers. He remarked, rather unsympathetically to missionary efforts:

> Great anxiety is displayed by the younger natives to acquire learning of any description, and in many kraals the usual hunting or love song has given place to dolorously rendered hymns, and on every Sunday may be seen the spectacle of processions of girls and young men wending their way to receive the ministrations of a local preacher who is generally possessed of more rhetorical and vocal power than theological knowledge.[71]

Evangelical work was not only introducing new habits, aspirations and values, but also in some instances the outward appearance of the young church-goers was changing. The same Native Commissioner, Jackson, reported in 1903:

> There are several native catechists or preachers . . . who hold services

& also give lessons in reading & writing. On Sundays numbers of Natives in dandy, ill fitting, civilized dress flock to the services & join in the singing of hymns most heartily.[72]

Apparently this intellectual and religious learning had its bad results, causing the barely literate youths to aspire to white collar occupations, to shun blue collar activities, probably to question their elders and to shed the submissiveness of an African child. As R. Lanning, the Native Commissioner of the Bubi district observed, the elderly natives complained that the missions were tending 'to demoralize their children, the children will not work and become disobedient and filled with ideas they would never entertain were it not for the missions'.[73] Be this as it may, it is clear that Christianity with its allied institutions was making a noticeable impact on the way of life of the people.

But it must be emphasised that the majority of the converts did not come from the old people but from the young. The missionaries explained that polygamy, beer drinking, beliefs in witchcraft and other customs and habits made the elders unwilling to make a clean break with their past.[74] The youths were, however, interested in schooling, so that if the missionary was to maintain this rate of growth he had to improve the standard of education. The fact that education remained rudimentary during these years soon frustrated many young people and caused much of the indifference to the Gospel that was reported in the latter decade. Even as early as 1906 many scholars were said to have 'generally reached the standard of attainment of the native teachers', and there was no longer any progress being made.[75] Many village schools offered teaching up to the equivalent of the present Zimbabwe Grade II. Since these classes were also the preparatory groups for baptism, students simply left school before they could be accepted into full Church membership. After 1910 the various missions, having experienced the high rate of lapsing into old habits of their first converts, raised the time of preparing for full membership. This increased the possibilities of pupils going out of the control of the missionaries before being baptised. This is vouched for by Neville Jones who complained that although the Church membership of the district was growing, the class membership was declining, because many people were leaving their homes to seek employment before they could be catechised and received into the Church.[76]

In addition to the stagnation of education, the rate of growth of the Church decreased because of the competition between the mission station and the centres of western economic activity. When the young people went to town and came in contact with loose life they lost much of their Christian training. John White, whose Bulawayo circuit coincided mostly with the mines and towns, said in 1917 that he was constantly cancelling names of defaulting members from the registers. He pointed out that where there was a large white community which was indifferent even to the externals of the Christian religion the young African Christians were easily influenced.[77] The fact was that much of what the missionaries regarded as 'all the vices of the white men' acquired in towns, was considered by these Africans as examples of sophistication. Consequently when boys came back from town to their homes they were markedly changed in their behaviour. They even went so far as to lead the rural girls into sexual immorality.[78] This was the problem posed by the dichotomy between Western religion and secular civilisation. There was nothing much the missionaries could do about it except to hope that a few of the Africans would have the moral strength to resist 'the temptations of our civilization'.[79]

The other problem which seemed to upset the relationship of the missionary with the people, and therefore to generate indifference to the Church, was that the missions were large landowners. The laws of the mission farms were perhaps stricter than on any other property. The tenants were not supposed to brew beer, to be polygamists, to worship their ancestors, and they were forced to send their children to school regularly. All this was on top of free labour to the station and mission fields, including what was described as a small tax.[80] The net result was that many people left with their children to go and live in the reserves; those who remained simply paid the required tax and felt no further obligation to the Church.[81] When the missionaries extended their fields to the reserves they found the same people who had either been driven from their original land by the white farmers or by the missionaries themselves and therefore perhaps still nursing bitter feelings against the Europeans. In any case these people were just as indifferent to Christianity as those living in the now white areas.[82] Apart from all these factors, the Gospel seemed to have the quality of a fashion. When first preached many people flocked to it, but after some time people simply grew uninterested.[83] Perhaps the demands of Christianity were too much, and, as we have already said, the thought of forsaking one's traditional way of life was often unbearable.

Although Church membership had by 1923 grown quite considerably, much of the power in the running of the stations was still in the hands of the white missionaries. The Brethren in Christ, the L.M.S. and the W.M.M.S. allowed the local congregation to discuss issues related to beer drinking, polygamy, and the best ways of combating such evils, but in the end it was the missionary who drew up the rules and regulations. The Wesleyans of course sat with their black assistant ministers at the Synod and they had as much say in the discussions as their white counterparts, except when the conduct of a white missionary was under scrutiny. Considering the state of education in western Zimbabwe, there is no doubt that devolution of power to local Christians was still a long way off. There is no evidence to indicate that the people at this time were seeking power in church matters. The white leadership was still accepted without much questioning.

Notes

1. Cf. M. Schoffeleers and I. Linden, 'The Resistance of the Nyau Societies to the Roman Catholic Missions in Colonial Malawi' in T. O. Ranger and I. N. Kimambo (eds.), *The Historical Study of African Religion with Special Reference to East and Central Africa*, London, 1972, pp. 256–7
2. L.M.S. B3/Reports: S.A. Report of Centenary, 4 March 1899; B58, S.A., Helm to For. Sec., 10 May 1900; Helm to Hawkins, 4 Sept. 1900; Rees to For. Sec., 4 June 1900; W.M.M.S. S/M, Rhodesia 1912–22; Minutes of the Rhodesian District Synod, 1913; *The Zambesi Mission Record*, iii, 38, Oct. 1907, p. 304
3. W.M.M.S. C. Mashona, 1891–9, Shimmin to Hartley, 25 Nov. 1891; Weavind to Hartley, 26 Oct. 1894; *The Zambesi Mission Record*, iii, 38, 1907, p. 303
4. W.M.M.S. S/M S.A., 1898–9, Mashonaland and Rhodesian District Synod Minutes, 1908; C. Rhodesia 1917–23, White to Hartley, 12 Nov. 1918; S/M Rhodesia 1912–22, Rhodesian District Minutes 1919; Dean R. Richland, 'Outlines of the Growth of the Evangelical Lutheran Church of Southern Rhodesia', undated typescript, p. 4
5. R. Masinga, 'Africa's Daughters', *The Book of Rachel and Ratna*, World Womanhood Series, L.M.S./c. 1921, pp. 1–16
6. T. O. Ranger, *The African Voice in Southern Rhodesia*, London, 1970, p. 50
7. L.M.S. B5/Reports: S.A. Report of Hope Fountain, 1915; L.M.S. S.A. 1915, 'Minutes of the Executive Committee, at Hope Fountain, 23–30 April 1915'

8. Of the ten evangelists brought to Rhodesia by W.M.M.S., two were killed in the uprisings of 1896–7, five returned home after a brief stay, and only three decided to make Rhodesia their permanent home. See C. Thorpe, *Limpopo to Zambesi*, London, 1951, p. 54

9. L.M.S. B58, S.A., Rees to For. Sec., 4 June 1900

10. *Ibid.*, Helm to For. Sec., 10 May 1900; B3/Report, S.A. Report of Centenary, 4 March 1899

11. W. H. Anderson, *On Trail of Livingstone*, Mount View, 1919, p. 24

12. *Ibid.*, p. 144

13. R.N.A. N3/5/1/7, Brown to C.N.C., 30 March 1922

14. *Ibid.*, N.C. (Selukwe) to S.N., 1 April 1922

15. *Ibid.*, C.N.C.'s minute, 12 April 1922; C.N.C. to S.N., 20 May 1922

16. *Ibid.*, N.C. (Selukwe) to S.N. (Gwelo), 4 July 1922

17. *Ibid.*, C.N.C. to Admin., 29 April 1922

18. *Ibid.*, C.N.C. Circular Letter No. 1, 939/22, 3 May 1922

19. W.M.M.S. S/M S.A., 1889–99, Mashonaland Rhodesia Synod Minutes, 1898

20. *Ibid.*, Jan. 1899 Rhodesia Synod Minutes, Dec. 1899

21. *Ibid.*, Rhodesia Synod Minutes, Dec. 1899

22. W.M.M.S. S/M S.A. 1900–5; Rhodesian Synod Minutes, Dec. 1901

23. W.M.M.S. S.A. 1906–11, Rhodesian Synod Minutes, Feb. 1907; see also the most illuminating paper on the institution by the Rev. W. R. Peaden, 'Nengubo Training Institution and the First Shona Teachers' in A. Dachs, *Christianity South of the Zambezi*, Gwelo, 1973, pp. 71–82

24. *Ibid.*, W.M.M.S. S/M Rhodesia 1912–22, Rhodesian Synod Minutes, Jan. 1915

25. W.M.M.S. C. Rhodesia, 1905–17, Brigg to Hartley, 2 Aug. 1915

26. *Ibid.*, Dr H. Haigh to J. K. Waddilove, 10 April 1917

27. W.M.M.S. S/M Rhodesia 1912–22, Rhodesian Synod Minutes, 1912

28. W.M.M.S. C. Rhodesia 1903–17, White to Goudie, 14 Aug. 1914; White to Hartley, 27 June 1915; S/M Rhodesia 1912–22, Inspector's Report, 10 Oct. 1916

29. R. McIntosh, Inspector of Schools, 'Waddilove Training Institution Nengubo Native School', 10 Nov. 1916; McIntosh Report, 5 Nov. 1915; J. Candy, Inspector's Report of Waddilove, 11 Nov. 1921; W.M.M.S. C. Rhodesia 1917–23; Stanlake to Hartley, 29 Aug. 1917

30. Cf. Hostetter, pp. 31–2

31. Candy's Report, 17 Nov. 1921; W.M.M.S. S/M Rhodesia 1912–22, Foggin to Stanlake, 24 Nov. 1921; Stanlake's Report, 1921

32. W.M.M.S. L1/1, Noble's Report, p. 16

33. W.M.M.S. S/M Rhodesia 1923–33, H. Carter's Report of Bulawayo Circuit, 1921

34. L.M.S. B3/Reports, S.A. Wilkerson to Cousins, 27 Jan. 1898

35. *Ibid.*, Wilkerson's Balance Sheet and Report of the Institute, 1902

36. *The Chronicle of the L.M.S.*, 1904, p. 72

37. *The Bulawayo Chronicle*, 30 Nov. 1894

38. L.M.S. B3/Reports, S.A. Wilkerson to For. Sec., 14 Jan. 1903

39. L.M.S. B3/Reports, S.A. Wilkerson to Cousins, 12 Jan. 1907

40. L.M.S. B59, S.A. 'Supplementary resolution of MDC', encl. in Helm to For. Sec., 23 Oct. 1901; B4/Reports, S.A. Williams, Report on Education, 1906
41. L.M.S. B4/Reports, S.A. Williams, Report, 31 Dec. 1909
42. L.M.S. B3, S.A. Williams to Directors, 1 Jan. 1906
43. L.M.S. B4/Reports, S.A. Williams, Report, 31 Dec. 1909
44. *Ibid.*, Inyati Report, 1909; Carnegie to For. Sec., 7 Jan. 1909; Carnegie to For. Sec., 25 Jan. 1909
45. *Ibid.*, Williams, Report, 31 Dec. 1909
46. L.M.S. B5, Hope Fountain Report, 1917; S. A. 1915, 'Minutes of the Executive Committee at Hope Fountain, 23–30 April 1915'
47. L.M.S. B5/Reports, S.A., Report of Hope Fountain, 1917; Report of H.F.G.B.S., 1918; Report of H.F.G.B.S., 1921; S. de J. Lenrestey, Inspector's Report of Hope Fountain, 5 March 1921; B6/Reports, S.A. Report of H.F.G.B.S., 1923; Report of H.F.G.B.S., 31 Dec. 1923; Simmonite's Report of H.F.G.B.S., 31 Dec. 1923; Masinga
48. L.M.S. B5/Reports, S.A. Balance Sheet of H.F.G.B.S., 1918
49. R.N.A. FR2/2/1, reminiscences of Ivon Fry
50. W.M.M.S. C. Mashona, 1891–9, Eva to Hartley, 12 Dec. 1896
51. *The Popular Edition of the L.M.S.*, 1918–19, p. 26
52. Masinga, pp. 9–10; L.M.S. B6/Reports: S.A. Reports of H.F.G.B.S., 1921; Simmonite's Report of H.F.G.B.S., 31 Dec. 1923
53. Hostetter, p. 32
54. *Ibid.*, pp. 114–5
55. *The Zambesi Mission Record*, iv, 51, Jan. 1911, p. 163
56. P.H. 'Empandeni Bro D.', Fr E. Biehler, Notes for the Resident Commissioner [c. 1922]
57. *Ibid.*
58. Father Biehler's achievements at Empandeni compared favourably with his work at Chishawasha, Shonaland. See L. Vambe, *An Ill-fated People*, London, 1972, pp. 145–7
59. *The Foreign Field of the Wesleyan Methodist Church*, iv, pp. 233–4
60. C.O. 417/617, South Africa, Resident Commissioner to High Commissioner, 10 March 1919
61. R.N.A. N3/5/1/7, C.N.C. to Director of Education, 10 Sept. 1922
62. S.P.G. E. Series, Broderick's Report, Dec. 1920
63. L.M.S. B4/Reports of Inyati, 1910; Helm to Joint Sec., 14 Feb. 1911; W.M.M.S. S/M S.A. 1900–5, Statistics, 1901; S/M Rhodesia 1912–22, Statistics, 1911
64. *The Zambesi Mission Record*, iv, 50, Oct. 1910, p. 141
65. L.M.S. B4/Reports: S.A., Report of Hope Fountain, 1906
66. L.M.S. B60, S.A., Rees to For. Sec., 25 Jan. 1902; W.M.M.S. S/M S.A. 1906–11; Report of Bulawayo, 1909
67. L.M.S. B62, Mtabeleland and Bechuanaland, Report of Inyati, 1903
68. L.M.S. B3/Reports, S.A., Carnegie to For. Sec., Dec. 1911, 1901; L.M.S. B39, Matabeleland and Bechuanaland, Carnegie to For. Sec., 24 June 1901
69. L.M.S. B2/Reports, S.A., Rees to For. Sec., 1894
70. *The Foreign Field of the Wesleyan Methodist Church*, iv, 336

71. R.N.A. NB6/1/3–4; H.M. Jackson, Report, 31 March 1902
72. *Ibid.*, M. Jackson, Report, 1 April 1903
73. *Ibid.*, R. Lanning, Report, 1903
74. W.M.M.S. L1/1 Noble's Report, p. 15; S/M S.A. 1906–11, Report of Bulawayo Circuit, 1908
75. L.M.S. B3/Reports: S.A. Williams, Education Report, 1906
76. L.M.S. B6/Reports: S.A., Report of Hope Fountain, 1921; W.M.M.S. S/M S.A., 1906–11, Bulawayo Circuit Report, 1906
77. W.M.M.S. B8, Biographical, Bulawayo Native Circuit Report, 1917
78. L.M.S. B4/Reports, S.A., Carnegie to For. Sec., 7 Jan. 1909
79. W.M.M.S. B8, Biographical, Bulawayo Native Circuit Report, 1917
80. W.M.M.S. C. Rhodesia, 1905–17, White to Hartley, 24 July 1917; P.H. Empandeni Bro. D., The Agreement with Tenants, 1911
81. W.M.M.S. B8, Biographical, Report of Tegwani, 1922
82. L.M.S. B6/Reports, S.A. Report of the Shangani Reserve, 1918
83. *Ibid.*, Report of Hope Fountain, 1921

7

Conclusion

To assess the significance of the missionary enterprise in western Zimbabwe from 1859 to 1923 it is helpful first to relate it to studies that have been carried out regarding other parts of Africa. The striking features contrasting western Zimbabwe from much that occurred north of the Zambezi are the absence of the slave trade and slavery and the nature of the political insecurity facing the Ndebele. Professor Oliver, studying a much larger region than Ndebeleland (East Africa), has broadly distinguished three types of African societies, both in terms of their response to missionary propaganda and their accessibility to missionaries. The first category is that of the 'freedmen and refugees' over whom the missionaries established 'political dominions'. The second includes well-organised chiefdoms or kingdoms where 'free missions' were set up. In between these two extremes was the type of situation where missionaries made journeys to the surrounding districts, a pattern similar to that of the Berlin Mission in the Ndebele tributary chiefdoms in the 1880s.[1]

It is the first two that must now interest us here. Professor Oliver points out that it was among the communities made up of liberated slaves, people with tribal cohesion broken up by neighbouring raiders, or individuals dissatisfied with their own way of life and hence forced to seek security among the missionaries, that spectacular Christian achievements of the pioneer period were realised. In more specific terms Dr Wright refers to Rungwe in the Southern Highlands of Tanzania, where the Moravians found 'the refugees who had infiltrated from the raid-torn rift corridor and formed a reservoir of relatively ready workers to compensate for the refusals of the self-sufficient Kukwe villages'. The readiness to go to the missionaries derived from their realisation that the mission stations 'provided a substitute corporate life for them'. These refugees came from such peoples as the Nyiha, Safwa and Ndali, all victims of the powerful raiding states of the Ngoni, Hehe and Sangu. Perhaps even more amenable to the Christian teachings and apparently the first nucleus of the converts that were later to carry the Gospel to the out-stations from the central stations were the liberated large group of females and children 'from one of Mlozi's caravans . . . [who were] distributed . . . among the missionaries at Rungwe, Wangemannshoh, and Manow', by Baron von Eltz of the Anti-Slavery Expedition, stationed at Langenburg as Military Administrator in 1893.[2] This same process was observable in West Africa, though it operated in a slightly different manner. There it was what Professor J. F. Ade Ajayi calls the exiles or emigrants (again freed slaves) from Sierra Leone, Brazil and Cuba, some of whom had already made great strides in the assimilation of Christianity, education and other cultural ideas and skills of the West, that furnished the first black missionary agency. Moreover, these people were the first nuclei of converts at the famous Nigerian centres of real aggressive missionary enterprise, such as Lagos, Ibadan, Calabar, Creek Town, Duke Town and Ake.[3]

The western Zimbabwe situation bore similarities and contrasts to the situations already outlined. Slavery and the slave trade, factors that so encouraged the early westernisation of East and West Africa, were somewhat lacking in western Zimbabwe. Although nineteenth-century European observers sometimes described the capturing of the Shona and the Hole as the equivalents of slave raiding and slavery, the Ndebelised indigenous people never felt their social position so precarious as to make them seek security among the missionaries. The Jesuits, who attempted to set up the Tati mission station as a centre for Hole refugees, were disappointed to find that none came. Nor did the conversions accomplished by Thomas at the Shiloh station with the majority of persons of Shona origin mean anything more than that these people formed the majority of Ndebele population. To be sure, even after the collapse of the Khumalo regime at the turn of the present century, it was often found that the former Hole such as chief Tshitshi were far less amenable to western culture in general than the Zansi Gambo and Ngege. Perhaps if missionary enterprise had been afforded a similar strategy as in East Africa, where, as Dr Wright says, the Christian teachers 'championed the aspirations of people whose autonomy was lost or threatened . . . by the strong Sangu, Hehe, and Ngoni states', or in the south the Tonga who were preyed upon by the Ngoni, and concentrated on the Kalanga and the Shona in general, all victims of the Ndebele raiding activities, things might have turned out differently. In the event the Ndebele authorities prevented any continuous missionary activity among their subjects, reducing the whole enterprise to spasmodic contacts.[4]

Elsewhere in Africa, however, sometimes external political threats helped the missionaries to gain a firm foothold in an African state, as in the case of Ganda that developed 'the outstanding prototypes' of 'free' missions. There King Mutesa sought after the white teachers to counter the 1869–79 Egyptian expansion. This point is described fully by J. V. Taylor in his book, *The Growth of the Church in Buganda*. He says the Kabaka looked upon the Europeans as the most powerful ally to have within his borders. 'To welcome [the white men's] religion', Taylor goes on, 'might be incidental to being initiated into all his other wisdom.' The western people were to the Ganda ruler the source of all advanced technological skills as well as manufactures and they were therefore more formidable than the Arab traders, who were mere carriers of western material products. The king thus accepted the missionary and his religion to avail himself of western wisdom and military secrets. Coupled with political insecurity in the face of the Egyptian imperialist advance was the Gandas' general disillusionment with their traditional religion. It was at this point that the Catholics and the Church Missionary Society penetrated the state; and between 1878 and 1884, in the first three years with the active support of the Kabaka and later in spite of his indifference as well as of his somewhat anti-Christian rituals, the missions managed to lay Church foundations – a stage described as the 'congruence' by Taylor. Although the Church was still in its nascent state, its newly acquired followers were of remarkably strong fibre, being prepared to be 'burned alive in one great pyre at Namungongo' by the Kabaka Mwanga, the successor of Mutesa.[5]

It is not only external pressures that proved decisive in the expansion of Christianity in a state. McCracken has discovered that a combination of external pressures and internal insecurity forced the Ngoni ruler, Mbelwa, to accept Livingstonia missionaries.

First the Ngoni state of Mbelwa was declining militarily and could no longer with impunity raid its neighbouring agricultural societies which defended themselves in prepared stockaded villages and with firearms. Internally, Mbelwa lived in perpetual fear of his state being broken up by segmentation. His authority was also being undermined by his councils consisting mainly of people of ability who had been incorporated north of the Zambezi. Some of his chiefs also apparently challenged his paramountcy. All these factors compelled Mbelwa to accept the missionaries with the hope that Christianity would unify his kingdom. Once accepted, the Livingstonia missionaries put to good use their strategy of combining commerce, religion and industrial training and eventually achieved spectacular results.[6]

In all these respects, the Ndebele state presents an interesting and striking contrast to the Ganda kingdom and the Ngoni. First the Ndebele and Ganda kingdoms were equally well organised politically. The element of external danger was ever present, if not more pressing in the minds of the Ndebele rulers. From the inception of the Ndebele state its existence was threatened at different times by the Zulu, the Boers, the British and the Portuguese. In view of this one would have expected the Ndebele rulers to adopt the solutions of the Kabaka, or, indeed, that of their own neighbours the Ngwato of Khama, who welcomed the missionaries. Yet the Ndebele rulers never showed anything more than spasmodic interest in the missionaries, which, moreover, was not accompanied by the conversion of courtiers or many ordinary people as in the case of the Ganda.

Four things seem to explain the Ndebele anomaly. First, the Kabaka and Khama were confronted by two racial groups, the former by the Arab imperialists and European missionaries, and the latter by the black Ndebele raiders and white teachers. The rulers of Ndebeleland were mostly face to face with the problem of religious and political expansion being championed by one racial group. Secondly, while traditional religion in the Ganda state was causing some disaffection, the Ndebele religion was growing in prestige on account of its fusion with the Shona one and also through borrowing ideas from Christianity. In Ndebeleland, moreover, the missionaries were not the only representatives of Western wisdom and technology because of the presence of white traders. Finally, unlike the Ngoni, the Ndebele state was united and Lobengula and Mzilikazi were secure in their positions.

Having sketched out some of the salient features contrasting the Ndebele state with other African areas of missionary enterprise, it is essential to make a few remarks about the significance of the period 1859–1923 in terms of the religious development and social changes of the peoples of Ndebeleland in particular and Zimbabwe in general. From the religious point of view, it was during this period that the people moved from religious conflict on the social level to what might be called in Professor Murphree's terminology the 'synthetic' stage.[7] The spiritual hostility that had partly accounted for the alliance of the Ndebele king with the izinyanga, the izangoma and the izanusi, that had prompted Nina kaPansi to stage a confrontation with the Jesuits at Empandeni, and that had presumably motivated some of the Mwari cult officials to come out in full support of the risings, was to some extent eliminated by the end of our period. The peoples of western Zimbabwe began to accept the presence of European culture as something that had come to stay and with which they had to come to terms. The Mwari cult priests apparently continued to elaborate upon the concept of their high god and theology to the extent that today Mwari is also known as the Holy Spirit (*Mweya Mtswene* or *Umoya ongcwele*).[8] As one Ndebele informant pointed out, the missionary God has become identical with Mwari, although the two ways of approaching Him still persist, i.e. through the Church and through the mountain shrines.[9] The outcome of this syncretic attitude was that the people resorted to the missionaries for medical treatment as well as to the Christian God in times of drought with as much ease as they turned to the indigenous Mwari.

Moving down the scale from the territorial situation to the family and individual levels, we enter a much more complicated area. Although there were people like Mhlope who abandoned indigenous beliefs and practices and embraced Christianity, the missionaries found it difficult to eradicate traditional religion during the period. Indeed, in view of the tenacious hold of traditional beliefs on the people, the settlers doubted whether it was ever possible 'to make genuine converts of the South African Natives; if their so-called conversion is not mere sham'.[10] The missionaries asserted that it was almost impossible to persuade the old people to do away with their ancestor worship. But they said that it was easy to educate the young ones to adopt Christian habits, such as honesty, refusal to participate in the ancestor-worship ceremonies and rituals, abandoning the use of bad language, and becoming less materialistic and less selfish. Yet even the youths could not cast away the fear of the abathakathi (witches) and imikhobo (ghosts). In short, the result was that first there was age selectivity in conversion to Christianity – with the youths filling the churches and the old ones refusing direct or actual acceptance of the new faith; and secondly while the old ones were imperceptibly expanding their theology through borrowing ideas from the new religion, the young Christians were bringing indigenous beliefs to Christianity.

In 1907 Fr O'Neil declared that even those who professed to be Christians believed in witchcraft, a superstition he said that was so ingrained in the minds of the Africans that it could not be effaced easily by Christianity.[11] Actually the situation does not seem to have changed even today in Zimbabwe, if not in most parts of Africa. In Zimbabwe it is not uncommon for teachers with Junior Secondary School Certificate, or with higher academic and professional qualifications, who are in fact the African elite of the rural and urban societies, to go to an inyanga for protective medicines against enemies or for magic to guarantee security and promotions in jobs.

That the persistence of African traditional beliefs in orthodox Churches is not a peculiarity of Zimbabwe emerges from the Rev. Dr E. Fashole-Luke's fascinating and most revealing paper on Christianity and Islam in Freetown. Fashole-Luke demonstrates that the Freetown Christian lives a real double life; he holds 'firmly to the doctrines of the Church, but hold[s] equally firmly the traditional beliefs of . . . [his] Fathers'. The Church's refusal to accept and integrate African beliefs and practices into its own doctrines, coupled with its impotence to efface these systems from the minds of the Africans, Fashole-Luke aptly tells us, 'has succeeded in making the majority of her members in Freetown lead a Jekyll and Hyde existence'.[12]

In Zimbabwe the persistence of traditional beliefs expressed itself through the failure of Christian marriages as well. The general tendency of our fathers was to become Christians when they were still going to school and to marry according to Christian rites and then to revert to polygamy as they grew older and acquired more property. This is not to say monogamous marriages failed completely, as mission employees in particular adhered to them for the rest of their lives.

All these forms of persistence of African beliefs and customs had important implications for the development of Christianity in Zimbabwe, and in Africa in general. First, they gave birth to the type of orthodox African Christian who leads a double existence: surreptitiously adhering to the religion of his fathers and publicly worshipping in the church. It was a position that was perhaps difficult to maintain in the early days, when polygamy was still a way of life. Such a public expression of adherence to African customs could not be adopted by a Christian without being expelled from the Church.

Secondly, the continuance of African beliefs among Christians portended the growth of independent Churches. During these early days, as Professor Ranger has shown in one of his papers, independent Churches were still a foreign influence in Zimbabwe, dominated by Malawians, South Africans and a few Zimbabwean migrant labourers who had worked in South Africa.[13] The movement had not yet acquired the indigenous character that it has since achieved. Zimbabwe had not yet got the 'highly Christianized atmosphere' in which Christian independency flourishes.[14] Within the next few decades, however, Zimbabwe witnessed a sprouting of independent Churches, some of which displayed a genius for integrating the old and the new forms of religious expression. They borrowed old techniques of dealing with social problems and recast them in a Christian context. They acknowledged the existence of the ancestral spirits, and while they took a stand against them they also evolved Christian ways of dealing with them.[15] In fact Sr Mary Aquina, who has studied some independent Churches in Zimbabwe, has been struck by the similarities of some features of the new Churches with those of the old systems of religion to the extent that she sees 'the manifestations of the charismata of the Holy Spirit' as revealing 'a fusion between pagan and Christian beliefs in spirits'.[16] Whether the process has been one of merely amalgamating the old and the new or, in the words of Fisher, it has been one of evolving 'a higher religious awareness which transcends and subsumes current religious formulations',[17] is a question to which students of independency have still to address themselves. For our purposes, suffice it to say that the religious pluralism of such people as Gambo, Ngege, including many of the early converts who failed to make a clean break with the traditional religious systems, and perhaps the continual universalisation of Mwari by the cult's priests, pointed to the development of independent Churches.

Such a study as the present one must necessarily take into account two recent stimulating and thoughtful discussions of the phenomenon of African conversion to the two world religions, Christianity and Islam, by Robin Horton and Humphrey J. Fisher. Horton's 'thought-experiment' describes African religious development outside the Christian and Islamic contexts but in the presence of other modern factors. With the crumbling or weakening of the microcosms, Horton argues, people apparently begin to lose confidence in the lower tier of their cosmologies, consisting of the lesser spirits, and start to elaborate upon their concept of the high god and to develop a moral code for the wider world (macrocosm) with which the supreme being becomes closely associated. In this context, the people are impelled to embrace Christianity and Islam by other features of the modern world as much as by the activities of the missionaries, a process reducing the world religions to 'the role of catalysts – i.e. stimulators and accelerators of changes which were "in the air" anyway; triggers for reactions in which they do not always appear amongst the end-products'.[18]

Horton's argument appears to me to fit more the behaviour of the unconverted than that of the converted. It seems, indeed, to apply to the religious efforts of the traditional leaders, such as Lobengula and the Mwari cult's priests. These were the people, as we have seen, who used Christianity as a source of ideas and were apparently stimulated by it to elaborate their beliefs and practices in order not only to resist conversion, but also to develop a satisfactory system of explaining the new changes wrought in particular by the European presence. Indeed, it is more fitting to imagine the unconverted pluralists, such as Gambo, Ngege, Tjingababili (people with firm roots in the old beliefs and practices but holding some aspects of Christianity to be good and desirable), as likely to make an effort to develop their cosmologies by borrowing aspects of Christianity which happen to coincide with what they want than to think of such stalwart converts as Makaza, Shisho Moyo, Mhlope, Matambo as well as the youths that filled the schools and churches as making such efforts.

Turning to Horton's argument regarding the recession of the lesser spirits, we find that it is not substantiated by our study. While the missionaries by the early twentieth century no longer had much difficulty with the territorial cult of Mwari they still had problems in divesting their converts of the beliefs and practices associated with the microcosms, such as ancestor spirits, diviners, and witchcraft. In fact, it seems to me that in Zimbabwe it was the people's efforts to adapt Christianity to the beliefs and practices of the microcosms that partly produced independent Churches. Fisher, however, has some insights that are applicable to our case. Fisher bases his discussion on the history of Islam in Africa, whose presence on this continent is much longer than Christianity's. He postulates three stages of African conversion to Islam, two of which fit satisfactorily the Zimbabwe situation. The three stages are quarantine, mixing, and reform. Without being pedantic about the Islamic context of Fisher's discussion, we can say the quarantine stage covers the period when Christianity is represented by the missionaries; the mixing when converts come in large numbers; the reform when people try to purify their religion after the mixing stage. The last stage does not concern us here, because it emerges out of several centuries of mixing.[19]

The Ndebele kingdom, however, presented a classic example of the quarantine stage. For a long time the missionaries and a dozen or so converts represented Christianity in its orthodox form. The converts were people who passed into the missionary world in that they were ostracised by their own society and found refuge as employees of the missionaries or left the country to go and live in South Africa. Indeed, as Fisher correctly suggests, it does not appear that the first converts in western Zimbabwe sought 'a new dignity and self-respect' in Christianity. It was only at the turn of the present century when reading and writing had acquired a certain amount of value that the literate converts achieved any respect in the eyes of the people of western Zimbabwe. On the other hand, Fisher, by drawing upon the evidence regarding the slave trade and slavery situations, has over-estimated the carrying-over of traditional practices, beliefs and rituals to Christianity by the quarantine converts. In a situation like the Ndebele one, the converts were placed in such a situation that they could not participate safely in both the Christian and the traditional worlds. They literally left their homes to go and live at the mission station with the missionaries: they became, as Carnegie complained, the missionaries' people. There is no need to discuss the mixing stage which we have already mentioned as constituting part of the moulding process of independency.

From the intellectual point of view, however, that intense thirst for education which is so characteristic of Zimbabwe black youths today was during these early years a thing of the future. People like Gambo, Ngege and some of the Kalanga chiefs might show a desire for their children to go to school. But many children were prevented from the full benefit of missionary education by the almost indefinable opposition of their parents to missionary activity. When a mission station was first built in a place the people manifested an 'undercurrent of antagonism, on account of ancient customs and religions'.[2] After some time this silent hostility would degenerate into indifference, an attitude which caused many parents to have no scruples about prohibiting their children from going to school in order to drive cattle to the dip-tanks, to go and scare away the birds from the ripening crops in the fields, to mind the babies while the mothers hoed the gardens or harvested the crops, or to take messages to distant relatives. It was an attitude which certainly emanated both from lack of appreciation of the value of formal education and from an unfortunate clash between traditional economic activity and schooling. The ploughing, cultivation and harvesting seasons all coincided with school days. And throughout these periods the young boys were supposed to look after cattle.

But it is possible to exaggerate the latter cause. Indeed the magnitude of the problem faced by those who were trying to bring western education to the Africans demonstrates that it was rooted in the general hostile attitude of the people towards western culture. The amendment of the Education Ordinance in 1903 stipulated that a pupil could earn an annual grant if he attended school for 150 days for four hours daily. In 1909 the western Zimbabwe school registers showed that 2,040 children came to school at the beginning of the year, but that only 886 (forty per cent) of them had satisfied the 150 days' requirement.[21] In 1921 the L.M.S., Brethren in Christ, Presbyterian Church, the S.D.A. and the Church of Sweden Mission had 6,836 pupils enrolled in their schools, yet only 4,324 (fifty-seven per cent) remained in school for 150 days.[22] It is clear that the indifference of the parents to education was far from being overcome in the period 1898–1923.

However, this perennial hurdle in the adjustment of the Africans to western influence was removed when those who were the first pupils became parents. These half-educated parents, having experienced the unfortunate state of being relegated to the labouring class in the white men's world, the difficulties of trying to find a job with a good salary when one is uneducated, resolved that their children must be better educated than themselves. Unlike their own parents, this new class of fathers and mothers looked after the cattle in the mornings when their children went to school and they also went to the dip-tanks. In this way irregular attendances at school were greatly reduced.

The African pioneer builders, carpenters, cooks, evangelists, agricultural demonstrators, tailors, teachers and leather repairers, unlike their counterparts in southern Nigeria, were not politically articulate. They did not use the church as a place of political education, but they accepted the leadership of their white missionaries. Indeed, one searches for what might be interpreted as militant nationalist consciousness in vain. The two major complaints of both the students and the teachers of these early days were about more money and a sound type of education which would enable them to find better jobs in towns, on the farms and in mining compounds. They repeatedly demanded to be taught English, which seemed to them to be the passport to better employment.[23] Three things would seem to account for the mild political activity of these people of western Zimbabwe. First the Administration tried as much as possible to keep out South African Ethiopian influences. Secondly, the missionaries showed a great reluctance to employ teachers from South Africa, relying on their own products. Finally, the shattering experience of being twice defeated in battle by the whites caused the people to change their tactics. As the Ndebele themselves said, it would not be their old spears, shields, clubs and traditional regiments that were going to liberate them, but the children with missionary education. Of course the education of these early days was far from being propitious to the production of articulate indigenous protest movements. The most highly educated people of western Zimbabwe were those who learned at Waddilove and Tigerkloof in the Cape. And these never went beyond standard five with some ministerial, teacher, or other training. Such people who were further carefully sealed off from outside influences could not be expected to develop any meaningful nationalist ideas. Indeed they might protest against low wages and perhaps join their elders in complaining about shortage of land, or sign protest letters to the Administration with the missionaries, but they could not furnish any meaningful leadership to their people in a liberation movement. All this was still in the future. For the moment then the pressing need was to learn as much as possible from the white missionary in order to lead a good life in the rapidly changing environment. In short, adaptation to western culture through the help of the missionary was the issue that was paramount in the minds of the early twentieth-century peoples of western Zimbabwe.

Finally, much of the explanation of the backwardness of African education before 1923 lies in the attitudes of the settlers and the B.S.A. Company Administration towards missionary enterprise. The whites did not favour literary education for Africans and so gave very little financial support to the missionaries. Nor did the Administration attempt seriously to co-ordinate the various mission- ary educational efforts. In fact the whole situation was well summed up by the Director of Native Education who said that before 1928 African education 'was an appendage of the European Education Department; the step-child inevitably receiving the crumbs from the table of the accredited education family'.[24]

Notes

1. R. Oliver, *The Missionary Factor in East Africa*, London, 1952, pp. 50–80
2. M. Wright, *German Missions in Tanganyika*, Oxford, 1971, pp. 66–7
3. J. F. Ade Ajayi, *Christian Missions in Nigeria, 1841–1891: The Making of an Elite*, London, 1965, pp. 25–52; in Malawi too, K. J. McCracken says, 'In the early years therefore, and particularly at Cape Maclear most mission dependers were to some degree dispossessed and lacking in close ties with any tribal society'. See his 'Livingstonia as an Industrial Mission' in W. M. Watt (ed.), *Religion in Africa*, Edinburgh, 1964, p. 10
4. Wright, p. 21; see also D. N. Beach, 'The Initial Impact of Christianity on the Shona, the Protestants and the Southern Shona' in A. Dachs (ed.), *Christianity South of the Zambezi*, Gwelo, 1973, pp. 25–40; K. J. McCracken, 'Religion and Politics in Northern Ngoniland, 1881–1904' in B. Pachai, *The Early History of Malawi*, London, 1972, p. 216
5. See Oliver, pp. 67–8, 103–5; and J. V. Taylor, *The Growth of the Church in Buganda*, London, 1958, pp. 29–44
6. McCracken, 'Religion and Politics', pp. 217–20; K. J. McCracken, *Politics and Christianity in Malawi 1875–1940. The Impact of the Livingstonia in the Northern Province*, Cambridge, 1977, pp. 85–99
7. This does not mean that Murphree sees the 'categorical', 'layer' or 'veneer' and the 'synthetic' approaches as analytic models to be applied on sequential developments in space and time. On the contrary, he tells us that these are conceptual frameworks in anthropology capable of being applied to one case of study by different schools of thought. Nevertheless this study leads me

to suspect that some of these techniques are more applicable to particular periods in history than others. For instance the categorical can be profitably used to study the Christian and traditional religious confrontations in the nineteenth century, while the layer or veneer can suit the Shona-Ndebele religious fusion. Moreover some of the first few converts of the early twentieth century belonged more to the layer type than the synthetic. See M. W. Murphree, *Christianity and the Shona*, London, 1969, p. 2

8. Daneel, *The God of the Matopo*, p. 37
9. Interview with Ndiweni
10. *The Zambesi Mission Record*, v, 73, July 1916, pp. 374–7
11. *Ibid.*, iii, 33, Jan. 1907, p. 188
12. E. Fashole-Luke, 'Christianity and Islam in Freetown', *The Sierra Leone Bulletin of Religion*, ix, 1, 1967, pp. 10–11
13. T. O. Ranger, 'The Early History of Independency in Southern Rhodesia' in W. M. Watt (ed.), *Religion in Africa*, Edinburgh, 1964
14. T. O. Ranger, 'Christian Independency in Tanzania' in D. Barrett (ed.), *African Initiatives in Religion*, Nairobi, 1971, pp. 122–43
15. M. L. Daneel deals with this point in several of his works including his monumental study, *Old and New in Southern Shona Independent Churches, Background and Rise of the Major Movements*, The Hague, 1971; 'Shona Independent Churches in a Rural Society' in A. Dachs (ed.), *Christianity South of the Zambezi*, Gwelo, 1973, pp. 159–88; 'Shona Independent Churches and Ancestor Worship' in D. Barrett (ed.), *African Initiatives in Religion*, Nairobi, 1971, pp. 160–70
16. Sr Mary Aquina O.P., 'The People of the Spirit: An Independent Church in Rhodesia', *Africa*, xxxvii, 1967, pp. 203–19; see also Marie-Louise Martin, 'The Mai Chaza Church in Rhodesia' in Barrett, *African Initiatives in Religion*, pp. 109–21
17. H. J. Fisher, 'Conversion Reconsidered: Some Historical Aspects of Religious Conversion in Black Africa', *Africa*, xliii, 1973, p. 27
18. R. Horton, 'African Conversion', *Africa*, xli, 1971, pp. 102–4
19. Fisher
20. R.N.A. 12/1/40, N.C. (Belingwe) to C.N.C., 14 Nov. 1903
21. Calculations based on the figures in *Southern Rhodesia Report of the Director of Education, for the Year ended 31 December 1909*
22. *Southern Rhodesia Report of the Director of Education for the Year 1921*
23. There were of course some educated Ndebele who joined hands with the Mfengu (for example the teacher from Gwelo, Ernest Dube, and 'the Chairman of the Gwanda Branch [of R.B.V.A.], Mawagelana, a builders' labourer') to voice African grievances. See T. O. Ranger, *The African Voice in Southern Rhodesia*, London, 1970, pp. 92, 95, 100
24. *Southern Rhodesia Report of the Director of Native Education for the Year 1928*, p. 1

Note on archival sources

The following missionary and government archives were used for this book: National Archives of Rhodesia in Salisbury; Public Record Office in London; London Missionary Society Archives in London; Wesleyan Methodist Missionary Society Archives in London; Society of Jesus Archives in London and Prestage House in Salisbury; Society for the Propagation of the Gospel in Foreign Parts Archives in London.

In the Public Record Office I went through Series C.O.417 (Africa, South, 1884–1925).

For a brief description of the holdings of Rhodesia Archives and published guides to part of these the reader is referred to the 'Note on Archival Sources' in Robin Palmer, *Land and Racial Domination in Rhodesia*, Berkeley and Los Angeles, 1977. Nearly all my citations come from the Chief Native Commissioner (N), Chief Native Commissioner, Matabeleland (NB), the Administrator (A). From the Historical Manuscripts Collection I used the following: C. Alexander Bailie (BA 10/2/1); Berlin Mission (BE2/1/1), translated by Dr and Mrs Julian Cobbing; Alexander Boggie (BO 1/2/2); Henry John Borrow (BO 11/1/1); Ivon Fry (FR 2/2/1); Mary Margaret Carnegie (MISC/CA5); Frederick William Sykes (MISC/SY 1/1/1); Benjamin ('Matabele') Wilson (WI G/2); R. F. Windran (WI 8/1–2); Thomas Morgan Thomas (TH 2/1/1). I also had the opportunity of going through the Delineation Reports. These are generally not available to researchers, but their crucial importance in studying African history in Zimbabwe is best described by Dr D. N. Beach in his thesis (see Bibliography). I consulted the reports relating to the following districts: Charter, Que Que, Gwelo, Selukwe, Bubi,

Wankie, Nyamandlovu, Gwai, Plumtree, Gwanda, Belingwe, Essexvale, Insiza, and Filabusi.

By far the largest amount of the data used in this study came from missionary records. The London Missionary Society Archives in London hold incoming and outgoing correspondence, reports from the mission field and the Matabeleland District Committee minutes. The correspondence from headquarters is found in boxes marked 'Africa South Outgoing letters'; letters from missionaries are in boxes 1, 2(i) and 2(ii) 'Matabeleland', 58, 59, 60, 61, 62, 64, 71, with either the label 'Bechuanaland & Matabeleland' or 'South Africa'. The reports I used are contained in boxes 1 to 6 marked 'Reports, South Africa' and dating from 1866 to 1926. Supplementing this material are the mission's publications, *The Chronicle of the London Missionary Society* and *The Popular Edition of the London Missionary Society.*

The Wesleyan Methodist Missionary Society Archives in London also hold outgoing letters from the Secretaries and these are in boxes 8, 9, 11, 12 and 20. The reports are found with the Synod minutes arranged as follows: S/M South Africa, 1889–99; S/M South Africa, 1900–05; S/M South Africa, 1906–11; S/M Rhodesia, 1912–22; and S/M Rhodesia 1923–33. The incoming correspondence is in C. Mashonaland, 1891–9; C. Mashonaland, 1899–1904; C. Rhodesia, 1905–17; and C. Rhodesia, 1917–23. Under Biographical, Rev. S. Douglas Gray's papers are useful and are contained in boxes 8, District Reports; 10, Early Days; and 15, Medical, Educational, and Evangelists. The mission's publications included *Wesleyan Missionary Notices, Worker and Workers,* and Bulletins.

Most of the holdings of the Society of Jesus Archives in London on western Zimbabwe have been published in M. Gelfand (ed.), *Gubulumayo and Beyond,* London, 1968, and further consist of copies from Prestage House in Salisbury. In any case they are classified under BY/1, Title Deeds; C/3, A. Weld, S.J. Assistant 1873–83; C.K., letters of the Zambesi Mission and Extracts from Father Law's Diary 1879–80; TQ/6, letters from Fr Law; TR/6, Fr Law's Journal 1879–80; U/1–9 correspondence with the B.S.A. Company officials. In Prestage House the material for the period 1900 onwards was tentatively classified under 'Embakwe, Semokwe. Wankie, Gwanda, Bembesi (Bro Dioc.)' and 'Empandeni Bro D', The mission's publications were *Letters and Notices* and *The Zambesi Mission Record.*

The Society for the Propagation of the Gospel in Foreign Parts Archives in London contain annual reports marked E Series and the Bishop's letters marked D Series. *The Mission Field* was their publication.

Missionary sources are directly useful in understanding the origins and expansion of Christianity in western Zimbabwe. They throw light upon the lives of the missionaries, sometimes give statistics of converts and those who dropped out of the Church, offer histories of mission stations, tell us about the lives of the converts, the finances of the different missions, the type of education the missionaries were instituting, and the relations between the missions and the British South Africa Company Administration. From the African point of view, missionary records tell us about the culture and religious beliefs and institutions of the societies they sought to convert.

The latter information is, however, presented as descriptions of the problems the missionary encountered in his evangelical work. Such information tells us very little about the theology, rituals, organisation and socio-political aspects of African religious institutions. To overcome this problem one has to turn to published works on the territorial and local cults. Even these are not extensive. More extensive oral data collection than I was, and still am not, able to do is likely to enable us to give a balanced picture of the interaction between Christianity and 'traditional' religion in western Zimbabwe. I still feel that the present study, which relies heavily on missionary and government records, contributes significantly to our understanding of the religious and educational history of western Zimbabwe.

I interviewed the following people: Elija Dube, Inyati Mission, aged in the mid-sixties, interviewed on 16 June 1971; Nqagwana Khumalo, Ntabazinduna, aged about eighty, interviewed on 21 June 1971; Mpeta Mambambo, Inyati Reserve, aged well over eighty, interviewed on 17 June 1971; Agripa Mdzamiri, Nyawidzi African Purchase Area, aged about eighty, interviewed on 6 June 1971; Mancube, Inyati Mission, aged late seventies, interviewed on 17 June 1971; Mampala, Hope Fountain Mission, aged about eighty, interviewed on 14 June 1971; Mrs Machiva Ndiweni, Hope Fountain Mission, aged well over eighty, interviewed on 14 June 1971; Miss Fipa Nyoni, Inyati Mission, aged late sixties, interviewed on 16 June 1971; Kakaka Tshabangu, Inyati Mission, aged late seventies, interviewed on 17 June 1971. Most of these people were converted to Christianity in the early 1900s and were also among the first Africans to go to school. They are therefore in a position to tell about their difficulties in embracing Christianity and to give first-hand information about the type of education they received.

Bibliography

PRIMARY SOURCES

Unpublished Manuscripts

Diary of U. I. S. Driver 1896–7, a Native Commissioner in the Gwelo area, Add. Ms. 42, 174, British Museum.

RICHLAND, DEAN R., 'Outlines of the Growth of the Evangelical Lutheran Church of Southern Rhodesia', typescript, n.d.

THOMAS, CELT THOMAS, 'Thomas Morgan Thomas Pioneer Missionary 1828–1884', presented to the L.M.S. in 1960.

Unpublished Theses

BEACH, D. N., 'The Rising in South-Western Mashonaland, 1896–7', Ph.D., London, 1971.

BHEBE, N. M. B., 'Christian Missions in Matabeleland 1859–1923', Ph.D., London, 1972.

CARTER, F. V., 'Education in Uganda 1894–1945', Ph.D., London, 1967.

HASSING, P. S., 'The Christian Missions and the British Expansion in Southern Rhodesia, 1888–1923', Ph.D., The American University, 1960.

HOSTETTER, J. N., 'Mission Education in a Changing Society: Brethren in Christ Mission Education in Southern Rhodesia, Africa, 1899–1959', D.Ed., State University of New York at Buffalo, 1967.

MASHINGAIDZE, E. K., 'Christian Missions in Mashonaland, Southern Rhodesia, 1890 to 1930', D.Phil., York, 1973.
MTUTUKI, M. J., 'The Mwali Cult in Northern Botswana – Some Oral Traditions c. 1893–1976', B.A., University College of Botswana, 1977.
PARSONS, Q. N., 'Khama III, Bamangwato and the British 1895–1923', Ph.D., Edinburgh, 1973.
RENNIE, J. K., 'Christianity, Colonialism and the Origins of Nationalism among the Ndau of Southern Rhodesia, 1890–1935', Ph.D., Northwestern University, 1973.

British Parliamentary Papers

1877–8	C.2220
1885	C.4588
1886	C.4643
1888	C.5363
1889	C.5524
1890	C.5918
1893–4	C.7171
1896	C.8130
1897	C.8547
1917	Cd.8674

Southern Rhodesia Documents

Report of the Chief Native Commissioner, Matabeleland, 1903–12.
Report of the Chief Native Commissioner, Southern Rhodesia, 1913–23.
Southern Rhodesia Education Reports, 1903–27.
Report of the Education Committee, 1908.
Report of the Native Affairs Committee of Enquiry, 1908.
Southern Rhodesia Education and Developments, 1928–34.
Report by H. S. Kiegwin, Esq., Native Commissioner, on Suggested Industrial Development of Natives, 1920.
Report of the Commission Appointed to Enquire into the Matter of Education in all its bearing in the Colony of Southern Rhodesia, 1925.

Newspapers

Rhodesia Herald.
Bulawayo Chronicle.
The (Grahamstown) Journal.
The Diamond Fields Advertiser.

SECONDARY SOURCES

ABRAHAM, D. P., 'The Roles of "Chaminuka" and the Mhondoro-cults in Shona Political History' in E. Stokes and R. Brown (eds.), *The Zambesian Past*, Manchester, 1966.

AJAYI, J. F. ADE, *Christian Missions in Nigeria 1841–1891: The Making of a New Elite*, London, 1965.

and AYANDELE, E. A., 'Emerging Themes in Nigerian and West African Religious History', *Journal of African Studies* (U.C.L.A.), i, 1974.

ANDERSON, W. H., *On Trail of Livingstone*, Mount View, 1919.

ANDREWS, C. F., *John White of Mashonaland*, London, 1935.

ATKINSON, N. D., *Teaching Rhodesians: a History of Educational Policy in Rhodesia*, London, 1972.

AYANDELE, E. A., *The Missionary Impact on Modern Nigeria 1842–1914: A Political and Social Analysis*, London, 1966.

A.W., 'The Expulsion of Nkulumane', *Nada*, 1935.

BADEN-POWELL, R. S. S., *The Matabele Campaign 1896*, London, 1897.

BEACH, D. N., 'Ndebele Raiders and Shona Power', *Journal of African History*, xv, 1974.

BECKER, P., *The Path of Blood*, London, 1962.

BHEBE, N. M. B., 'The Ndebele and Mwari before 1893', Lusaka Conference on the History of Central African Religions, unpublished, 1972.

'A Critical Review of our Knowledge of the Mwari Cult', University of Rhodesia, Henderson Seminar, 1973.

'Missionary Activity among the Ndebele and Kalanga: A Survey' in A. J. Dachs (ed.), *Christianity South of the Zambezi*, Gwelo, 1973.

'Ndebele Trade in the Nineteenth Century', *Journal of African Studies* (U.C.L.A.), i, 1974.

'Some Aspects of Ndebele Relations with the Shona in the

Nineteenth Century', *Rhodesian History*, iv, 1973.
'Ndebele Politics During the Scramble', *Mohlomi* (National University of Lesotho), 1977.
Lobengula of Zimbabwe, London, 1976.
BLAKE-THOMPSON, J. and SUMMERS, R., 'Molimo and Mwari, Notes on a Native Religion in Southern Rhodesia', *Nada*, 1956.
BOGGIE, A., *From Ox-Wagon to Railway*, Bulawayo, 1897.
BOGGIE, J. M., *First Steps in Civilizing Rhodesia*, London, 1940.
BROWN, R., 'The Ndebele Succession Crisis 1868–1877', *Historians in Tropical Africa*, Salisbury, 1962.
'The External Relations of the Ndebele Kingdom in the Pre-partition Era' in Leonard Thompson (ed.), *African Societies in Southern Africa*, London, 1969.
'Aspects of the Scramble for Matabeleland' in E. Stokes and R. Brown (eds.), *The Zambesian Past*, Manchester, 1966.
BRYANT, A. T., *The Zulu People*, Pietermaritzburg, 1949.
BULLOCK, C., *The Mashona and the Matabele*, Cape Town, 1950.
CARNEGIE, D., *Among the Matabele*, London, 1894.
CHAPMAN, J., *Travels in the Interior of South Africa*, 2 vols., London, 1868.
CHIRGWIN, A. M., *The Blood-Brother: The Story of Cullen Reed*, London, c. 1930.
COCKROFT, I. G., 'The Molimo (Mwari) Cult', *Nada*, 1972.
COBBING, J., 'The Evolution of Ndebele Amabuto', *Journal of African History*, xv, 1974.
'The Absent Priesthood: Another look at the Rhodesian Risings', *Journal of African History*, xviii, 1977.
COILLARD, F., *On the Threshold of Central Africa*, translated by C. M. Mackintosh, London, 1897.
COLVIN, I., *The Life of Jameson*, 2 vols., London, 1912.
COOPER-CHADWICK, J., *Three Years with Lobengula*, London, 1894.
CRAWFORD, J. R., *Witchcraft and Sorcery in Rhodesia*, London, 1967.
DACHS, A. (ed.), *Christianity South of the Zambezi*, Gwelo, 1973.
DANEEL, M. L., *The God of the Matopo Hills*, The Hague, 1970.
Old and New in Southern Shona Independent Churches, Background and Rise of Major Movements, The Hague, 1971.
'Shona Independent Churches in a Rural Society' in A. Dachs (ed.), *Christianity South of the Zambezi*, Gwelo, 1973.
'Shona Independent Churches and Ancestor Worship' in D. B. Barrett (ed.), *African Initiatives in Religion*, Nairobi, 1971.

DECLE, L., *Three Years in Savage Africa*, London, 1898.

DUPLESSIS, J., *A History of Christian Missions in South Africa*, London, 1911.

DURKHEIM, E., *The Elementary Forms of Religious Life*, translated by J. W. Swain, New York, 1965.

ELLIOTT, A. W., *Gold From the Quartz*, London, 1910.
Notes for a Sindebele Dictionary, Bristol, n.d.

FINDLAY, G. G. and HOLDWORTH, W. W., *The History of the Wesleyan Methodist Missionary Society*, London, 1922.

FISHER, H. J., 'Conversion Reconsidered: Some Historical Aspects of Religious Conversion in Black Africa', *Africa*, xliii, 1973.

FLOOD, D. G. H., 'Industrial School at Inyati', *Nada*, 1970.
'The Contribution of the London Missionary Society to African Education in Ndebeleland' in A. Dachs (ed.), *Christianity South of the Zambezi*, Gwelo, 1973.

FORTUNE, G., 'Who was Mwari', *Rhodesian History*, iv, 1973.

FRANKLIN, H., 'Manyusa', *Nada*, 1932.
'Nyaningwe', *Nada*, 1928.

FRIPP, C. E. and HILLER, V. W. (eds.), *Gold and the Gospel in Mashonaland*, London, 1949.

GANN, L. H., *A History of Southern Rhodesia: Early Days to 1934*, London, 1965.

GARBETT, G. K., 'Religious Aspects of Political Succession among the Valley Korekore (N. Shona)' in E. Stokes and R. Brown (eds.), *The Zambesian Past*, Manchester, 1966.

GELFAND, M. (ed.), *Gubuluwayo and Beyond: Letters & Journals of the Early Jesuit Missionaries to Zambesia (1879–1887)*, London, 1968.
The African Witch, London, 1967.
'Medicine and the Christian Missions in Rhodesia, 1857–1930' in A. Dachs (ed.), *Christianity South of the Zambezi*, Gwelo, 1973.

GLASS, S., *Matabele War*, London, 1968.

GOODALL, N., *A History of the London Missionary Society*, London, 1954.

GRAY, R., *The Two Nations*, London, 1960.

HAILIE, A. J., *A Brief Survey of the London Missionary Society in Southern Africa*, Bulawayo, 1951.

HEMANS, H. N., 'History of the Abenanzwa Tribe', *Rhodesia Science Association*, xii, 1912.

HLAZO, T. J., 'The Naming of the Hill Intaba Yezinduna', *Nada*, 1934.

HOLE, H. M., *Lobengula*, London, 1929.
'The Rise of the Matabele', *Rhodesia Science Association*, xii, 1912.
'Notes on the Batonga and Batshukumbi', *Rhodesia Science Association*, v, 1905.

HOLUB, E., *Seven Years in South Africa*, 2 vols., London, 1881.

HONE, PERCY F., *Southern Rhodesia*, London, 1909.

HOOPER, H. D., *Africa in the Making*, London, 1922.

HORTON, R., 'African Conversion', *Africa*, xli, 1971.

HUGHES, A. J. B., *Caste and Nation among the Rhodesian Ndebele*, Manchester, 1959.

JACKSON, H. M. G., 'A Boer Invasion of Rhodesia', *Nada*, 1924.
'A Sketch of Lobengula', *Nada*, 1932.

KEIGWIN, H. S., 'An Educational Experiment', *South African Journal of Science*, xxviii, 1926.

KRIGE, J. E., *The Social System of the Zulus*, Pietermaritzburg, 1950.

KUPER, H., HUGHES, A. J. B., and VAN VELSEN, J., *The Shona and The Ndebele of Southern Rhodesia*, London, 1954.

LATOURETTE, K. S., *A History of the Expansion of Christianity in the Americas, Australia and Africa*, Vol. v, London, 1943.

LEWIS, D. G., 'Molimo', *Nada*, 1934.
'Lobengula's regiments: Recruiting and Lobola', *Nada*, 1956.
'The Shangani Fight', *Nada*, 1934.

LIVINGSTONE, D., *Missionary Travels and Researches in South Africa*, London, 1858.

LOVETT, R., *History of the London Missionary Society*, 2 vols., London, 1899.

LYALL, C. H. (ed.), *Twenty Years in Khama's Country*, London, 1895.

LYE, W. F., 'The Ndebele Kingdom South of the Limpopo River', *Journal of African History*, x, 1969.

MACKENZIE, J., *Ten Years North of the Orange River*, Edinburgh, 1871.

MACKINTOSH, C. W., *Coillard of the Zambezi*, London, 1907.

MADZIYIRE, S. K., 'African Religious Practices and Christianity among the Shona People' in A. Dachs (ed.), *Christianity South of the Zambezi*, Gwelo, 1973.
'Heathen Practices in the Urban and Rural Parts of Marandellas Area and their Effects upon Christianity' in T. O.

Ranger and J. Weller (eds.), *Themes in the Christian History of Central Africa*, London, 1975.

MAGABA, E. B., 'African Customs Connected with the Burial of the Dead in Rhodesia' in A. Dachs (ed.), *Christianity South of the Zambezi*, Gwelo, 1973.

MAHLANGU, P. S., *Umtwakazi*, Cape Town, 1957.

MANDY, F., 'Matabeleland: The Future Gold Fields of the World. Its People and Resources, 1891', *Rhodesia Pamphlets*, i, 1, bound privately by the Commonwealth and Foreign Office Library.

MARTIN, MARIE-LOUISE, 'The Mai Chaza Church' in D. B. Barrett (ed.), *African Initiatives in Religion*, Nairobi, 1971.

MASINGA, R., 'Africa's Daughters', *The Book of Rachel and Ratna*, World Womanhood Series, L.M.S., c. 1921.

MASON, P., *The Birth of a Dilemma*, London, 1958.

MCCRACKEN, K. J., 'Livingstone as an Industrial Mission, 1875–1900: A study of Commerce and Christianity in Nyasaland' in W. M. Watt (ed.), *Religion in Africa*, Edinburgh, 1964.
'Religion and Politics in Northern Ngoniland, 1881–1904' in B. Pachai, *The Early History of Malawi*, London, 1972.
Politics and Christianity in Malawi 1875–1940: The Impact of the Livingstonia in the Northern Province, Cambridge, 1977.

MHLAGAZANHLANSI, *Early Days and Native Ways in Southern Rhodesia*, Bulawayo, 1944.
My Friend Khumalo, Bulawayo, 1947.

MOFFAT, R., *Missionary Labours and Scenes in South Africa*, London, 1842.
'A Visit to Moselekatse's Country, King of the Matabele', *Royal Geographical Society Journal*, xxvi, 1859.

MOFFAT, R. U., *John Smith Moffat*, London, 1921.

MURPHREE, M. W., *Christianity and the Shona*, London, 1969.

MWANZA, R., 'Mwari, The God of the Karanga', Lusaka Conference, 1972.

'MZIKI', *Molimo* (written in 1911).

NIELSEN, P., *The Matabele at Home*, Bulawayo, 1913.

NOBBS, E. A., *Guide to the Matopo*, Cape Town, 1924.
'Native Cattle of Southern Rhodesia', *South African Journal of Science*, xxiv, 1927.

NOBLE, W. J., *A Report of the Secretarial Visit to Rhodesia and the Transvaal District of South Africa September 20–March 30*, London, 1930.

OLIVER, R., *The Missionary Factor in East Africa*, London, 1952.
OATES, G. E. (ed.), *Matabele and the Victoria Falls*, London, 1898.
O'NEIL, J., *A Phrasebook in English and Sindebele with a full Vocabulary for the Use of Settlers in Matabeleland*, London, 1910.
PALMER, ROBIN, *Land and Racial Domination in Rhodesia*, Berkeley and Los Angeles, 1977.
PARKER, F., *African Development and Education in Southern Rhodesia*, Ohio, 1960.
PASCOE, C. F., *Hundred Years of the S.P.G.*, London, 1901.
PEADEN, W. R., 'Missionary Attitudes to Shona Culture 1890–1923', *Central African Association Local Series*, 27.
'Nengubo Training Institution and the First Shona Teachers' in A. Dachs, *Christianity South of the Zambezi*, Gwelo, 1973.
POSSELT, F. W. T., 'Nkulumane', *Nada*, 1923.
'Chaminuka', *Nada*, 1926.
'Some Notes on the Religious Ideas of Natives of Southern Rhodesia', *South Africa Journal of Science*, xiv, 1917.
'The Rise of the Amandebele', *Rhodesia Science Association*, xviii, 1918.
Fact and Fiction, Bulawayo, 1935.
Upengula. The Scatterer, Bulawayo, 1945.
PRELLER, G. S., *Lobengula*, Johannesburg, 1963.
RANGER, T. O., *Revolt in Southern Rhodesia*, London, 1967.
The African Voice in Southern Rhodesia 1898–1930, London, 1970.
'State and Church in Southern Rhodesia 1919–1939', *Historical Association Rhodesia and Nyasaland*, Local Series, 4.
(ed.), *Aspects of Central African History*, London, 1968.
'The Role of Ndebele and Shona Religious Authorities in the Rebellions of 1896 and 1897' in E. Stokes and R. Brown, *The Zambesian Past*, Manchester, 1965.
'Christian Independency in Tanzania' in D. B. Barrett (ed.), *African Initiatives in Religion*, Nairobi, 1971.
'The Early History of Independency in Southern Rhodesia' in W. M. Watt (ed.), *Religion in Africa*, Edinburgh, 1964.
and KIMAMBO, I. N. (eds.), *The Historical Study of African Religion: With Special Reference to East and Central Africa*, London, 1972.
and WELLER, J. (eds.), *Themes in the Christian History of Central Africa*, London, 1975.

RAYNER, W., *The Tribe and Its Successors*, London, 1962.
REA, W. F., 'The Missionary Factor in Southern Rhodesia', *Central African Historical Association, Local Series*, 7.
RICHARDS, J. P., 'The Molimo', *Nada*, 1942.
ROSENLHAL, E. (trans.), *The Matabeleland Travel Letters of Marie Lippert*, Cape Town, 1960.
ROTBERG, R. I., *Christian Missionaries and the Creation of Northern Rhodesia 1880–1924*, Princeton, 1965.
SAMKANGE, S., *Origins of Rhodesia*, London, 1968.
On Trial for my Country, London, 1966.
SCHAPERA, I., *The Bantu Speaking Tribes of South Africa*, London, 1937.
Rainmaking Rites of the Tswana Tribes, London, 1971.
SCHOFFELEERS, M., 'The History and Political Role of the M'Bona Cult among the Mang'anja' in T. O. Ranger and I. N. Kimambo (eds.), *The Historical Study of African Religion With Special Reference to East and Central Africa*, London, 1972.
'An Organizational Model of the Mwari Shrines', paper presented at the University of Rhodesia, Faculty of Social Studies, 1973.
and LINDEN, I., 'The Resistance of Nyau Societies to the Roman Catholic Missions in Colonial Malawi' in T. O. Ranger and I. N. Kimambo (eds.), *The Historical Study of African Religion With Special Reference to East and Central Africa*, London, 1972.
SELOUS, F. C., *Travel and Adventure in South-east Africa*, London, 1893.
Sunshine and Storm in Rhodesia, London, 1896.
SILLERY, A., *Bechuanaland Protectorate*, Oxford, 1952.
Botswana: A Short History, London, 1974.
SMITH, E. W., *The Way of the White Fields*, London, 1928.
STENT, V., 'How We Made Rhodesia, March 12, 1926', *South African Pamphlets*, iv, (Commonwealth and Foreign Office Library).
SUMMERS, R., *Zimbabwe: A Rhodesian Mystery*, Johannesburg, 1963.
and PAGDEN, W., *The Warriors*, Cape Town, 1970.
SUNDKLER, B. G. M., *Bantu Prophets in South Africa*, 2nd ed., London, 1961.
SYKES, F. W., *With Plumer in Matabeleland*, London, 1897.
TABLER, E. C., *The Far Interior*, Cape Town, 1955.
Pioneers of Rhodesia, Cape Town, 1966.

TAYLOR, G. A., 'The Matabele Head-ring and some Fragments of History', *Nada*, 1925.

'The Amandebele and other Tribes of Matabeleland', *Rhodesia Science Association*, vi, 1906.

TAYLOR, J. V., *The Growth of the Church in Buganda*, London, 1958.

The Life and Labours of the Reverend J. B. Radasi, Gisbone, 1966.

THOMAS, T. M., *Eleven Years in Central South Africa*, London, 1873.

THORPE, C., *Limpopo to Zambesi*, London, 1951.

VAMBE, L., *An Ill-fated People*, London, 1972.

VON SICARD, H., *Ngoma Lungundu*, Uppsala, 1952.

Zwakaitika Kare Mukereke YaMarutere, vol. 1, Gwelo, 1970.

'Die Initiation in Monomutapa-Reich', *Ethnos*, Stockholm, vi, 1941.

'Karangemas Maniskouppfatting', *Svensk Missionstidskrif*, (Uppsala), xl, 1952.

'Mwari, der Hochgott der Karanga', *Kolomane Völkerkunde* (Wiener Beiträge zur Kulturgeschichte und Linguistik. Herausgegeben von H. Baumann), i, 1944.

WALLIS, J. P. R. (ed.), *The Northern Gold Fields Diaries of Thomas Baines*, 3 vols., London, 1946.

Matabele Mission of J. S. and E. Moffat, London, 1945.

Matabele Journals of Robert Moffat, 2 vols., London, 1945.

The Southern African Diaries of Thomas Leask 1865–1870, London, 1945.

WEBER, M., *The Sociology of Religion*, 4th ed., Boston, 1963.

WEINRICH, A. K. H., *Black and White Elites in Rural Rhodesia*, Manchester, 1973.

'The People of the Spirit: An Independent Church in Rhodesia', *Africa*, xxxii, 1967.

'Zionists in Rhodesia', *Africa*, xxxiii, 1968.

WILLOUGHBY, W. C., *Race Problems in New Africa*, Oxford, 1923.

WILSON, M., *Communal Rituals of the Nyakyusa*, London, 1959.

Religion and the Transformation of Society: A Study in the Social Change in Africa, Cambridge, 1971.

WOOD, J. G., *Through Matabeleland*, Cape Town, 1893.

WRIGHT, M., *German Missions in Tanganyika*, Oxford, 1971.

Index

A.C.A.C.Z., 108–9
Abraham, D. P., 78
African preachers, 67–70, 105, 107, 108, 109, 120–2, 146–7, 153; advantages of, 130; colonial authority and, 108–9, 133–4; complaints against, 133; dangers of foreign, 131; and literacy, 148, 150–1; recruitment, 130–1; training, 132, 134–7
agriculture, 11–12
Ajayi, J. F. Ade, *xi*, 158
ancestor spirits (*amadlozi*), worship of, *xii*, 13, 14–16, 18, 22, 29, 32–3, 54, 55, 70, 78, 94, 110, 152; Kalanga, 122–3
Anderson, W. H., 132
Anglo-Ndebele war, 1893, 75, 79, 85, 90, 91, 97
anthropology, *xi*
Anti-Slavery Expedition, 158
Aquina, Sr Mary, 163
Ayandele, E. A., *xi*

Baines, Thomas, *quoted*, 52–3
Baker, H. J., 107
Beach, Dr D. N., 67, 90–1
Berlin Mission, 47, 66–7, 69, 157
Bick, Fr Charles, 120
Biehler, Fr, 123, 144
Boers, 27, 32, 68; Trekkers, 2, 51
Bonner, P. L., 92
Brady, J. B., 140
Brethren in Christ, 107, 131, 143, 153, 166

British South Africa Co., 58, 90, 107, 117, 131, 168
Brown, Holman, 132
Bulawayo mission station, 58–9, 89, 96, 98, 106

capitalist economy, growth of, 105
Carnegie, David, 62, 64, 82, 83, 87–8, 105, 148, 165; *quoted*, 65, 84, 114
Carnegie, Mary Margaret, 40, 62, 87
Carter, H., 138
Cenda, chief, 69
Centenary mission station, 105
Chibi, chief, 52, 68
Chingoma, chief of Imbahuru, 68, 69
Chirisamhuru, Mambo, 3
Chitawudze, chief, 69
Christian Catholic Apostolic Church in Zion, 108–9
Christianity: borrowing of ideas from, *xii*, 13; fails to offer practical answers, 43–4; growth, 97–100; Mwari identifies with, 20, 69–70, 76, 161; pluralist attitudes to, 115–19, 162–4; 'quarantine' phase, 100, 165; resistance to, 17, 57; traditional religion as obstacle to, 28, 29–30, 40–1, 48, 57–63; *see also* missionaries
Church of England, *see* England, Church of
Church Missionary Society, 159
Church of Sweden, *see* Sweden, Church of

clan structure, 5
Clarkson, trader, 56
Cobbing, Dr Julian, 90–3
Cockin, Joseph, 54, 56, 77, 81
Coillard, Francis, 47, 68
colonial rule, 65, 75; and black preachers, 108–9, 133–4; laying missionary foundations for, 69; Lobengula and, 80–5; missionaries and, 82–4, 168; Mwari and, 70, 80–81, 83, 89–90; and social traditions, 112–13
cosmologies, two-tiered, *xi–xii*, 13, 164
Croonenberghs, Fr, 59

Depelchin, Fr, 48
divination of witches, *xii*, 17, 23, 57; colonialism as eradicator of, 80, 85; as political weapon, 47–8, 50, 56, 87; as weapon against Christianity, 17, 86, 119, 122
Dombodema mission station, 99, 105, 120, 140
Dube, Elija, 115
Dyembewu, Rozvi chief, 4

Education Ordinance (Amended), 1903, 166
Elliott, W. A., 84
Embakwe mission station, 106, 110, 120 1
Empandeni mission station, 58, 99, 106, 110, 114, 120–1, 125, 148; school, 143–4
England, Church of, 107–8
Epworth mission station, 136
Ethiopianism, 106, 134, 167
ethnic groups, amalgamation, *xi*, 1–5; effect on religious beliefs, *xii*, 1, 4, 6, 12–13, 18, 22–3, 47, 65–6, 92, 94, 160; Shona identify with Ndebele, 9

Fashole-Luke, E., 162
Fisher, Humphrey J., 100, 163–5
Free Church of Scotland, 108
Fry, Ivon, 142
Fute Dlamini, 141

Gambo Sithole, Ndebele chief, 80, 116–19, 158, 163–4, 166
gold mining, 83, 107, 112
Gumbo, Baleni, early convert and composer, 64
Gwai mission station, 132

Harpur, C. W., 118–19
Hartmann, Fr Andrew, 106
Hehe people, 158–9
Helm, C. D., 83–4, 105; wife of, 149
Hlegisane, Mfengu doctor, 51–2, 85–6
Hobasi, Ndebele soldier, 80–1
Hobile Hlabangana, 141
Hole people, 5–7, 79, 158; converts, 64; doctors, 9, 23; legal discrimination against, 11; missionary work among, 58; political importance, 48–9; status, 7–11
Hope Fountain mission station, 51, 60, 61–3, 89, 99, 105, 131, 148, 149; Girls' Boarding School, 130, 137, 141–3; training institute, 139–40
Horton, Robin, 100, 164
Hostetter, J. N., 143

Impande people, 58
independent churches, *xiii*, 163, 165
Ingwenya mission station, 108
Inqobo people, 60–1
Inyati mission station, 28, 30, 35–6, 97–8, 105, 147, 149
Islam, 164–5

Jackson, H., 150
Jameson, Dr L. S., 106
Jesuits, 47, 52, 54, 58–60, 105–6, 120, 123–4, 125, 143, 148, 158
Johannes, evangelist, 67–70
Johnson, Frank, 50 1
Jones, Neville, 99, 130, 133, 140–1, 151
Joyi, convert and preacher, 109
Juba, P., 133
Jukwa, rain-doctor, 55–6

Kabu Bebebe, rebel leader, 98
Kagubi, spirit-medium, 91

186 *Index*

Kalanga people, 4–5, 6–7, 9, 58, 93, 97, 110, 159; agricultural expertise, 12; attitudes to missionaries, 119–24, 146; religious beliefs, 77; Shumba cult, 122–3
Kanda, 60
Khama, king of Ngwato, 80, 116, 160
Khumalo, Mirriam, 141
Khumalo, Mtompe, 55, 99
Khumalo, Muyengwa, 149
Kitwe mission station, 106
Knothe, C., *quoted*, 9, 68
Kololo people, 6
Kwena people, 27

Langalibalele, Nguni chief, 68
language, 9, 19, 108, 119, 145
Lanning, R., 151
laws: Code of Native Law, 113; Ndebele state, 11
Lee, John, *quoted*, 54
Leya people, 6, 58, 67
literacy, *xiii*, 32, 37–8, 41, 59, 62–3, 114–15, 129–30; African evangelists and, 148, 150–1; Lobengula, 50–1; Mzilikazi and, 38, 40
Livingstone, David, 27
Livingstonia mission station, 41, 159–160
Lobengula, king of Ndebele, 7, 17, 20, 91, 94, 160, 164; attitude to white colonisation, 80–5; and divination, 47–8, 50, 56, 57; and missionaries, 50–2, 58, 61–2, 75, 82–3; political dependence on traditional beliefs, 48–9, 52, 59, 65–6; poverty, 49; *quoted*, 53; and rain-making, 47, 49, 52–3, 54–5; religious beliefs, 50, 51–53, 75–6
Lomaqele, early convert, 63–4
London Missionary Society, 27, 33, 35, 37, 41, 47, 51, 54, 60, 63, 64–5, 82–4, 110, 126, 131–3, 138–40, 146, 150, 153, 166; expansion, 105–6; ordination of ministers, 62; quarrels within, 39
Lotshe Hlabangana, adviser to Lobengula, 34, 56, 80, 83

Loziba, wife of Mzilikazi, 32, 33
Lye, W. F., 7

Mabiletsa, P. M., 108
McCracken, Dr John, 159; *quoted*, 41
Mackay, J. R., *quoted*, 111
Mackenzie, John, 39–40
Madindire, chief, 69
Maduna, chief, 109
Mafa Sibindwana, 133
Mafule, Moyo, 99
Magatshana, cousin of Lobengula, 56–57
magic, belief in, *see* witchcraft
Mahura, chief of Tlaping, 27
Majila, chief, 120
Makubila, convert and preacher, 109
Malaba, chief, 120
Mambos, 3, 19–20
Mandy, Frank, 60
Mankonyana, rain-doctor, 55
Manqeba, adviser to Mzilikazi, 33–5
Mapiravana, chief, 69
marriage, 43, 112–13, 149–50, 152, 162
Masibi, Baleni, early convert, 64, 88
Masinga, Rachel, 130–1, 141–3
Matambo, convert, 97–8, 164
Matambo, Hilda, 141
Mate, chief, 122
materialism, Ndebele, 30, 37, 41, 44, 63, 80, 110, 124
Matibe, chief of Pfumbi, 67–9
Matopo mission station, 107, 143
Maund, E. A., *quoted*, 12
Mazaka Nkala, convert, 98–9, 164
Mazibuko, Letta, 141
Mbelwa, king of Nguni, 41, 159–60
Mbiko, rebel, 60
Mbikwa Ncube (Malaba), Venda priest, 76
Mbiza, 62
Mbulali, Mfengu doctor, 51–2, 85
medical work, missionaries, 23, 34, 43, 56–7, 59
medicine men (*izinyanga*), 6, 9, 16, 23, 28, 31, 40, 56–7; attitude to whites, 85–7; Mbulali and Hlegisane, 51–2
mediums (*amajukwa*), 76, 79, 125

Menzo, rain-doctor, 55
Merere, king of Safwa, 82
M'fazi, Moses, 107, 118, 122
Mfengu people, 131
Mfezela, proposed king of Ndebele, 95
Mgoma, Jonathan D., 109
Mgugu, J., 133
Mhlahle, chief, 116
Mhlatshwa (Petros), convert and preacher, 109
Mhlope, Inja, catechist, 120–2, 148, 161, 164
military recruitment, 4–5, 6–7, 10, 90
Milner, Sir Alfred, 117
missionaries: arrival of first, *xii*, 21, 27–8; blamed for Ndebele misfortunes, 30–3, 44; Catholic-Protestant differences, 110–11; conversions, 63–4, 69, 100, 109, 148–9; disregard for Ndebele customs, 33, 43, 124; early failure, 35, 44; expansion of coverage, 105–9; influence by proximity, 97–8; later attitudes to, 114–126; and literacy, *xiii*, 32, 37–8, 41, 59, 62–3, 114–15, 129–30; Lobengula and, 50–2, 58, 61–2, 75, 82–3; medical work, 23, 34, 43, 56–7, 59; Mwari cult and, 69–70, 124–5; Mzilikazi and, 27–31, 33, 35–7, 39–43; Ndebele fears of, 27; preaching, 29–30, 35–7, 43; role in fall of Ndebele state, 75; schools, *xiii*, 37–38, 41, 42, 58, 110, 114, 120–2, 129, 132, 134–45; self-justification, 53; Shona and, 66–7, 119; and social traditions, 111–14; successes, 61–2, 63–4, 69, 97–100; types of response to, East Africa generally, 157–68; view of traditional religion, 109–13; and white colonisation, 82–4, 97, 168
Mkanya mission station, 106, 123
Mkupuvula mission station, 132
Mkwati, Mwari official, 91, 92, 93–4, 96
Mncumbata, adviser to Lobengula, 48–9, 51, 149
Mnene mission station, 107

Mngcengence (Nina), sister of Lobengula, 56
Modimo (Molimo), Sotho-Tswana high god, 17–18
Moffat, John Smith, 30, 33, 36, 39, 57, 64–5, 86; *quoted*, 40, 58
Moffat, Robert (Mtshete), 18, 27, 28–29, 32, 34, 53
monotheism, 1, 70, 76–7
Monyakanya, chief, 39
Moravian Brethren, 157
Morgan, T. M., *quoted*, 10
Moses, early convert, 64
Moyo, Shisho, early convert and preacher, 62, 87–9, 164
Mpangala, Venda chief, 23
Mpini, chief, 120
Mpose, chief of Remba, 67–9
Mpotswana, adviser to Nyamanda, 95, 96
Mtamjana, 94
Mtinhima, Rozvi chief, 4
Mtshabezi mission station, 107, 143
Mtutuki, M. J., 93–4
Mulugulu, chief, 94–5
Murphree, Professor M. W., 161
Musingavika, high priest, 69–70
Mutesa, Kabaka of Ganda, 159
Mwanga, Kabaka of Ganda, 159
Mwanza, R., 81
Mwari, Shona high god, *xii*, 1, 13, 54 60–1; and colonisation, 80–1, 83, 89–90; cult, 19–22, 30, 47, 54–6, 75–79, 161; and missionaries, 69–70, 124–5; priests, 19, 49, 55, 76, 89, 95–6, 164; and risings, 1896–7, 90–100; shrines, 19–20, 54, 56, 96–7
Mwelane, T. M., 108
Mzila, father-in-law of Lobengula, 50, 56
Mzilikazi Khumalo, king of Ndebele, 1–2, 5, 9, 77, 91, 92, 160; death, 48; and literacy, 38, 40; and missionaries, 27–31, 33, 35–7, 39–43; policies towards Rozvi states, 3; as protector, 6; religious beliefs, 18, 21

Naka Pasi, 93–4

Nambia people, 5
Nanzwa people, 5, 6, 58, 67
nationalism, African, 131, 167
Native Charitable Fund, 141
Native Marriages Ordinance, 1901, 112
Native Tax Ordinance, 1904, 112
Nawa, rain-doctor, 55
Ncube, Priscilla, 141
Ndali people, 158
Ndebele people, 2, 4, 9, 12, 110; and concept of God, 42–3; difficulty of evangelising, 57, 59–60; fear of invasion, 68; fear of missionaries, 27; later attitudes to missionaries, 114–19, 146; martial spirit, 52; materialism, 30, 37, 41, 44, 63, 80, 110, 124; rebellion, 90; understanding of Mwari, 75–9; *see also* risings
Ndebele state, *xi–xii*; fall of, *xii*, 75, 105; formation, 1–5; laws, 11; political structure, 4–5, 80–6, 157, 160; resistance to, 3–4; social structure, 5–11, 30, 161–3; trade, 11–12; *see also* religious beliefs
Ndiweni, Machina, 8, 149
Ndungu, convert and preacher, 109
Nehanda, spirit-medium, 91
Nemakonde people, 81
Nembire, leader of proto-Shona, 78
Nengubo (Waddilove) training school, 134–7, 141, 146, 167
Ngege, chief, 108, 111, 115–16, 158, 163–4, 166
Ngono, John, 133
Nguni people, *xi–xii*, 2, 4, 5, 6, 13, 41, 92, 131, 158–60; religious beliefs, 17, 47, 49
Ngwane people, 92
Ngwato people, 5, 28, 160
Nhla people, 5–6, 49, 79; converts, 64; religious beliefs, 13, 17–18, 22–3, 77; religious functions, 6
Nina kaPansi, spirit-medium, 125, 161
Nkani Sibanda, 7
Nkulumane, hair-apparent to Mzilikazi, 48, 60
Nkulunkulu (Somandla), Zansi high god, 13–14, 18; Mvelengangi, his wife, 13; as name for God, 116
Nkungusi, wife of Lobengula, 50
Ntogwa, 94
Ntuli, Adelaide, 141
Nxobe, Mika, convert, 88
Nyai people, 6, 158
Nyamanda, king of Ndebele, 91, 95
Nyamazana, queen of Swazi, 2, 3
Nyanganyoni Mhlope, 95
Nyoni, Fipa, niece of Mazaka, 98–9, 149
Nyoni, Weary, 146–7
Nyubi people, 4, 12

Oliver, Professor R., 157
O'Neil, Fr J., 110, 120–4, 162

Paris Missionary Society, 47, 66
Pasipamire, spirit-medium, 76
Pedi people, 7
Pfumbi people, 67
pluralism, in religious beliefs, 115–19, 162–4
political structure, Ndebele state, 4–5, 80–6, 157, 160
polygamy, 43, 112–13, 152, 162
preaching, effects of, 29–30, 35–7, 43
Presbyterian Church of Scotland, 111, 166
Prestage, Fr Peter, 58–60, 96, 106, 112

Radasi, John Boyan, 108, 116, 122
rainmaking ceremonies (*mutoro*), 16–17, 21, 33, 60–1; Lobengula and, 47, 49, 52–3, 54–5; missionaries and, 116, 118
Ramhushu, Josiah, 130
Ranger, Professor T. O., 79, 90–2, 94, 96–7, 163
Reed, Cullen, 99, 105
Rees, Bowen, 97–9, 105, 126, 132, 148–9; wife of, 98
religious beliefs, traditional: king's role, 6; Lobengula, 50, 51–3, 75–6; Lobengula's dependence on, 48–9, 52, 59, 65–6; missionaries, view of,

109–13; Mzilikazi, 18, 21; Nguni, 17, 47, 49; Nhla-Sotho-Tswana, 17–18, 22–3, 47; as obstacle to Christianity, 28, 29–30, 40–1, 48, 57–63; pluralist attitudes, 115–19, 162–4; role in fall of Ndebele state, 75; Shona, 13, 19–23; Zansi, 13–17, 18–19, 22–3; *see also* Mwari
Remba people, 67
Rhodes, Cecil John, 49, 83–4, 112, 116
risings, 1896–7, *xii*, 75, 79, 90–100, 105, 117, 142
rites, religious, 15–16
Rozani people, 4
Rozvi confederacy, 1, 20; replaced by Ndebele rule, 2–5
Rudd Concession, 1888, 49, 75, 83–6, 97, 105

Safwa people, 82, 158
St Aidan mission station, 107
St Columba mission station, 107
St Joseph mission station, 106
Salugazana, goddess, 77, 96
Salugazana, spirit-medium, 54, 55, 81
Samuel, evangelist, 67–70
Sangu people, 158–9
Schapera, Professor, *quoted*, 18
schools, mission, *xiii*, 37–8, 41, 42, 58, 110, 114, 120–2, 129, 132, 134–45
Scott, Mr, 138
Sebitwane, chief of Kololo, 6
Selous, Frederick Courteney, 78
Sendika, early convert, 64
Sendla, chief, 108
September, J. L., 131
Setshele, chief of Kwena, 27–8, 34
Seventh Day Adventists, 99, 106, 131–134, 166; complaints about, 133
Shiloh mission station, 37, 63, 88, 158
Shimmin, Isaac, 106
Shologulu, father of Mwari, 78
Shona people, *xi–xii*, 2, 6, 159; identification with Ndebele, 9; independent chiefdoms, 2, 3, 67, 90; and missionaries, 66–70, 119; proto-Shona, 78; rebellion, 90; religious authorities, 49; religious beliefs, 13, 19–23, 47; subjection to Ndebele, 2–5, 66–7, 158
Shonaland, occupation, 75, 80
shrines, 19–20, 54, 56, 96–7
Siama, interpreter, 33, 35
Sibindi, son of Gambo, 118–19
Sibongo, early convert, 64
Siginyamatshe (Siminya), medium, 79
Sihulukulu, rain-doctor, 55
Silima mission station, 106
Simmonite, Jessie, 141
Sindisa, chief, 58
Sitjumi, diviner and convert, 148
Sitomo, medicine man, 56–7
slavery, absence of, 157, 158
social structure, Ndebele state, 5–11, 30, 161–3
social traditions, missionaries attempt to change, 111–14
Society of Jesus, *see* Jesuits
Solusi mission station, 99, 106; school, 132
Sotho-Tswana people, *xi*, 2, 5, 6, 22–3, 27, 68, 92; religious beliefs, 17–18, 47
spirit possession, 20, 57; mediums, 76, 79, 125
spiritual consciousness of Ndebele people, 109–10
Stanlake, Mr, 118
supreme being, existence of, in cults, *xii*, 13, 18, 76–7
Sweden, Church of, 107, 108, 130, 166
Sykes, Frederick William, 62
Sykes, Fr Richard, 113
Sykes, William, 28, 36–8, 39–40, 50, 60–1, 83, 97; *quoted*, 41, 42

taboos, 9, 19
Tama, early convert, 64
Tati mission station, 158
Taylor, J. V., 159
teacher training, 137, 140
Tegwani mission station, 106, 118, 120, 136, 149
Temple, C. H., 106, 109–10
Thabayezinduna crisis, 48

Thomas, Thomas Morgan, 33, 36–7, 39–40, 47, 56–7, 63–4, 76, 88, 92–3, 158; *quoted*, 42, 52, 63, 86, 93, wife of, 33, 37
Thompson, Francis, 84
Thonga (Tonga) people, 5, 41, 159
Tigerkloof school, 110, 140, 141, 167
Tjingababili, chief, 120, 164
Tlaping people, 27
Tobela, Venda chief, 6
Tohochipi, Mambo, 3, 67
totems (*isibongo*), 5, 9
trade, 11–12, 27, 29
Tshaka, king of Zulu, 2
Tshakalisa, son of Lobengula, 148–9
Tshitshi, chief, 120–2, 158
Tshoko, wife of Mzilikazi, 115

umuhlehlo (Ndebele earmark), 9
Unlugulu, Ndebele priest, 91

Vaughan-Williams, Lt-Col, 55
Venda people, *xi–xii*, 2, 4–5, 6, 12, 19, 23, 93
Virwa people, 5
von Eltz, Baron, 158

Waddilove, J. K., 136; school, *see* Nengubo
Wanezi mission station, 107
Wankie mission station, 132
Wesleyan-Methodist Missionary Society, 106–7, 130, 132, 134–6, 146, 148, 153
westernisation, 48–9, 56, 117; acting against Christianity, 152; hostility to, 166–7; missionaries wish to impose, 111, 144–5; Ndebele uncertainty about, 75
White, John, 106–7, 134, 152
white men, relations with, 49, 51, 56, 58, 65, 68, 159; blamed for misfortunes, 30–3, 44, 95–6; Lobengula's attitude, 80–5; Mwari and, 70, 89–90; paramount issue, 75
Wilkerson, George J., 138–9, 145
Williams, Richard C., 139, 145
Willoughby, W. C., 110
Wilson, Major, 117
Wilson, Professor Monica, *quoted*, 13
Windram, R. F., 50
witchcraft, belief in, *xii*, 14, 16–17, 28–29, 86, 162; *see also* divination
women, attitudes to, 136–7, 142
World War I, 108, 118, 125
Wright, Dr Marcia, 82, 157, 159

Xwailile, wife of Lobengula, 56

Zachariah, convert and preacher, 109
Zambesi mission, 47, 48, 58, 96, 105, 113; *Zambesi Mission Record*, 113
Zansi people, 5–6, 48, 51, 79, 105, 158; converts, 64; religious beliefs, 13–17, 18–19, 22–3, 77
Zondo, diviner, 57
Zulus: migration to Transvaal and Zimbabwe, 1–2, 17; revolution, 1
Zuzumba mission station, 106–7, 122
Zwangendaba, king of Nguni, 2